Why Federations Fail

An Inquiry into the Requisites for
Successful Federalism

Edited by Thomas M. Franck

Thomas M. Franck
Gisbert H. Flanz
Herbert J. Spiro
Frank N. Trager

Why Federations Fail

Studies in Peaceful Change, No. 1

Prepared Under The Auspices of
The Center For International Studies, New York University.

New York: New York University Press
London: University of London Press
1968

To SAMUEL RUBIN, *Champion of the Center for International Studies and of Better International Understanding*

Errat

WHY F

Page

Page :

Contents

INTRODUCTION

On Federalism

by Frank N. Trager

Herein we are concerned with four "cases," four experiments in creative federalism, each occurring at the end of the same imperial connection. Our purposes in this examination are twofold: to provide the basic data necessary to an understanding of each case in all its uniqueness; and to explore the possibilities for comparability and inductive generalization.

The end of empire, especially since World War II, has been accompanied by the extraordinary theoretical popularity of the idea of federalism-as-panacea. It has been prescribed and applied as a remedy for a great variety of political, economic, social, cultural, and other ailments and at all levels of organization—from metropolitan areas, to Europe (by the European Union Movement), to the world (by the United World Federalists, among others). It was a principal topic of discussion at one of the triennial congresses of the International Political Science Association, held in Geneva, in 1964. Among all the newly independent countries in Asia and Africa, only in Indonesia has the concept, after a brief experience with it, been overtly rejected and condemned. For, in those special circumstances, it has been regarded—perhaps not without

reason—as a device by which the former imperialist power
sought to limit Indonesian sovereignty.

But Indonesia is exceptional in its ideological rejection of
the federal ideal. In a highly stimulating monograph, Professor William H. Riker pointed out that in 1964 well over half
the land mass of the world was ruled by governments that,
with some justification (however slight), described themselves
as federalist.[1] In this present study, we are concerned with
political systems which appeared to want to apply a federal
solution to their problems—unlike Indonesia—but failed, and
which turned from federalism towards separatism—again
unlike Indonesia, which rejected federalism in favor of a more
centralized union.

What is federalism, and why do federations form and
fail? Can we discern factors that make for success or failure
of federal srtuctures? What role, for example, is played by the
constitution itself, its formula for dividing power between the
center and the units? What relative importance should be attached to the nonconstitutional factors: religion, culture, language, distribution of resources? What weight is to be given
to personal and psychological factors: charisma, commitment,
friendships, rivalries, and personal ambitions?

What we mean by federalism is not a fixed point on a
map, but a tendency which is neither unitary nor separatist.
In Aristotelean terms, it is the median between these two polar
positions, and thus their true opposite. A federalized state is
one in which the several units and their respective powers are
constitutionally or otherwise legally united under the ultimate
power of a central state and government.[2] But it is also an

---

[1] William H. Riker, *Federalism: Origin, Operation, Significance*
(Boston: Little Brown & Co., 1964), p. 1. Riker cited Argentina, Austria,
Australia, Brazil, Canada, Congo, Ethiopia, West Germany, India,
Malaysia, Mexico, Nigeria, Pakistan, the Soviet Union, Switzerland, the
United States, Venezuela, and Yugoslavia. I am in general agreement
with Riker's analysis.

[2] At least two federalized constitutions, the Soviet of 1936, and the
Burmese adopted just before independence in 1948, contained provisions
affecting the right of subordinate units to secede. These unusual provisions are operationally meaningless. The Burmese constitution was
abrogated by the action of the Revolutionary Government after the military take-over in 1962.

essential mark of a federalized state that the subordinate units retain or have reserved some irreducible powers operative within the same territory and regulating the same population over which the federal authority also applies with respect to other matters or different aspects of the same matter. As George Washington observed, it is difficult to draw with precision this median line, nor is the "mix" necessarily fixed by a federation at the moment of its creation for all time. The citizens' freedom to alter the "mix" of federal and state power to meet the exigencies of changing circumstances may be essential to the system's ability to endure, always provided that some significant degree of power remains both at the center and with the units.

This process of balancing is illustrated by the decision in 1872 in *Tarble's Case* which refused the states permission to issue writs of habeus corpus for federal prisoners, where it was said that "there are within the territorial limits of each State two governments, restricted in their sphere of action, but independent of each other, and supreme within their respective sphere. Each has its separate departments; each has its distinct laws, and each has its own tribunals for their enforcement. Neither government can intrude within the jurisdiction, or authorize any interference therein by its judicial officers, with the action of the other." But it is as noteworthy that judicial decisions defining central power are not infrequently altered by other judicial decisions in different instances and circumstances, as for example, in the cases affecting child labor where the 1918 decision in *Hammer* v. *Dagenhart*[3] was overruled by the 1941 case, *United States* v. *Darby*.[4] In short, man-made law finds way of utilizing the triadic separation of powers in a federal system to subtract from or add to the powers of the center or of the units. In the United States, for one, the powers of the center have progressively grown at the expense of the units—but not, and never, totally or finally if the United States is to remain a federal system.

In 1787 John Adams, then in London, started to write as

[3] 247 U.S. 251 (1918).
[4] 312 U.S. 100 (1941).

a series of letters, *A Defence of the Constitutions of Government of the United States of America Against the Attack of M. Turgot in his Letter to Dr. Price.* His defense lay in what he repeatedly called "the balance" and which he defined as "a total separation of the executive from the legislative power, and of the judicial from both . . . three independent, equal branches . . . perhaps the three only discoveries in the constitution of a free government, since the institution of Lycurgus."[5] More than a thousand pages later, closely argued, frequently polemical, historically illustrated, he brings his work to a conclusion "with unexpected dignity"[6]; for there had appeared "The Report of the Convention at Philadelphia, of the 17th of September 1787." This *Report,* of course, with few changes was engrossed as the Constitution of the United States and was signed in the Convention on that date. In commenting on the *Report,* Adams writes, "The former confederation of the United States was formed upon the model and example of all the confederacies, ancient and modern, in which the federal council was only a diplomatic body. . . . The magnitude of territory, the population, the wealth and commerce, and especially the rapid growth of the United States, have shown such a government to be inadequate to their wants; and the new system, which seems admirably calculated to unite their interests and affections, and bring them to an uniformity of principles and sentiments, is equally well combined to unite their wills and forces as a single nation." He allows that the "result of accommodation cannot be supposed to reach the ideas of perfection of anyone . . . that it may be improved is not to be doubted, and provision is made for that purpose in the Report itself."

Adams here succeeds in distinguishing the central difference between confederal and federal systems—in the former, ultimate power or sovereignty resides in the individual units making up the confederation, their interrelationships are "diplomatic"; whereas in the federal system there is a non-

---

[5] My edition is the third, 3 volumes, Philadelphia, 1797. See the Preface, p. ii.

[6] *Ibid,* Volume 3, p. 505. All other quotations in this paragraph are to be found on pp. 505–506.

absolute subordination of the parts to the principles and sentiments of a "single nation." He also provides a set of geopolitical and socio-economic conditions which help to bring a
federalized state into being.

George Washington as President of the Convention, had
already offered his own clarification as between the two systems. In his letter to the Convention, September 17, 1787, he
recognized the essence of federalism as a balancing of "rights
(i.e., powers) which *must be* surrendered" to the central government, and "those which *may be* reserved" to the several
states, or parts of the central government. (Italics added.) But
he insisted that the "greatest interest of every true American,
the consolidation of our Union" led to the "concession[s]"
which the "political situation rendered indispensable." And
Washington, perhaps more keenly aware than most of the
problems involved, added to the usual set of socio-political and
geopolitical conditions for federalism that of "safety" (the
security, "perhaps [of] our national existence").[7]

Though no contemporary political leader would seriously
advance the often-quoted statement of Gladstone to the effect
that the U. S. federal constitution was "the most wonderful
work ever struck off at a given time by the brain and purpose
of man," no modern or contemporary federalized constitution
has failed to acknowledge or to reflect in more or less degree
what Adams called "the balance" and what Washington called
the "line" between the central and subordinate parts of a
federalized government—and the new states have sought this
balance and this line for reasons, among others, similar to
Washington's and Adams'.[8]

What, then, makes people, tribes, colonies, nations, want
to join in a federation? Federal states come into being because

[7] The letter, usually available in standard collections of U.S. Constitutional documents, is printed, along with the *Report* as part of *Ibid*,
pp. 507–28; especially pp. 526–27. Riker, pp. 18, 20, briefly calls attention
to Washington's preoccupation with the military weakness of the government under the Articles of confederation, especially, in connection with
Kentucky's interest in joining Spanish America!

[8] In this connection it is still profitable to reread "The Federal
Constitution," Chapter VIII in Volume I of Alexis de Tocqueville, *Democracy in America*.

people conceive or acquire and support an interest which, they believe, is better served in such a political entity. Riker effectively argues that what he calls the federal "bargain" is "always" attended by two necessary conditions for its occurrence. These are the desire to aggregate or expand territory without the use of force and to ready its government for some military-diplomatic threat or opportunity.[9] In this aggregation or expansion the additional factors enumerated by Adams and Washington play critical roles. The aspiration for economic development and utilization of complementary or otherwise enhanced resources, the restoration of a historical past with its connotations of a restored or regained fatherland, the ideals of a common cultural tradition, the hope of creating a new patriotism, new loyalties to a politics capable of evoking satisfaction and pride—all these and more are aspects of the political drives which cause men to seek a federal solution.

This incomplete list which derives from the "classical" literature of the late-18th and 19th centuries makes no claim to essentiality.[10] Moreover, our Western-centered experience relevant to the causation of federalism does not tell us all about newly-independent Asia and Africa. Each experiment with federalism shares something with all other federal experiences; and in each there is much that is both unique and relevant, perhaps even of the essence. The Malayan Federation—which precedes the Malaysian Federation by at least six years—will in all probability endure whether or not the Malaysian Federation, even without Singapore, lasts. It will endure because the unique Malay character of the Malay States, even excluding Sabah and Sarawak, has more tangibles and intangibles to cause the federation to remain together than to separate, as in the remote past, into minor sultanates

---

[9] De Tocqueville, pp. 11–13. The "bargain," he writes, is "between prospective national leaders and officials of constituent governments for the purpose of aggregating territory, the better to lay taxes and raise armies." The rest of this short book is an analysis of relevant data and demonstration of the "necessary" propositions.

[10] For a contrasting approach *see* Karl Deutsch, *Political Community in the North Atlantic Area* (Princeton: Princeton University Press, 1957), p. 58. The Deutsch list is less extensive than the one I have suggested.

now obviously incapable of individual survival. I cannot
"prove" such a proposition. It is at best a value judgment
drawn out of experience with the "interests" of the Malays in
the Malayan Federation.

Or, to take another example, one not treated in this book:
I cannot *prove* that a Thai federalism will not emerge from
the agitation in the Lao-Thai provinces of the Northeast. But
judging by the absorptive capacity demonstrated by Thailand
in the past, I would say that in time it will find a means of
accommodating the Lao-Thai without transforming its unitary-
state system into a federal one. But, similarly, without proof,
I am reasonably confident that the Busman—the majority
group in Burma—will accept some new form of ethnic-linguis-
tic federalism with the Chins, Kachins, Karens and Shan.

In the final analysis we cannot *know*—in the scientific
sense—all the "essential" elements which hold the "cement"
of a system together or cause it to fissure and break. We do
know that because the "village," or the "city-state" or perhaps
even the small state is no longer viable or self-defensible, some
form of federal institution is a useful choice for political systems searching out a middle way between the two polar perils
of imperium and anarchy.

It is in this sense that we would of course rather have had
the federations studied in this work succeed than fail. As they
did fail, it does their memory honor to conduct a post-mortem
in the hope of gaining knowledge necessary to prevent other
failures.

Why
Federations Fail

CHAPTER 1

East African Federation

by Thomas M. Franck

INTRODUCTION

There is and was no East African Federation.

And so this chapter differs from the others in that it touches not upon the failure of what was, but of what might have been.

What might have been and what *ought* to have been. If ever the right political galaxies appeared to be in propitious conjunction, it was in East Africa in the summer of 1963. Here four nations—Tanganyika, Zanzibar, Kenya, and Uganda —come of age with historic, functional, political and personal ties so strong that their failure to seize the moment seems, at first glance, almost a flouting of destiny.

It is, in fact, a near-classic example of political wrecking: of personal ambitions and ego triumphant over the logic of history. In place of a great federation a handful of politicians created, instead, an illusion of identity between the national interest and their personal ambitions. As a class, and with important exceptions, *nouveau puissant* behaved exactly like

3

nouveau riche in the ostentatious display and excessive protection of their new resource.

A superficial glance at East African attempts at federation are likely to confirm the worst nihilistic theories of modern history, of nations and destiny as random playthings of a tiny political power-elite.

But before concluding that unprincipled, self-serving political ambition—political subjectivism, to borrow the Russian expression—is the locomotive of history (and remembering that contemporary African events are anyway probably somewhat *sui generis*) it is first necessary to evaluate the real strength of the social, economic, and historic forces which tended to make for East African unity and which were defeated in 1964 and 1965. If these factors were all along overrated, then the significance of the triumph of political subjectivism is also likely to be over-rated, as with the proverbial French tailor whose reputation for invincibility stemmed from the townspeople's failure to ascertain that the seven he was said to have slain at one blow were not men but only flies.

It must, however, be admitted that in December, 1963, federation seemed a sure thing and an ideal to which not only the technicians, the economists, the civil servants, but also the political leaders had dedicated themselves.

"We, the leaders of the people and governments of East Africa . . . pledge ourselves to the political Federation of East Africa" they unequivocally declared in Nairobi on June 5, 1963, "This is our day of action in the cause of the ideals that we believe in and the unity and freedom for which we have suffered and sacrificed so much."[1] Significantly, the word "unity" in the Declaration takes precedence even over "freedom."

Thereafter, who would doubt that Kenya, Uganda, Tanganyika and Zanzibar would federate? Every piece of scenery was in place and the cast seemed well rehearsed in the carefully prepared script. Skeptics were merely subversive or obdurate.

The British Government gave a very senior man the relatively minor diplomatic role of High Commissioner to Kenya in the understanding that the unfolding play would soon make him High Commissioner to a united East Africa. He quit when he found the well-set piece suddenly careening to grotesque Pirandelloesque improvisation.

But the High Commissioner's disappointments were those of an outsider, a European, a "neo-colonialist." When East Africans had little else about which to boast or with which to comfort themselves, they feigned to rejoice in the failure of East African federation as a frustration of British-American hopes and "schemes" rather the way some college students quickly learn to convert the sawdust of academic failure into the currency of social protest and nonconformity. Yet the hope of federation was fundamentally East African; the benefits would have accrued entirely to East Africa: and the failure, although not quite so entirely, was also East Africa's.

Perhaps 10 per cent of the population of East Africa is genuinely literate. The locomotive of history hurtles with great speed along this narrow-gauged track, and event after event, policy after policy, is reached and passed with very little public discussion outside the inner circles of the politically-privileged class. Momentous changes in previously accepted, fundamental policy are undertaken with no meaningful public discussion. This is not a defect of the African personality, it is a defect of teaching democracy through a colonial system, a project as impossible as teaching a bed-ridden man the theory of riding a bicycle and then expecting him actually to *do* it when he is let up.

In any event, the hopes of federation faded with the same spectacular speed and lack of informed public participation as they had come. By April, 1964, Prime Minister Obote of Uganda had already made it clear that the chances of federation in East Africa were now "extremely thin."[2] By August, President Kenyatta of Kenya announced that he was not about to "kneel to Nyerere" and Tanganyika. He also said that federation had all along been less a serious objective than a ruse to win speedy independence from Britain.[3] This was news not only to London but also to Dar es Salaam.

In May, 1965, there was a political "happening" neither explicable nor surprising in the tortuous context of East African affairs. Kenya police seized seventy-five tons of

Chinese arms and forty-seven soldiers infiltrating its territory en route from Tanzania (Tanganyika and Zanzibar)—to where? To Uganda, said the governments in Dar es Salaam and Kampala. In Nairobi, darker intentions were being attributed to the delivery. It was said the guns were not just passing through, but were destined for Kenya's disaffected Luo elements around Lake Victoria. President Kenyatta publicly accused his two neighbors of "an act of criminal folly"[4] and privately, of plotting a tribal, Communist-supported coup against him. The Central Legislative Assembly of the East Africa Common Services Organization found it understandably awkward to meet in this poisoned atmosphere.[5] At the same time, Nairobi refused to ratify its earlier understanding with Uganda and Tanzania (the Kampala Agreement) on an equitable allocation of new industry resulting from the customs union, and Tanzania in reprisal or self-defense began to dismantle the East African common market by imposing quotas on imports from Kenya, and ended the East African currency union by minting its own coin and establishing its own Central Bank.[6]

In the place of federation, East Africa now had its own "little cold war." In April, 1966, President Kenyatta accused two Tanzanian ministers of entering Kenya to plot his overthrow with the new left-wing opposition which was forming around former Vice-President Oginga Odinga. The suspicion was in general, if not in every detail, justified although Kenyatta should have known from personal experience that in East Africa (and, of course, elsewhere) the capers of individual ministers need not be in accord with their government's official policy. Yet it is also true that the governments of Tanzania and, to a lesser extent, Uganda have ill-disguised their belief that the Kenyans have "sold out" to the British and Americans, while, from the rarified heights of Nairobi, Tanzania increasingly seemed a steamy political jungle infested with Chinese advisers and intriguing Zanzibaris in search of revolution. East Africa had gone in two years from the threshhold of federalism to bickering, suspicion, and cynicism in its *inter se* relations. Watching from the Rhodesian battlefront, President Kaunda of neighboring Zambia wrote the East African leaders, ". . . you inspired us during our struggle for independence. . . . We have been saddened greatly by recent events."[7]

And yet, among East Africans the mystique of unity remains a reality still vividly perceptible to the political senses: an *élan* of historic common achievement, an aura of Swahili culture, a wisp of the "old boy" circuit among the leaders, Makerere College, London University, the Pan-African Federation, the Africa Bureau, Bayswater's "one-night cheap hotels."[8] So it was altogether natural to East Africans at the end of May, 1965, when the crisis had temporarily eased and Kenyatta had agreed to release Uganda's seized arms, lorries, and men, that Prime Minister Obote should thank him for a decision "in keeping with his character as a worker for African unity."[9] The East African Central Legislative Assembly met again to do its postponed work, and the three heads of state conferred genially at Mombasa and agreed to set up a commission to try once more to rationalize and develop the required system of cooperation and integration. In opening his new Central Bank, President Nyerere of Tanzania said, "It would have been much to our heart's desire if it were a federal president officiating at the inauguration of a federal central bank—and I must say quite candidly that I would have been ready, and, in fact, happier to be in the audience to watch him."[10] Most important of all, in 1967, the three East African governments signed an agreement, effective December, 1967, which continued and to some extent strengthened the common market, common institutions, common communications infrastructure, and common planning which they had gradually developed during the colonial era (and which is discussed below).

It was a good thought, if not one profusely shared by other East African politicians. Yet, evidently, if the idea of East African federation has indeed been submerged in the flood of political personalism and artificially-created nationalism, it yet remains a lost Atlantis that continues to exert a dimly perceived but persistent tug on the political memory of East Africans. This, in itself, distinguishes the East African federal experiment from most other broken political marriages.

Familiar is the dissolution leading to profoundly poisoned relations among former partners like Britain and Ireland, Northern and Southern Rhodesia, or India and Pakistan. Less familiar but not uncommon is the *sang*-Freudian correctness with which civilized Scandinavians disguise their mutual alienation. But East Africa fits neither of these polar stereotypes, resembling more those peculiar ex-lovers who, having broken up, still continue to meet and engage in love-hateful domestic bickerings that end sometimes in sex but never again in marriage.

Some failures seem natural: the deprived boy from the slums who takes to crime, or the federation imposed on angry masses by a power-hungry racial elite which ends in revolution and break-up (what in the chapter on Central African Federation is called the facile "Hollywood" presumption). By any such standard, the failure of East Africa to federate was an unnatural failure, astounding in the deftness with which it snatched defeat from the jaws of victory.

THE ROOTS OF EAST AFRICAN UNITY

There are deep, dividing scars across East Africa: the topography of the Rift Valley, the ethnography of tribalism, the modalities of climate and agriculture. But few of these approximate the chalk lines drawn for reasons largely irrelevant to African conditions by nations themselves only for an instant relevant to African history. One of the factors most frequently cited in support of the logic of East African unity is the lack of logic of its dividing boundaries.

Zanzibar joined British East Africa in an exchange for Heligoland in the North Sea[11] and in a set of transactions earlier the same year, much of what became the boundary between Kenya and Tanganyika was first drawn to divide the Sultan of Zanzibar's mainland marches into German and British spheres of influence. Negotiated colonial spheres of influence also account for the boundary between Tanganyika and Nyasaland; and between Tanganyika and the Congo.[12]

Within a single colonial empire, states, called "territories" in East Africa, were created and altered in response to administrative convenience. It was to simplify administration of the railway running from Mombasa into the interior, and to surround the line of rail with a fertile agricultural hinterland tended by white settlers that the entire eastern province of Uganda was in 1902 transferred to Kenya by the colonial administration.[13] And it was a European war, fought to a decision in Europe, which brought Tanganyika under British administration by the award, in January, 1920, of a League of Nations mandate. As late as 1963, Britain was still tidying up the last territorial transaction in East Africa, one which sensibly transferred residual title to the so-called coastal strip from the Sultan of Zanzibar to Kenya.[14]

Although several such efforts at twelfth-hour rationalization were made by the colonial powers, what had been done by them in their ascendancy they generally could not undo in their decline. Those territories, like Northern and Southern Rhodesia or Rwanda and Burundi, which colonial interests had rent asunder, decolonization could not again join together. In any event, the natural condition of East Africa without national boundaries is not one of international or regional unity but of tribalism. Thus the East African nations came to independence—Tanganyika in 1961, Uganda in 1962, Kenya and Zanzibar in 1963—with their divisive and arbitrary boundaries substantially intact. (In a few instances, Ruanda-Urundi, for example, decolonization provoked even more fragmentation.) Britain might have tried to insist on East African unification as the *condition-precedent* for independence, but the diasterous consequences of imposed federalism had been exposed in the Rhodesias and Nyasaland. Her self-restraint was justified by the collapse of colonially imposed federalism in newly independent French West and Central Africa.[15]

The colonial boundaries, left unamended, cut with fine indifference through various ethnic groupings: the Masai shifted around by colonial winds of whim which antedate the winds of change, find themselves in both Kenya and Tanganyika; Luos are both in Kenya and Uganda; the Shifta tribesmen of Kenya's Northern Frontier District are ethnically part of

Greater Somalia, the Nyasas are in both Tanganyika and Malawi, the Karasuk spill over from Uganda into Kenya. This mix is further compounded by large-scale migration, at first prompted by Arab slave trading, later by the British mercantilist policy of "free flow" which allowed largely unrestricted migratory movement of labor across East African boundaries, and most recently by the forced flight of refugee masses from the Southern Sudan, Rwanda, and Mozambique into Uganda and Tanganyika.

Nor is the topography and economy of the region better served than ethnography by existing boundaries. The northern highlands of Tanzania are on both counts naturally a part of the Nairobi—rather than the Dar es Salaam—orbit, just as the southern highlands of Tanzania are more nearly of a geographic piece with Zambia; Kenya's Northern Frontier District merges with Somalia; so too the Equatoria province of the Sudan with the Acholi district of Uganda and the Turkana region of Kenya with the Karamojong part of Uganda.

Not only does traditional productivity, crops, cattle, marketing, tend to follow geographic contours rather than the artificial boundaries, but the overall similarity of soil and climate has led to similar cash and export crops. Thus, the three leading commodities, coffee, cotton, and sisal, together account for 42 per cent of Kenya's, 58 per cent of Tanzania's and 77 per cent of Uganda's exports.[16]

These facts emphasize the superficiality, irrationality, and instability of the existing regional boundaries that divide East Africa—they do not necessarily argue for regional unity, although the two are too readily confused. The same conditions may as readily cause border incidents and raids, irredentist "liberation movements," chauvinistic repression of minorities and other familiar ingredients of intra-regional animosities. Thus, if the factual ingredients of irrational and unstable boundaries argues at all for regional federation, it is less because unity is the concomitant of unstable borders than because the alternatives to unity are so likely to be irritation, nagging, tribalist provocation, and conflict. In East Africa, this is exactly what has happened. The point about these irrational national boundaries is not that their lack of ethnic, geographic and economic logic makes them easier to remove but rather that, unless these improvident barriers *are* removed, they are almost certain to cause the new nations serious trouble. Unless, for example, the East African countries develop and sell their three staple crops cooperatively, they are in danger of falling into mutually destructive competition for world markets. Unless federation minimizes the significance of boundaries, divided tribes will almost certainly try to ignore or redraw them. But the argument which proceeds from illogical frontiers is one of reason, not one of necessity. That boundaries are unfounded in economic, geographic or ethnic reality makes it *wiser*, but not necessarily *easier*, to remove them.

There are other factors making for unity in East Africa which have similarly been overrated, such as the role of the two common languages. True, English is the working language in most of the region. But not in Zanzibar, and less and less in Tanganyika which is being swahiliized. But Swahili is not universal either. It is the *lingua franca* of Tanzania, and is spoken by about half the people of Kenya. But it is on the wane in Uganda where the Baganda, at least, consider it inadequate philologically, and socially inferior. Other tribes simply see no need to impose still another alien tongue.

Kenya, Uganda, Tanganyika, and Zanzibar also share the common legacy of British colonial rule. This includes a common tradition of bureaucratic procedures and forms and a degree of statutory uniformity far exceeding that which exists today between the states of the United States.[17] The British left behind a system of tax law, criminal law, evidence law, law of professional qualifications, commercial law and British common law which only to a minor extent varies in usage among the four territories. But this was the unity of empire. As soon as the East African states became independent, they set about destroying this alien unity, passing divergent laws without even mutual consultation in the same jovial wrecking spirit with which the royal crowns were lopped off courthouses and imperial inscriptions sanded from public cornerstones.

Less readily effaced is East Africa's gradually developed *habit* of cooperation and unity. This had many origins. The struggle for independence in Kenya, Uganda, and Tanganyika was essentially a common struggle waged cooperatively by friends. At the time when many of East Africa's senior leaders of today were graduating from their secondary schools, there was but one institution of higher learning serving all East Africa: Makerere College in Uganda which, in 1949, became a constituent overseas college of London University.[18] President Nyerere of Tanzania; Zanzibar's Minister of State, Aboud Jumbe; Kenya's Minister of Finance, James Gichuru; Uganda's Milton Obote and Basil Bataringaya and many others were all more-or-less contemporaries who began at Makerere a habit of lifelong political cooperation. Joseph Nye in a recent study reports that, in 1960, eleven of thirty Uganda Legislative Council members were Makerere alumni, as were eight of seventeen Tanganyikans and seven of the fourteen elected members of the Kenya Legislature. Altogether in 1963, twenty of the forty-nine cabinet ministers in the three countries were graduates of Makerere,[19] which thus may be seen as a political incubator somewhat like Balliot and Magdalene Colleges at Oxford.

Similarly, cabinet minister, politicians, trade unionists like Kambona of Tanganyika, Abdulla Hanga of Zanzibar and Tom Mboya of Kenya worked closely together in England, sometimes rooming together, campaigning for African liberation at the same London meetings, being encouraged and sustained by the same handful of enlightened Labour Party Members of Parliament, in some cases attending London University, the Inns of Court or taking a course at Ruskin College.

The habit of cooperation among East African leaders had also its institutional side. At first, this did not take a particularly East African form. Jomo Kenyatta was one of the convenors of the Sixth Pan-African Congress in Manchester, England, in 1945, which marked the opening shot in the successful post-war campaign to win in Africa the freedom for which the Allies had successfully fought Hitler. The Pan-Africanist Congress was, however, dominated by the leaders of the continent's much more developed and sophisticated West

Coast. So was also its successor in 1958, the Accra-based All-African Peoples Organization. In natural response to their shared and special interests, the young nationalist leaders of British East and Central Africa organized their own mutual assistance organization: the Pan African Freedom Movement for East and Central Africa (PAFMECA). Its coming into being as an association of the like-minded East and Central African political parties gave the region an institutional basis of shared purpose, struggle and cameraderie which no other part of Africa could match.[20] Fraternal PAFMECA saw its constituent parties attain power in Zambia, Tanzania, Kenya, and Uganda. It promoted the defeat not only of colonialism but of rival African factions. By 1962, PAFMECA expanded to include the South African liberation forces (causing a change of name to PAFMECSA) as well as the governments of Somalia and Ethiopia. At its crest, PAFMECSA included governments as well as political movements. Not until September, 1963, when its remaining tasks of liberation were assumed by the newly formed Organization of African Unity (OAU), was PAFMECSA dissolved.[21]

PAFMECA, harnessing the amiable turbulences of common struggle and personal friendship generated the federalist movement of the 1960's. In a policy statement to the Conference of Independent African States at Addis Ababa in 1960, Julius Nyerere, as the leader of the East African country closest to independence, took the lead in linking the idea of Federation with African nationalism, anticolonialism and Pan-Africanism. His remarks followed extensive consultation with his PAFMECA colleagues and he was able to announce that "Many of us agree without argument that Federation of the East African States would be a good thing. . . . We have said and rightly so, that the boundaries which divide our countries were made by the imperialists, not by us, and that we must not allow them to be used against our unity. . . ."[22] We must confront the Colonial office with a demand not for the freedom of Tanganyika, and then for Kenya and then Uganda and then Zanzibar," Nyerere declared, "but with a demand for the freedom of East Africa as one political unit."[23]

Nyerere's initiative was soon ratified. At the January,

1961 meeting in Nairobi, PAFMECA unanimously resolved
that federation was essential to the political, social, and economic betterment of East Africa.[24]

But the importance of PAFMECA, too, has been over-
estimated. As a force for federation, it suffered from two
significant limitations. In the first place, its base was only a
highly personalized coincidence of the personal visions and
ambitions of a very small handful of leaders. It never succeeded in becoming a mass movement in any sense, although
it ran alongside—but never tried to harness—a vague, popular
ethos of unity. And so, when the visions and ambitions of the
few dozen leaders began to diverge, the ethos crumbled.

In the second place, PAFMECA did not resolve certain
political rivalries which arose as the spoils of the anticolonial
struggle came within reach. Even during the early, euphoric
days of freedom fighting, the apparent unanimity of the East
African elite was only a relative one, with the leaders dis-
cernibly grouping in circles, the outer of which included such
more socially conservative movements as the Zanzibar Nationalist Party (ZNP) led by wealthy Arabs, the Kenya African Democratic Union (KADU) which preached tribal
autonomy, and the Democratic Party of Uganda (DPU) which
was basically Catholic-traditionalist. These parties cared less
about East African unity and more about preserving or re-
storing precolonial prerogatives of native chiefs, sultans, and
kings. In the inner circle were the four more radical parties
of East Africa. These were the Tanganyika African National
Union (TANU) of Nyerere; the Kenya African National
Union (KANU) of Gichuru, Odinga, and Mboya—and, later,
Kenyatta; the Uganda People's Congress (UPC) of Obote;
and Zanzibar's Afro-Shirazi Party (ASP) of Abeid Karume.
By 1961 this "inner four" had begun to support each other
without excessive regard for the niceties of nonintervention.
Dogmatic assertions about what might have been are pre-
sumptuous, but this much can be observed: the optimum con-
dition for federation would have been one in which the four
East African countries had reached independence at the same
moment, which might have been December, 1961, and under

the leadership of governments led by the four inner-circle parties.

As luck and colonial policy would have it, the crucial months following the Nairobi PAFMECA meeting saw an "outer-circle" party take power in each East African country except Tanganyika. The outer-circle party not only was less a part of the East African *élan* but was also in each case a party of the minority. In Kenya, for example, KANU won 590,661 votes to KADU's 143,079. Yet KADU was invited to form a government with the help of independents and others representing racial minorities because the colonial governor and KANU could not reach agreement on the Kenyatta issue—the sticking point being the former's arbitrary insistence on four months' delay in authorizing the release of someone he considered irretrievably evil. The resultant detour in Kenya's march to independence meant that the optimum moment and the optimum condition had been lost. Largely because Britain, or local colonial administrations found them more compatible, outer four parties were also returned to office without majority support in Uganda and Zanzibar during this critical period. Later, of course, they had to be turned out.

It was only Tanganyika which was ready at the optimum moment, another case of St. Mark's injunction: for although Tanganyika was last in all the "essential" ingredients of effective statehood—literacy, per capita income, investment, trained personnel—she was first into *uhuru* [freedom]. If the other East African countries, with their superior human and natural endowment were unready it was more because *Britain* was unready—unready to sit down at the Lancaster House table to bargain with Peter Koinange and others suspected of a Mau Mau past, psychologically unready to release Kenyatta and restore him to political life, unready to abandon the loyal tribal minorities to majority control,[25] unready to see prosperous industry and agriculture transferred to inexperienced hands, and unready to abandon the principle of Westminster parliamentary democracy as the model for Africa. The indecent haste and zeal, the *schadenfreude,* with which Belgium turned a totally unprepared Congo over to independence and

certain chaos after a transition of only a year from absolute
colonial authoritarianism is the other extreme of the British
insistence on punctilious "standards," on explicit constitutional
guarantees, on so long classifying the ban on the return of
Kenyatta and his friends to public life as "not negotiable," on
transitional racial electoral rolls, on reserved seats, on crossing
each "t" and dotting each "i" when time was of the essence.
(The "t's" and "i's" in any event became uncrossed and un-
dotted right after independence.)

But a much more serious consequence of the delay in
Kenya's and Uganda's independence was its effect on the
ethos of unity. Ambitious political leaders soon discovered
that, while it is one thing to fight together for power, it is
quite another to share power once it is won. Political unity
could only have been achieved at the moment of transition
from colony to nation, while the leaders were still in the battle
dress of comrades-in-arms. That this feat could not be arranged does not make the cameraderie of the fighting days
less real, despite its significance. On the contrary. In the years
before independence, the inner circle of East African leadership developed a spirit which strongly resembled the youthful
élan and cameraderie of the Kennedy administration. It is not
so much that Obote was young or Kiwanuka old; certainly
Kenyatta was nearly as old as KADU leader Ronald Ngala *and*
the British Governor together. But in early 1960 the inner
circle of PAFMECA (Kaunda, Nyerere, Kambona, Obote,
Nboya, Kenyatta, Gichuru) had a youthful restless spirit, a
lean and hungry intellect, an integrity, an indifference to
tradition—both African and Western—an idealistic, intelligent
inventiveness; a fondness for innovation, for the probe and
thrust, which is not a creed or ideology so much as *style*. Had
they been able to translate that *élan* into a political union,
there would have been nothing comparable on the African
continent. But they could not, for *élan* was not enough.

The cause of East African unity suffered from bad tim-
ing, but also from the singular failure to develop an ideology
of unity. Kaunda, Nyerere, Mboya, and Obote are men of intellect, imagination and vision. Yet, while they attracted to
their cause many skillful political pragmatists, they produced

no ideologists to develop and enunciate a systematic blueprint for East African unity, a grand design to fire the imagination and quicken the pulse.

In 1961, Dr. Nyerere offered to delay his own country's independence so that the optimum moment and conditions might coincide.[26] "To those people who would wait until the countries are separately independent," he had warned in 1960, "I say that they do not know human nature. You must rule out the question of federation after we take our seats as sovereign states in the United Nations."[27] But Nyerere's singularly altruistic offer was at once repudiated by his associates in the TANU executive. And in almost every other instance East African unity seemed to be espoused by politicians only for as long as they were not in office.

There were other institutional elements in the East African "habit" of working together. These include the common services (rail, telegraph, telephone, harbors, etc.), the customs and currency union, the Central Legislative Assembly and the interterritorial university. All this functional unity had been built up gradually and pragmatically over a period of almost half a century, so that, in 1963, there was in East Africa a substantially greater degree of economic and functional integration than in the better-advertised European Economic Community. But, like the unity of the law, the unity of common services was an alien, if benevolent invention administered by colonial bureaucrats. It was a good thing, but it captured no imaginations. Moreover, its very success in bringing, or seeming to bring most of the benefits of federalism without any sacrifice of sovereignty made the argument for federation less persuasive, less urgent.

Functional unity in British East Africa began almost at the same time as colonial rule itself. Sir Harry Johnson as early as 1901 had urged the merger of Kenya and Uganda. His recommendation was followed only in part—by the transfer of Uganda's eastern region to what later became Kenya. But a postal union between the two territories was initiated in 1911, followed in 1917 by a customs union. In 1923, after Britain had assumed mandated responsibility for Tanganyika, the external tariffs of the three territories were equalized and an internal common market for local produce was decreed[28] which was extended by 1927 to include imports. The Court of Appeal for Eastern Africa came into being in 1902, and in 1920 the East African Currency Board took over the issuance of a common decimal coinage.[29] In 1933, the postal union between Uganda and Kenya was extended to Tanganyika[30] and at about the same time a common telegraph service went into operation.

East African air services were established in 1937, and during this same period governmental research, statistical operations, meterological services, courts and income tax collection all came under regional administrations.[31]

In 1947 these and other services were consolidated into an East African High Commission.[32] The High Commission was reorganized into an East African Common Service Organization (EACSO) by agreement among the governments of Kenya, Uganda and Tanganyika.[33] EACSO was comprised of a Common Service Authority exercising executive powers by unanimity and consisting of the Prime Minister of Uganda and the Presidents of Kenya and Tanzania. A number of subsidiary committees in such fields as communications, finance, commerce and industry, labor, research and social services,[34] were set up to assist the Authority. Each was composed of the relevant cabinet ministers from the three territories. Limited legislative power was located in a Central Legislative Assembly (CLA) made up of a speaker appointed by the Authority, ministerial members of the subsidiary committees, two members of the secretariat—the Secretary General and the Legal Secretary—and twenty-seven members representing the three territories, nine from each, elected "by the legislative house of the Territory in such manner as that legislative house may prescribe by its rules of procedure."[35] Whenever new territorial elections took place new CLA members for their territory were to be chosen.[36]

The CLA's legislative powers were conceived to be recommendatory with its legislation to come into effect upon the unanimous approval of the three-member Authority.[37] On the other hand, once that approval is given, it automatically becomes the internal law of each territory.[38]

EACSO inherited from its predecessor, the High Commission, twenty operative departments: agriculture and forestry research, customs and excise, desert locust survey, civil aviation, freshwater fisheries research, income tax, industrial research, information services, malarial disease institute, leprosy research, literature bureau, marine fisheries research, meterology, posts and telecommunications, railways and harbors, statistics, trypanosomiasis research, veterinary research, and virus research.[39] In addition, the East Africa Currency Board was continued into the new period, although it is not a part of EACSO, and so also the University of East Africa. An appellate court for Uganda, Kenya, Tanganyika and Zanzibar, as well as several other smaller territories was reconstituted under EACSO authority.[40]

Much of this elaborate infrastructure of common service has been self-financing; the telephone, telegraph, railways and harbors administrations, for example. Other services are not, and for these EACSO was empowered to derive its revenue by a formula, devised by commission under the chairmanship of Sir Jeremy Raisman, which proposed in 1960 the establishment of a "distributable pool" of central revenues made up by taking 6 per cent of the yield from customs and excise levies and 40 per cent of the income tax charged to companies on profits from manufacturing and finance.[41] The distributable pool was created for two purposes. Half the amount therein was designated for the non-self-sustaining services. The other half was assigned back to the territories, but in equal shares and not according to origin. Thus the distributable pool also introduced an element, albeit a small one, of fiscal equalization and redistribution into the East African community.

EACSO did not constitute a federation. It was not conceived to be even a truly super-national economic community because its law-making power depended upon tripartite unanimity of the member governments. But in practice, East Africa had, by the end of 1961, inched a long way toward an integrated system of communications, marketing, finance, research, higher education, adjudication and currency control. British Colonial Secretary Ian Macleod remarked in 1961 that "federation for East Africa, if it comes, should be a grass

roots movement which the people of East Africa themselves
want, and not something which we impose on them from
Westminster."[42] In this he may have been reflecting British
experience in Central Africa and the West Indies. But also,
"I think all the gates to a possible federation (have been) left
ajar,"[43] and "In due course, the institutions of the organization
could well become the basis of an even wider and more general
form of association."

And so they well could. But they didn't.

WHY FEDERATION FAILED

Despite so many superficially auspicious factors in its
favor—the irrationality of East Africa's dividing boundaries,
the *élan* which had developed among its leaders, the common
Swahili culture, the common British traditions, and the long
record of functional cooperation—East Africa utterly failed to
turn inchoate unity into actual federation.

East Africa approached the 1963 target date for federation with great faith in the ability and willingness of its
leaders to translate the personal cameraderie of the fighting
years into a federal political institution. It soon became apparent, however, that beneath the inscrutable concept of
federalism lay many different and mutually contradictory
ideas which, having never been previously explored, could not
now, suddenly, be reconciled. This is not to say that even a
highly developed East African ideology could not also have
crumbled under the dead weight of personal political ambition
—but probably not quite so quickly or so ignominiously and
perhaps, if the ideology had been used to enroll a wider public
commitment, it might have triumphed over personal ambition
and schism.

As it was, the mutually antagonistic concepts hiding behind the conceptual facade of "federalism" included the following: 1. Mercantilist federalism, 2. Centrifugal federalism,
3. Regional federalism, 4. Pan-African federalism.

It is, even now, nearly impossible to find a politically

s not favor federalism. But what
l is the lack of any fundamental
urpose and scope of federalism
lism" was but a vague, unenun-
s a convenient goal—a positive
iity of anticolonialism. This was
twar decolonizing world, and it
rica. Vaguely aspirational goals
i form of stimulator and unifier
nce a society has progressed to
me real and immediate, if the
ne sharp ideological definition
ew long-range goals) they tend
riding, confusing and thus im-
ess. When "federalism" ceased
... aspiration and ventured to become reality, it resembled the African spider which "carries its numerous young
so neatly packed on its back that when you see it on a wall it
looks like a single unified entity; but when you approach it too
closely, it suddenly fragments itself and scatters in many
different directions."[44]

In the East African instance, the scattering took place
almost as soon as the decision to federate was announced by
the political leaders of Kenya, Uganda and Tanganyika on
June 5, 1963. Their Nairobi Declaration, after pledging the
three states to federation by December, established a working
party to "prepare a framework of a draft constitution for the
Federation of East Africa. It will report back to a full conference of East African Governments. In its work it will
consult with the three governments and with their consent
may co-opt constitutional or other experts. The EACSO will
be associated with these deliberations.

"In the third week of August a full scale conference will
be convened to consider the proposals of the working party."

In the optimistic spirit of the moment it was believed by
many, both in East Africa and London, that from the unified
core of Kenya, Uganda, Tanganyika [Tanzania] and Zanzibar
would grow a wider federation to include Somalia, Ethiopia,
Rwanda, Burundi and, in time, Northern Rhodesia [Zambia]

and Mozambique. As Tanganyika's foreign minister, Oscar
Kambona, had said, "You know our attitude to federation—
the bigger the better."

The cabinet-level working party first met in Dar es
Salaam on June 9. It consisted of Messrs. Binaisa and Kakonge of Uganda; Mboya and Murumbi of Kenya; and Kambona and Jamal of Tanganyika. They soon co-opted their
respective legal and constitutional advisers, but the meetings
were small, informal, and very secret. At the end of two days
in Dar, Mr. Mboya announced that agreement had been
reached "on every issue."[45] Even the site of the federal capital
—at Arusha—seemed to have been decided. The attorneys-
general were instructed to draft the constitution in time for
the next meeting of the working party at Kampala eighteen
days later. The UN was asked to—and did—provide experts
to assist in arranging fiscal and civil service matters. Mr.
Kambona was meanwhile sent to Nyasaland and Northern
Rhodesia to keep the leaders of those countries informed.
Other members of the working party went to Uganda where
they met the hereditary rulers of Toro and Buganda, the
Omukama and the Kabaka. "It is quite obvious," reported
Tom Mboya, afterwards "that everyone wants unity." Mr.
Kakonge publicly felt certain that the Kabaka and the Omu-
kama "want to come with us."[46] At this seemingly happy
moment, however, things seemed suddenly to fall apart.

The Kampala meeting of the working party was the first
real bargaining session at which the members dealt with the
actual problem of drafting concrete terms for federation. It
ended ominously without ritual expressions of optimism and,
indeed, without even an agreed communiqué. Two days later,
Prime Minister Obote said publicly that the Nairobi Declaration did not actually commit Uganda to Federation and that
the terms of the relationship were still only in the exploratory
stage.[47] Ominously, too, the Kabaka of Buganda failed to attend the meeting arranged between the political leaders and
the Uganda hereditary rulers following the Kampala meeting.[48] It was also considered somewhat an ill omen by the
other participants that Uganda had added to its working party
group Mr. Adoko Nekyon, the Minister of Broadcasting and

Tourism, who was widely considered to be committed to little more than a functional mercantile league between the East African nations.

During July the working party continued to meet in Nairobi and in Zanzibar, which, having had its election, now entered the negotiations. The deep secrecy in which the meetings continued to be shrouded prevented the East African community from realizing how badly the talks were going. Secrecy was supposed to prevent foreign governments from exploiting differences or otherwise interfering in the bargaining process. As it turned out, however, this is exactly what it failed to do. Secrecy did, however, underline the total independence of what was going on behind closed doors, the bargaining and bickering, from any regional ideological mass movement. At its death as at its inception, East African federalism remained a small personal understanding, or, as it turned out, a misunderstanding involving, at its core, no more than at most, four dozen persons. Indeed, after the federation's failure, a commission was set up to try to make the best of it and salvage what it could. A year after it had completed its work, that report, too, was still top secret. It is hard to say whether this extraordinary secrecy is due to the fact that no one in the public cares, or, conversely, whether the public has ceased to care because of all the secrecy with which the elite, like members of a Masonic lodge, surround the petty rituals of government.

In August, the working party met again in Dar es Salaam. This time, Mr. Nekyon, disregarding the negotiators' vow of silence, publicly disclosed the state of deadlock for the first time in an address to Ugandan students at University College in Dar, citing as irresolvable some matters which the others thought had been agreed before he joined the working party. He also bluntly stated that federation could not come that year. Uganda needed first to study "exactly where she is going . . . and to whom we are to surrender our powers," and must have "certain guarantees" lest it be thrown "into darkness."[49]

Mr. Nekyon's surprising statement did reveal the fundamental chasm which had probably always existed but had been obscured by the term "federation" for as long as it was

no more than a vaguely aspirational goal. Mr. Nekyon took
the position that federalism was a method of securing certain
mutual "businessman's" advantages to the participating countries who were its shareholders, and that its powers should be
limited strictly to those essential to the securing of the desired
advantages. Most of the Kenyan and Tanganyikan negotiators
had vaguely assumed an ideological commitment to federalism,
that its benefits need not to be proven but only hypothesized,
and not in an accountant's terms of immediate advantages to
the individual territories but rather in the political visionary's
ideals of manifest destiny for greater East Africa. Indeed,
Tanzanian leaders were the most anxious for a close federation although, in economic terms, they had the most reason to
fear the industrial and commercial domination of Kenya and
the competitive advantage of Uganda's highly developed power
and transport grid.

But beyond the vague idea that federalism was not what
Mr. Nekyon thought it was, the Kenyans and Tanganyikans
had little inspiration to offer each other. This became apparent
when efforts were made to force Uganda's hand by proclaim-
ing a union of Kenya and Tanganyika which could landlock
the Ugandan economy. A contingency plan for such a union
had earlier been favored by the "good East Africans":
Nyerere, Mboya, Murumbi and Kambona, but at the moment
when it might have been implemented, Prime Minister Kenyatta preferred to keep the door of negotiations open and
himself started to have second thoughts about the entire
federal project.[50] Although it was conceded at the outset by
the other East African leaders, that, as the senior "freedom
fighter," Kenyatta was entitled to the Federation's presidency,
the Mzee himself was not particularly interested in a role
which seemed to him to resemble that of constitutional mon-
arch. He began to suspect that Julius Nyerere, as number
two man, would wield the real political power.

For five weeks after the Dar es Salaam breakdown, efforts
were made to get the talks unstuck by convening a new summit
meeting. A date and place were finally agreed and Nyerere
and Kenyatta awaited Mr. Obote on September 19, in Nairobi,
the Kenyan being, as usual, reluctant to fly. By this time, how-

ever, the *élan* was gone. Nothing about it had been so ephemeral as its death. At the last moment, Prime Minister Obote simply decided not to attend and sent his Minister of Communications instead—with temperamental consequences which can readily be imagined.

We may reasonably end our account at this point. Completeness requires us to glance forward to December, 1967, for the enactment of the Treaty for East African Co-operation in which the three governments not only preserved much of the common institutions and economic unity of EACSO, but actually added some new ones, including a Common Market Tribunal and created an "East African Community." This, however, was a functional association, a *"quasi*-federal" relationship which might, again, give rise at some propitious future time to efforts for political federation. But for the time being, genuine federalism of the classical models engineered in the West—Canada, the United States, Australia—is dead in East Africa. In 1964 East Africa came within reach of such a federation. It is unlikely to try again unless and until success is far more sure than it was at that time.

Among the specific issues which had remained unresolved in 1964, were such questions as whether East Africa would constitute one nation or four, for purposes of conducting foreign relations and particularly for membership in the United Nations. Uganda strongly objected to any diminution of the voting power of East Africa at the UN and rather irrelevantly cited the example of the "three Soviets"—Russia, Byelorussia, and the Ukraine—which are allowed separate membership in the world organization. Zanzibar, supported by Uganda, had proposed a powerful upper chamber of parliament similar to the Senate of the United States in which, analogously, each of the four territories would have equal representation. There were also disagreements about international borrowing rights for the territories which Uganda insisted on retaining.[51]

These differences, and a few more, are, however, merely the tip of the iceberg. The very fact that this tip looms so large will cause the observer rightly to wonder what ever made the parties agree to embark on federation in the first place? The answer is that they did not. There never had, in essence, been ideological agreement: only a personal, verbal one. In lawyer's terms, there had never been a "meeting of the minds," only a misunderstanding over a single word—federalism—used by many persons to mean different things.

Federalism, as Hughes points out, can be on the one hand a movement to unite separate political entities; or it can be a way of developing political power away from a center and toward loosening component parts.[52] It can be, to use Colin Legum's felicitous phrase, both *fission* and *fusion*. In East Africa, it had the bad luck to be used both ways at once. We will return to this problem shortly.

In addition, federation can be essentially an *ideology* or a *methodology*, that is, it may be either a perfect end in itself or it may merely be a means to the achievement of such limited objectives as cheaper railroad fares or a power grid. The methodological federalist pursues unity only so far as is necessary to achieve his limited objective. The ideological federalist pursues federalism as far as possible or conceivable. The objectives of the one may be—and in the case of East Africa *were*—incompatible with those of the other. We shall see that this is also the common component of failure in the other three federal experiments discussed below.

The origins of federalism in East Africa are not ideological but rather methodological or mercantilist. From the beginnings of British rule, the idea of a united East African colony has had appeal to two nonindigenous groups, imperial government officials and Kenya white settlers. They saw in federation a simplification of imperial administration, a strengthening of the building blocs of empire, and an opportunity for rapid economic development of the entire region to facilitate internal self-government under their control, as in Southern Rhodesia. By no means all, and probably not even a majority of either group were in any sense ideologically committed to federalism. Ever since they first heard of it in 1776, Britishers have had a slightly queasy feeling toward federalism as a political concept. But for its first sixty years, federalism in East Africa was rightly associated with the white "bwana" and was primarily seen by Africans as a device to develop a white mercantile hegemony throughout East Africa similar to the one in Kenya and, later, in the Federation of Rhodesia and Nyasaland.

The determined and persistent, if unsuccessful, mercantilist-federalist campaign reached its climax between 1925 and 1955 and therefore remains fresh in the East African memory. In 1924, the Ormsby-Gore Commission was the first of several teams of imperial experts dispatched to examine and make recommendations on closer union between the British territories of East and Central Africa. It toured Kenya, Uganda, Tanganyika, Northern Rhodesia, Nyasaland, and Zanzibar. Its report led to the establishment of a regular coordinating conference of five British governors and the Zanzibar Resident.[53] The first meeting was held in Nairobi in 1926 and included also the Civil Secretary of the Sudan.

In 1929, the Hilton Young Commission reported on the possibilities of establishing a federal council and certain common services for which Kenya's Governor Grigg had been actively campaigning. It reported that "there is a need for the coordination and so far as possible, central direction, of certain services such as communications, customs, defence and research."[54] No one was happy with the report. The Africans of Uganda and Tanganyika feared federation as a way of packaging them with Kenya's white settlers. Kenya's white settlers saw in the Hilton Young report no assurance that they would control events even in Kenya, let alone in the hypothetical federation. The Kabaka of Buganda wrote to London, "We see that the Commission recommends that our Kingdom of Buganda should be joined with those other countries in what is called a closer Union or Federation. There is no question, Sir, but that this matter is causing us great anxiety."[55]

The African fight against federation was at this time led by a white imperial official, Sir Donald Cameron, the Governor of Tanganyika, whose views on the motives of the white settler community of Kenya are probably the first definitive expression of East African nationalism. "You want to create here the same conditions as exist in the Union of South

Africa; and ultimate complete dominance for the white man
based on what you call 'responsible government,' " he wrote
in 1930.[56]

Between 1930 and 1945 the central theme of East African
politics was not independence or African freedom or socialism,
but the battle between the mercantilist-federalists and their
opponents, whose ranks included white, neo-Lugardian, anti-
mercantilist, "soft-nosed" civil servants and missionaries bent
on preserving the native in his splendid state of nature, as
well as the first of the more modern and politically minded
Africans who abhorred the "human game reserve" concept as
much as white hegemony. Many of the present generation of
African leaders cut their teeth on the politics of antifederalism.
When the Federation of Rhodesia and Nyasaland was imposed
in 1953 against vigorous African opposition in Central Africa,
and when the British Colonial Secretary, Sir Oliver Lyttleton,
made his unguarded remark about East Africa being the next
to incur the benefits of federalization, the battle was joined
and *federation*—meaning the mercantilist-colonialist methodological convenience—became a dirty word in the African
vocabulary from the Limpopo to the Horn.

In the event, federation was successfully prevented in
East Africa. The common services which were administra-
tively incorporated in an East Africa High Commission in 1948
were carefully isolated from politics and the British government was at great pains to give assurance that the Commission's role would be purely technical. Nevertheless, the High
Commission was at best tolerated by Africans. Jomo Kenyatta
opposed even this much[57] and the Kabaka of Buganda's continued suspicion of the colonial-mercantilists' federal aspira-
tions, seemingly confirmed by Lyttleton's indiscretion, led him
to demand Bugandan independence, which in turn evoked his
temporary deportation. Colin Legum, speaking of Lyttleton,
says, "What he did by his speech on East African Federation
was to pull the trigger that caused the explosion."[58] The
independence movement in Buganda, which was the first real
independence movement in East Africa, was therefore born
of a violent reaction *against* the possibility of federation.

By contrast, the 1960 Addis Ababa speech of Julius

Nyerere was the first important public rehabilitation of the concept of federation among Africans. This is doubly remarkable. In the first place, the legacy of common services described in the previous section, far from building up a mass following for pragmatic federalism, must be seen as something imposed on Africans by white mercantilists who believed that unity was an economically sound policy for East Africa and that the blacks would in time also come to see it that way. Under the circumstances, the common services were barely tolerated by African opinion. Much of what they did for East African growth was, itself, commendable. But the Services were forced to operate in an atmosphere of near-conspiratorial silence lest, in drawing attention, they might also draw fire.

Thus federalism was at first given a meaning in East Africa which was at once so limited as to be ideologically meaningless in any but a colonial-mercantilist society run by colonial bureaucrats and white-settler entrepreneurs, but it also evoked a response among the Africans which, for perfectly good cause, had no need to be anything but negative. One tends to forget that this condition persisted until a scant three years before Tanganyikan independence, and that this independence came to Tanganyika twenty years before its leaders had expected it. In 1958, Kenya was still the white man's country. By 1960 all that had changed completely. It suddenly became necessary for African leaders to throw all gears into reverse and to embrace the very federation which for 35 years had been anathema—not only to embrace it, but to give it a content more meaningful in the changed circumstances than "that mercantilist-colonialist conspiracy to which Africans are unalterably opposed."

There were less than two years between the Addis Ababa speech and Tanganyikan independence in which to unbutton the fixed ideas of two generations, and to make a clean, ideological distinction between the colonial-white-mercantilist federalism of the past and a new Africanized, unifying, ideological federalism of the future. In three countries the "wrong" African governments for this sort of ideological innovation were in power. Moreover, the ideology had to be one which somehow reconciled regional to Pan-African federalism. Given the crush of other urgent problems which faced East African leaders—negotiating independence, interparty politics, resurgent tribalism, and learning to manage the machinery of a sovereign state—it is not too surprising that no concerted attempt was made to create such an ideology.

Nor was the need for an ideology ever fully embraced by most East African leaders. In part over-confidently and in part insincerely, many professed that federation was little more than a problem of legislative drafting, that "all Africans are brothers" by operation of some ethnic natural law. Yet in Uganda, in particular, there had already developed a small but powerful indigenous middle class of farmers, business and professional men with an undisguised and not wholly unwarranted confidence in the superiority of their ability and their traditions over those of their East African "brothers." As for the masses, they neither knew nor cared about anything but the exciting, imminent prospect of national independence.

When the negotiations for East African federation began in 1963, it was wrongly assumed by Kenyans and Tanganyikans that mercantilist-federalism had been purely a whiteman's policy. This proved premature in the case of Uganda and Zanzibar. Baganda mercantilists now wanted no more than, to quote Mr. Nekyon, "minimal alterations of territorial constitutions"[59]—as much as necessary to continue and improve the common services and add to the common economic weal, but not enough to undermine the traditions and privileges of Baganda society. In Zanzibar, the Arab and Indian business and land-owning elite were of the same opinion. They were all for federalism, no doubt, but within this infinitely vague, elastic frame they meant to preserve almost complete political autonomy for the governments and economies they controlled.

The negotiations for federation thus revealed the lack of any explicit idea of regional federalism and disclosed powerful pockets of continued support for a nonideological mercantilist association, one which could call itself "federal" only because the concept had been given no meaning.

The negotiations also revealed an entirely different con-

cept which attacked the proposed regional federation on the
ground that East African unity would make more difficult
the unification of the whole of Africa. To the negotiators from
Tanganyika, this discovery, that certain East African leaders'
commitment to federalism was in practice a commitment
against an *East African* federation, came as a thunderbolt.
They professed to see behind the Pan-Africanist dialectic of
Prime Minister Obote the guiding Italianate hand of Dr.
Nkrumah. In this they were not entirely mistaken, although
they tended to jump to the simplistic conclusion that Dr.
Nkrumah had somehow—probably by bribery—induced Mr.
Obote's group to join a plot to preserve Nkrumahist hegemony
over Africa. It was but dimly realized that in Pan-Africanism
the Nyereres and Mboyas had encountered a relatively sophisticated, systematic ideology to which they had only the most
rudimentary, improvised responses: the debate between regional and Pan-African federalists, such as it was, proved as
unequal—and as meaningless—as a debate between the Pope
and a bush-Baptist.

That Prime Minister Obote should see federalism in Pan-
African rather than regional terms, and should thus favor
a regional association of the loosest kind, should in fact not
have caught by surprise those who had attended the 1963
Addis Ababa meeting of African Heads of State, where Obote
had stood alone in support of Kwame Nkrumah's plan for the
immediate implementation of an all-African federation.[60] His
support for the "Unite Africa Now" policy may be best understood both as an expression of a genuinely ambivalent feeling
about the usefulness of approaching African unity through
regional federations and as a careful hedging against certain
harsh domestic contingencies. At the time, Obote's prime
ministership depended on the support of the ultra-loyalist
Kabaka Yekka party of Buganda. It seems reasonable to assume that his thinking will have proceeded something like
this: "If Kabaka Yekka can be made to go along on East
African federation, well and good. If not, I can accommodate
myself to their anti-federalism without loss of face among
African leaders by holding out for the Nkrumah optimum of

continental unity." In June, 1961, the Buganda government, after fifty years of determined antifederalism, was still maneuvering indecisively to find a new stance.

Obote's seemingly contradictory endorsement, in a three-week span, of Nkrumahism at Addis Ababa and East African federation at Nairobi reflected that ambiguity, as well as the meaninglessness of federalism in the East African context. In June of 1961, the Kabaka was still impressing the working party with a willingness to support federation. But within a month Buganda's government had decided that, while it was willing to enter a federation, it would only do so not as part of Uganda but as a separate state.[61] Kabaka Yekka appeared to have the necessary leverage in the Uganda parliament to press such a claim to the point, if not of success, then at least of bringing down the Obote government.

When Buganda fastened on centrifugal federalism, Obote fastened on Pan-African federalism, and the two, though having little else in common, were at least both agreeably contrary to the regional federal solution to which Kenya and Tanganyika thought every one was committed in principle.

The opposition to regional federation, centered in Uganda, thus had three components—and *all of them could claim to be federalists*. There were Uganda-first mercantilists who, to protect their superior economy and culture, favored as little federation as possible and only as much as methodologically necessary to continue the kind of commercial services already being rendered by EACSO. Nevertheless, they were able to profess federalism because the concept had developed no East African meaning.

The second group of opponents were the tribal nationalists, of which the Baganda supplied the outstanding example. But there were similar rumblings out of the Masai and other Kenyan tribes who did not see why East African federalism should not be a union of many smaller states, rather than of the existing artificial, colonially created entities. These centrifugal-federalists repeatedly cited the example of Zanzibar—with its scant 350,000 persons—being allowed to negotiate an independent entry into federation while a similar right was being denied much larger tribal "nations" on the mainland.

Again, this position can be characterized as federalist, and to its exponents, the argument was not anti-federalist in the least. Yet in the context of the 1963 negotiations it posed a threat to existing national units which none of the three national governments was prepared even to discuss, but to which at least one, that of Dr. Obote, was politically compelled to be responsive.

The third group of opponents expounded the Pan-Africanist or Nkrumahist view. Looked at from Kampala, this was the only logical consequence of the African federal aspiration. Looked at from Dar es Salaam and Nairobi, it was Ghanaian imperialism. Throughout the summer of 1964, Dr. Nkrumah sent angry, imperious letters to President Nyerere, to Prime Minister Kenyatta, and even to Prime Minister Kenneth Kaunda. To emphasize his displeasure at regional federal negotiations, he all but closed his High Commission in Dar es Salaam, culminating in a bad, if accidental, fire started by the incineration of files, and concentrated his diplomatic strength in Uganda.

Whether in response to internal political exigencies, Ghanaian influences, pure idealism, or a combination of the three, important Ugandan leaders of the UPC party became the spokesmen for this third view, saying disingenuously, "We are committed to the idea of Pan-African unity and we are afraid that our economic interest in federation will clash with our ideological interest in African unity."[62]

In short, it was never possible to join the issue of federalism, for all sides and all interests were "federalist." And in at least some instances there was no reason to impugn the sincerity with which they pursued those very "federalist" policies which ensured the failure to federate.

The lack of a formulated, enunciated and popularly received ideology of federalism in East Africa meant that the East African masses were unequipped to play any role in the federal negotiations, that public opinion was not in the least a factor in the bargaining which took place behind locked doors in the summer of 1964. Yet public opinion *might* have been a powerful curb on the subjectivism and personal ambitions of the leaders; this much is at least suggested by the fact that no East African leader dared openly wreck the negotiations, that the opponents of federalism had to fight with federalist weapons, and that the door has even now not been formally closed. Thus we see, for example, that the East African states still do not exchange diplomatic representatives because to do so would be to acknowledge the permanence of their separateness. But the role of public opinion in East Africa never went beyond an airy advocacy of the vaguest "federalism" and it was not difficult for shrewd politicians with personal power prerogatives at stake to convince the public that federation-wrecking was in fact federation-building.

Hamilton wrote in *The Federalist* in 1787, speaking of another federal experiment which nearly failed, "Happy will it be if our choice should be directed by a judicious estimate of our true interests, unperplexed and unbiased by considerations not connected with the public good. But this is a thing more ardently to be wished than seriously to be expected. The plan offered to our deliberations affects too many particular interests, innovates upon too many local institutions, not to involve in its discussion a variety of objects foreign to its merits, and of views of passions and prejudices little favorable to the discovery of truth."[63]

He might almost have been speaking of East Africa today.

NOTES

1. Declaration of Federation by the Governments of East Africa, in: Hughes, A. J., *East Africa: The Search for Unity* (Baltimore: Penguin, 1963), p. 265.

2. London *Times*, April 13, 1964, p. 12.

3. London *Times*, August 3, 1964, p. 7.

4. London *Times*, May 22, 1965, p. 7.

5. *Ibid.*

6. East African *Standard*, June 15, 1966, p. 4.

7. London *Times*, May 27, 1965, p. 10.

8. A useful, concise account of this period is to be found in Colin Legum, *Pan-Africanism* (2nd ed.; New York: Praeger, 1965).

9. *Times*, May 27, 1965, p. 10.

10. East African *Standard*, June 15, 1966, p. 4.

11. Agreement between Great

Britain and Germany, respecting Zanzibar, Heligoland and the Spheres of Influence of the Two Countries, Berlin, July 1, 1890, 18 Hertslets Treaties and Conventions, 455 ff. (London: Butterworths, 1893). *See also these U.K. Parliamentary Papers*: Correspondence re Anglo-German Agreement on Africa and Heligoland, C. 6146, 1890; Anglo-German East African Boundaries Agreement, C. 7203, 1893–94.

12. Cf. Agreement between Great Britain and Congo Free State on Spheres of Influence in East Africa, C. 7358, 7390, 7549, 1894.

13. For various accounts of this transfer see: Nye, Joseph, *Pan-Africanism and East African Integration* (Cambridge: Harvard University Press, 1965), pp. 86–87; Ingham, Kenneth, *A History of East Africa* (New York: Praeger, 1965 ed.), pp. 207–209; Franck, Thomas, *East African Unity Through Law* (New Haven: Yale University Press, 1964), pp. 19–20, and authorities cited therein.

14. Kenya Independence Order in Council, 1963, S.I. No. 1968 of 1963; Kenya Coastal Strip, Joint Statement by the Secretary of State for the Colonies and the Chief Minister of Zanzibar, Cmnd. 1971, 1963.

15. "Thus there developed the clash between two conflicting sets of historical forces: between narrow nationalisms based on the traditional political, linguistic, racial and religious loyalties, and the wider nationalism of the westernized elites which had grown within, and wished to inherit the larger cohesive units created by British rule." R. L. Watts, *New Federations* (London: Oxford University Press, 1966), p. 42.

16. EACSO, Economic and Statistical Review (December, 1961), pp. 32–33.

17. For a fuller account of the cause and substance of this uniformity, cf. Franck, *East African Unity Through Law* (ch. 4).

18. Makerere College Act No. 2 of 1949, Cap. 16, 1951, Revd. Laws of the High Commission.

19. Nye, pp. 82–83.

20. Legum, *Pan Africanism*, p. 72. Nye, p. 31.

21. Legum, *Pan-Africanism*, p. 138.

22. Legum, *Pan-Africanism*, p. 74.

23. Hughes, *East Africa: the Search for Unity*, p. 231.

24. Hughes, pp. 232–33.

25. Cf. Hughes, p. 136–37.

26. Cf. *Manchester Guardian Weekly*, Nov. 29, 1962, p. 2.

27. London *Times*, Nov. 5, 1960, p. 6.

28. Report on Tanganyika Territory for the year 1922, H.M.S.O. 1923, p. 16.

29. Report on Tanganyika Territory, 1920–21, H.M.S.O. 1923, p. 46.

30. Report on the Administration of Tanganyika Territory for the Year 1932, H.M.S.O. 1933, p. 115.

31. Cf. Inter-Territorial Organization in Africa, 1945, Colonial No. 191, H.M.S.O., 1945, p. 2.

32. East Africa (High Commission) Order in Council, S.R. and O. No. 2863 (1947) with a permanent executive secretarial and headquarters located at Nairobi (Id., art. 4 (1)).

33. An Agreement Between the Government of Tanganyika, the Government of Kenya and the Government of Uganda for the Establishment of the East African Common Services Organization,

EACSO Gazette, 1 Jan. 1962, E.N.
10.

34. EACSO Constitution, G.N.
437/1961, Tanganyika Gazette,
Dec. 10, 1961, arts. 3, 4.

35. EACSO Constitution, arts.
16, 18.

36. EACSO Constitution, art.
19.

37. EACSO Constitution, arts.
7, 29–30.

38. Agreement, *supra*, art. 5
(b); Tanganyika, Ord. 52, art. 4
(i); Kenya, Cap. 4, art. 4(i);
Uganda, Ord. 22 art. 4 (i).

39. For a detailed discussion
see Franck, Chapter 3.

40. EACSO Constitution, *supra*, art. 45. Eastern Africa Court
of Appeals Order in Council, S.I.
(1961), No. 2323, art. 11(4) (a).

41. East Africa, Report of the
Economic and Fiscal Commission,
1961, Cmd. 1279, H.M.S.O. 1961, pp.
59–69. The proposals are incorporated in: EACSO Constitution,
supra, art. 37.

42. 645 H.C. Deb. 259, 25 July
1961.

43. *Ibid.*

44. Hardwicke Holderness,
Quoted in Franck, Thomas, *Race
and Nationalism* (Fordham University Press, 1960), p. 187.

45. Tanganyika *Standard*, June
11, 1963, p. 1.

46. Tanganyika *Standard*, June
15, 1963, p. 1. For this account I
draw on my own recollections and
two written accounts which are in
substantial agreement although
written from the two ends of the
East African spectrum: Nye, Chapter 6, and Franck, *East African
Unity Through Law*, Chapter 5.

47. Nye, p. 185.

48. *Ibid.*

49. Tanganyika *Standard*, August 21, 1963, p. 1.

50. Working in Dar, I formed
the clear impression that Nye is
wrong in saying that the two-
nation union was vetoed by Tanganyika. Cf. Nye, p. 187.

51. Some additional areas of
disagreement are suggested in Nye,
p. 186. It is interesting that Nye's
list, apparently reflecting Ugandan
recollection of events, is substantially longer than my "Tanganyikan" list.

52. Hughes, *East Africa: The
Search for Unity*, p. 227.

53. Report of the East African
Commission, 1925, Cmd. 2387,
H.M.S.O. 1925.

54. Report of the Commission
on the Closer Union of the Depen-
dencies in Eastern and Central
Africa, Cmd. 3234, H.M.S.O. 1929,
p. 142.

55. Letter from the Kabaka
of Baganda to the Secretary of
State for the Colonies, 1930,
Papers Relating to the Question
of Closer Union, p. 85.

56. Despatch of the Governor
of Tanganyika Territory to the
Secretary of State for the Colonies,
1930, Papers Relating to the Question of Closer Union, p. 113.

57. Tanganyika *Standard*,
April 25, 1947, p. 3.

58. Colin Legum, *Must we
Lose Africa?* (London: Allen and
Company, 1954), p. 92.

59. Nye, p. 186.

60. Legum, *Pan-Africanism*, p.
136.

61. Cf. Statement of the Kabaka's Minister of Education, Abu
Mayanja, Weekly News, Aug. 30,
1963, p. 17.

62. Nye, p. 196.

63. Alexander Hamilton, *The
Federalist* (Cambridge: Belknap
Press, 1961), p. 89.

CHAPTER 2

The Federation of
Rhodesia and Nyasaland

by Herbert J. Spiro

"The birth of new nations" and "Africa" had become almost synonymous during a certain period in the 1950's and 60's. Multiple births were commonplace, and one wit commented that Africa seemed to need nothing more than obstetricians. Since each federation must consist of at least two "nations" or other units, Africa could not give birth to as many federations as nations, but most of the new states— whether embryonic, infant, adolescent, mature, or senescent —were involved in efforts to join with others in larger federations or other types of associations.

The Federation of Rhodesia and Nyasaland was the longest lived of all the attempts so far to federate African territories. Southern Rhodesia, Northern Rhodesia, and Nyasaland functioned as a federal system from October, 1953, until December, 1963. As it happened, the birth of the Federation of Rhodesia and Nyasaland was supervised by an able medical man, Sir Godfrey Higgins (later Lord Malvern), who had been Prime Minister of Southern Rhodesia and who was to serve as Prime Minister for longer than any other person before him in the history of the British Empire and Commonwealth. However, the death of the Federation was certified—indeed, it was celebrated in a mock funeral—by another able physician, Dr. Hastings Kamuzu Banda, the Prime Minister of Nyasaland.

The Federation of Rhodesia and Nyasaland need not have failed, at least in the sense that its three member states need not have severed all governmental ties among themselves. One need not conclude that the Federation was doomed to failure, merely because the federal government headed by Sir Roy Welensky and the Southern Rhodesian government headed by Sir Edgar Whitehead blocked the revisions and reforms necessary to save it. Instead it would be more accurate to attribute failure to the fact that the group or groups headed by the two white prime ministers preferred the risks implied in disestablishment of the Federation to the risks to Southern Rhodesian white supremacy which would have followed had they agreed to constitutional equality among the three territories and to massive African participation in the politics of each of them.

Because the break-up of the Federation and the independence gained by Malawi (née Nyasaland) in July, 1964, and by Zambia (née Northern Rhodesia) in October, 1964, was then followed by the "rebellious" Unilateral Declaration of Independence (UDI) of Southern Rhodesia in November, 1965, one could easily jump to the conclusion that the "wily white settlers" had planned it that way all along—at least since their refusal to make the concessions needed in 1960 or, at the latest, 1962. This conclusion would be quite wrong, because two Southern Rhodesian elections intervened, in the course of which more than one complete turnover occurred in the governing teams. Both Welensky and Whitehead were opposed to the UDI just before it took place, for both principled and pragmatic reasons. It would have been just as wrong to jump backwards from the failures of 1960 to the original founding of the Federation and to condemn its principal protagonists as hypocrites in 1953, simply because they refused to make the sacrifices needed seven years later in order to save the essence of their foundation. The argument, *post hoc ergo propter hoc*, generally makes even less sense in politics than elsewhere, because consequences are so much more difficult to foresee than antecedents are to hind-sight.

These introductory remarks are not meant to whitewash hypocrisy on the part of the Rhodesian organizers of Federation. Already in 1953, grave doubts were justified about the commitment of white politicians to the most important single goal stated for the Federation in the Preamble to its Constitution, that Federation "in particular would foster partnership and co-operation between their inhabitants." This phrase, and especially the word *partnership*, was clearly and to everyone's knowledge intended to refer to race relations. Much ink and oratory was poured out during the decade of Federation in debates about the meaning of partnership, with serious reference to such metaphors as the "partnership" between rider (whites) and horse (Africans) or between the white and black keys of the piano.

Any study of the antecedents of federation and the discussions immediately preceding its establishment clearly shows that white Rhodesian advocates of federation were not interested in bringing about a partnership based upon equality between the white and black communities, and certainly not one based upon the overwhelming numerical superiority of the black Africans. Politically aware Africans were fully cognizant of this outlook of the protagonists of the federal scheme, which they therefore opposed from the beginning— indeed, from before the beginning. These Africans had realized, at the latest by 1933, that the joining of the two Rhodesias was being promoted for reasons at best unrelated to race relations and at worst likely to lead to stronger discrimination against themselves.[1]

Both Southern and, in large part, Northern Rhodesia were originally settled and administered by the British South Africa Company, that great commercial corporation chartered by a British government which did not always show as much gratitude to its founder and head, Cecil Rhodes, as he believed himself to deserve. In 1922, the almost exclusively white electorate of Southern Rhodesia was given the option, in a referendum, between joining the (essentially unitary, nonfederal) Union of South Africa as its fifth province, and a grant of "responsible government" as a colony under ultimate British control. The vote went in favor of responsible government, with the British-appointed governor retaining control of de-

fense and external relations and, in effect, a veto over legislation deemed to be discriminatory against the native Africans.
Two years after the referendum, Northern Rhodesia passed
from the control of the Chartered Company (which retained
ownership of, and/or mineral rights to, large tracts of land)
to that of the British Colonial Office. Soon thereafter, the development of Northern Rhodesia's Copperbelt was begun and
along with it arguments on behalf of the "amalgamation" of
the two Rhodesias. Counterarguments were almost immediately put forward by Africans. For example, the Ndola Native
Welfare Association (Northern Rhodesia) passed the following resolution in 1933:

> While this Association would welcome amalgamation
> with Nyasaland where laws and conditions are similar to
> those in this country, it humbly asks that the Government
> will not agree to the amalgamation of Northern and
> Southern Rhodesia. Such a step would be greatly to the
> detriment of the interests and legitimate aspirations of
> the native population of this country.[2]

Why did white Rhodesians advocate amalgamation of the
two Rhodesias? Why did black Africans oppose it and instead
favor amalgamation of Northern Rhodesia and Nyasaland?
How did federation of the three territories result from these
cross-cutting demands and oppositions? What were the overt
and what the covert intentions of the various participants
in the founding of the Federation of Rhodesia and Nyasaland?
To what extent were these intentions realized?

THE BACKGROUND

Amalgamation of the two Rhodesias was advocated before
and after World War II for obvious political reasons which,
as often, had their economic undertones. In Southern Rhodesia,
the white population of about seven per cent controlled the

government, for all practical purposes without British interference. In Northern Rhodesia, the white population of about two per cent was represented by appointed and elected members of the Legislative Council, but government was firmly controlled from London. This difference most obviously affected native policy in the two countries. Northern Rhodesia, along with Nyasaland and the East African colonies of Uganda, Kenya, and Zanzibar, was covered by the doctrine of native paramountcy, first stated in 1930 by the Socialist Colonial Secretary Lord Passfield, the political theorist better known as Sydney Webb:

> His Majesty's Government think it necessary definitely to record their considered opinion that the interests of African Natives must be paramount, and that if and when those interests and those of the immigrant races should conflict, the former should prevail.[3]

This meant that whites in Northern Rhodesia could not acquire farm land, could not control African agricultural and mine labor, and could not pass discriminatory legislation and regulations with the same ease as in Southern Rhodesia. Subjection to Colonial Office control made life, including its economic aspects, more difficult for Northern than Southern Rhodesian white individuals and corporations. Both private individuals and the great companies engaged in the economic exploitation and development of Northern Rhodesia could reasonably expect to gain from the amalgamation of the two Rhodesias so long as their joint existence would be governed by constitutional arrangements like those obtaining in Southern Rhodesia since 1923.

The British government, however, could not countenance such arrangements, because they would clearly violate the promise implied in the policy of native paramountcy. Politically conscious Africans in Northern Rhodesia opposed amalgamation, because they feared the extension of Southern Rhodesian native policies to their territory. They naturally preferred amalgamation of Northern Rhodesia and Nyasaland, both of which enjoyed the constitutional status of British Protectorates and the special promise of native paramountcy.

Both colonies, moreover, were under direct Colonial Office administration and therefore had very similar, relatively enlightened native policies.

Various proposals of "closer co-operation or association between Southern Rhodesia, Northern Rhodesia and Nyasaland" led the British government, in 1938, to appoint a Royal Commission, the Bledisloe Commission, to inquire into the desirability and feasibility of these plans. The Commission opposed any early association, largely on the grounds of differential native policies in the northern territories and Southern Rhodesia.[4] In 1941, Lord Hailey, a distinguished retired official of the Indian Civil Service who was to make extensive surveys of African affairs, arrived at similar conclusions after covering the same ground. In a confidential "note" to the British government, he pointed to the politically and socially inferior, though educationally and in some respects economically superior position of Southern Rhodesian Africans compared to their northern counterparts.[5]

After World War II, during which the mining industry on the Northern Rhodesian Copperbelt experienced considerable expansion, the movement toward amalgamation was resumed. Starting in 1941, the British government had set up an Interterritorial Conference to coordinate the war effort of the three territories. The Conference had its own secretariat and facilitated meetings of the three governors and their associates in government. In 1945, the Conference was superseded by the Central African Council, whose tasks extended in the main to technical cooperation. The Council also provided a common meeting ground for white politicians from the three countries. By 1949, these leaders—especially Prime Minister Huggins of Southern Rhodesia and Mr. (later Sir) Roy Welensky, who led the white settlers of Northern Rhodesia—realized that the British government, then controlled by the Labour Party, would not allow amalgamation of the two Rhodesias. They therefore decided to launch an all-out campaign for the next best thing to amalgamation, that is, federation of the two Rhodesias and Nyasaland. The white politicans held a private conference at Victoria Falls in February, 1949, followed in 1951 by a conference of British civil servants, which issued a report in favor of federation, provided that those government services directly affecting Africans in their everyday lives would be left in the hands of the territorial governments.[6]

This conference was followed by another one at Victoria Falls, in late 1951, at which the Colonial and Commonwealth Relations secretaries met with the white politicians and, on the insistence of the British ministers, with leaders of the African nationalist movements. This was finally followed by a conference at Lancaster House, in London, during April and May of 1952, which hammered out the basis for a federal compromise between the white settlers and the British government. Only two Africans attended this conference. Both were from Southern Rhodesia. African leaders from the two northern territories, who had been invited by their governments to attend, boycotted the conference. The final constitutional conference, which took place in London in January, 1953, was entirely boycotted by Africans. It produced the constitution that provided the formal framework of relations among the three territorial governments and the federal and British governments for the next ten years.

Throughout this period, African leaders opposed the plans to federate with increasing vigor and at all levels. Fear of federation substantially increased political awareness among the African populations of the three countries. The exclusion of Africans from the earlier conferences, and their boycotts of the later ones, was used as proof of the anti-African aims of the federalists and of the antifederal convictions of the Africans. At the same time, however, the British government and its overseas colonial officials also looked to federation as protection *for* Africans against the openly racist policies of the Afrikaner government of the Nationalist Party, which had come into office in the Union of South Africa in 1948. According to Robert I. Rotberg, "The Colonial Office even attempted unsuccessfully to persuade the Government of Northern Rhodesia to limit Afrikaner immigration."[7] In other words, it was possible to support federation from a variety of otherwise opposed political positions: that of the white set-

tlers who wanted mainly to get out from under Colonial Office
control; that of the Colonial Office civil servants themselves,
who wanted to protect the Africans against *apartheid* on the
South African model; or that of the mining companies and
the British South Africa Company, engaged at the time in a
dispute over mining royalties with the whites of Northern
Rhodesia, but intent upon intensifying, integrating, and developing their operations in the Rhodesias and, to a lesser
extent in, Nyasaland.

THE CONSTITUTION

When the same general objective is being pursued for
such a variety of different, and in part contradictory motives,
the outcome is likely to be a rather unwieldy compromise
which will, in the end, bring no one what he was after and may
indeed result in the opposite of what was intended. The federal constitution was certainly unwieldy.[8] It was designed as
a compromise not only among the various groups favoring
federation, but also between them and their African opponents.
It ran to fifty-five pages in the official edition cited above. It
was a typically "British" federal constitution, informed
throughout by contemporary understanding (or misunderstanding) of other federal constitutions in the Commonwealth,
especially those of Canada and Australia, and not so much
that of India whose problems come closer to being even re-
motely analogous to those of the Rhodesias and Nyasaland. It
was a wholly "Western" constitution in that it completely left
out of account the political tradition and practices of the
indigenous peoples of the three territories, some of whom
were known to have relatively old and sophisticated political
systems.

The federal constitution was unusual though not unique
in that it combined in one federation member states at rather
different stages of constitutional development. Southern Rhodesia had had responsible government for thirty years by
1953, while Northern Rhodesia was still governed by its
British-appointed governor, advised by some ministers enjoying the confidence of the elected majority of the Legislative

Council. Nyasaland was behind Northern Rhodesia. This kind of federal "mix" is not unique. For example, the German Federation (1871–1918) combined monarchies with the three republican Hanseatic city-states of Hamburg, Bremen, and Lübeck. But it made for unusual complications in the Central African case, because the main cause of differential constitutional advancement was different racial composition and its consequence, divergent native policies. This divergence, in turn, had generated the massive African opposition to the federal scheme with the result that the racial issue, usually formulated in constitutional terms, continued throughout the life of the Federation to dominate and finally to divide its politics and ultimately to lead to its dissolution.

That the federal constitution was a compromise not only between different advocates of federation, but also between its advocates and its African opponents, came out in its Preamble:

Whereas the Colony of Southern Rhodesia is part of Her Majesty's dominions and Northern Rhodesia and Nyasaland are territories under Her Majesty's protection;

And whereas Northern Rhodesia and Nyasaland should continue, under the special protection of Her Majesty, to enjoy separate Governments so long as their respective peoples so desire, those Governments remaining responsible (subject to the ultimate authority of Her Majesty's Government in the United Kingdom) for, in particular, *the control of land* in those territories, and for the local and territorial political advancement of the peoples thereof. . . . [Italics supplied.]

The fear of the Africans in the two northern territories that Southern Rhodesia's policy affecting native lands would be extended to them was thus addressed by the constitution-makers at the very outset of their work. And the (significantly plural) peoples of Northern Rhodesia and Nyasaland were assured that they would be allowed to "enjoy" separate governments under the special protection of the British Crown for as long as they desired—a statement that implied that some method might be desired in the future to ascertain popular

desires. That method would presumably have to involve a
franchise much broader than existed in 1953, and broader
than the white settlers on their own would have been willing to
grant the Africans.

This, then, was a standard British-type constitution, providing for a cabinet dependent upon the support of a majority
in the (unicameral) parliament. The inequality of the member
states was explicitly recognized in the differential parliamentary representation assigned to them: Southern Rhodesia was
to have seventeen members of parliament, Northern Rhodesia
eleven, and Nyasaland seven. The black and white races were
also accorded unequal and disproportionate representation:
two MP's from each territory were to be elected Africans.
One European MP from each territory was to be charged with
special responsibilities for African interests, the one from
Southern Rhodesia to be elected, the two from the other
territories to be appointed by their governors.

This make-up of the federal parliament was subsequently
changed by amendment of the Constitution. Under the new
arrangements, Southern Rhodesia had twenty-four elected
European members, Northern Rhodesia fourteen, and Nyasaland six; Southern Rhodesia was to elect four African MP's,
and Northern Rhodesia and Nyasaland two each; the two
northern territories had another two "specially elected" African members each; and the three European members with
special responsibilities for African interests were continued.[9]

The complications arising from the compromise become
particularly evident in Chapter III of the Constitution, which
deals with legislative powers within the Federation. The first
Article of Chapter III, Article 29, begins as follows:

> Subject to the provisions of this Constitution, the
> Federal Legislature shall have power to make laws for the
> peace, order, and good government of the Federation . . . .

The phrase, "peace, order and good government," also occurs
in the parallel passage of the British North America Act of

1867, Canada's federal constitution, and may be taken as one of many evidences of the influence British constitutional experience elsewhere in the Empire and Commonwealth. The scope of exclusive federal-legislative power and of concurrent federal-territorial-legislative power is defined by the Second Schedule annexed to the Constitution, but in order to assuage African fears of the extension of the Southern Rhodesian land policy to the Protectorates, Article 33 provided explicitly:

> Notwithstanding anything in this Constitution, the Federal Legislature shall not have power to make provision for the acquisition, whether compulsory or by agreement, of any African land or of interests in or rights over any African land, otherwise than in accordance with the provisions of any of the African land laws applicable to the land in question; and any power for the compulsory acquisition of land conferred by a law of the Federal Legislature shall, notwithstanding anything in that law, not be exercisable in relation to African land for the purpose of settling immigrants thereon.

Nothing could have been clearer, particularly in view of the Federal Legislative List in the Second Schedule:

> 24. In relation to Southern Rhodesia, agriculture, that is to say—
>> (*a*) agriculture in general, including animal husbandry, dairies and dairy-farming, horticulture, poultry-farming, bee-keeping, fish-farming, pounds and agricultural colleges;
>> (*b*) agricultural research, including pasture, tobacco, veterinary and tsetse research;
>> (*c*) the provision and use of specialist services in connection with agriculture and agricultural products, including veterinary services, and services dealing with chemistry, entomology and plant pathology; and
>> (*d*) conservation,

but not including forestry, irrigation or such agriculture as the Governor-General and the Governor of
Southern Rhodesia acting jointly shall by order have
designated as African agriculture. . . .

25. In relation to Southern Rhodesia, animal health, including animal pests and diseases.

26. In relation to Southern Rhodesia, plant pests and
diseases. . . .

30. Primary and secondary education of persons other
than Africans.

31. Higher education (including higher education of
Africans), that is to say, institutions or other bodies
offering courses of a university, technological or
professional character.

Article 31 of the Constitution itself provided that

The Legislature of Northern Rhodesia or the Legislature of Nyasaland may by a law of that Legislature provide that, in the application of the Concurrent Legislative
List . . . there shall be included in that list . . . any matter
so specified relating to—

(a) such agriculture as is defined by law as non-
African; or

(b) animal health, including animal diseases and
animal pests other than tsetse; or

(c) plant pests and diseases.

These provisions were clearly designed to keep the control
of African land, agriculture, and primary and secondary education in the hands of the territorial governments, that is, in
the cases of Northern Rhodesia and Nyasaland, under the
protection of the British Colonial Office until such a time as
the governments of these two territories became responsive to
their African populations. As a result of these safeguards,
legislative powers were divided not only on a functional basis
—e.g., citizenship and currency were federal functions, while

control of the movement of persons and regulation of road traffic were concurrent functions—but also on a racial basis —e.g., African agriculture in Northern Rhodesia was a territorial function, while European agriculture became a federal function; African education was a territorial function, European education (on which much more money was spent per student) was a federal function, as was *all* higher education.

This complicated division of powers was meant to satisfy all the conflicting demands and fears, but it resulted in fact in perpetuating and even exacerbating the original antagonisms. Historians of American federalism have said that adoption of the Constitution of the United States was made possible by the "great compromise" during the Constitutional Convention in Philadelphia. The federal Constitution of Rhodesia and Nyasaland, by contrast, was made possible by a series of petty little compromises which foreshadowed the brevity of its life.

The federal Constitution was based upon recognition of inequality of the two main races in the three countries and upon acceptance of the related inequalities among the three member states, not only with respect to their representation in the Federal Assembly, but also as reflected in the revenue from federal income or profits taxes, from which, according to Article 80,

> ... there shall be payable to the Territories amounts equal to the following percentages respectively of the proceeds of that tax remaining after the deduction of the cost of its collection, that is to say—
> - (*a*) to Southern Rhodesia, thirteen [amended to fourteen per cent in 1958] per cent;
> - (*b*) to Northern Rhodesia, seventeen [amended to eighteen per cent in 1958] per cent;
> - (*c*) to Nyasaland, six per cent.

This division was based in part upon the relative gross national products of the three member territories, largest in

Northern Rhodesia because of the Copperbelt, and in part on
the proportion of their populations subject to income taxes,
highest in Southern Rhodesia because of its relatively larger
European population. Throughout the life of the Federation,
this provision continued a divisive issue about which Northern
Rhodesians, both white and black, engaged in much recrimina-
tion, because they believed that their territory was being exploited by Southern Rhodesia.

Southern Rhodesia was favored over Northern Rhodesia
in another important matter (with respect to which Nyasaland was not even "in the running")—location of the federal
capital. Article 6 of the federal Constitution provided that

> The seat of the Federal Government shall be at such
> place as the Federal Legislature may by law provide, but
> unless and until that Legislature otherwise provides shall
> be at Salisbury in Southern Rhodesia.

No serious consideration was given to relocating the capital
in Lusaka, the capital city of Northern Rhodesia, which is
much more centrally located. A commission, on which served
constitutional lawyers from Australia and Canada, the two
white federations in the Commonwealth, made recommendations on this question. The main issue, however, was a dispute
between two Southern Rhodesian claimants—Salisbury and
Bulawayo, with the former emerging victorious as the capital
both of the Colony, and the Federation. Salisbury served as
dual capital for the entire ten years of the life of the Federation, and continues to serve as the capital of Southern Rhodesia today.

One reason why Africans objected to having the federal
capital anywhere in Southern Rhodesia was its native policy
which was generally more discriminatory than that of the
Colonial Office Protectorates. Paragraph 3 of Article 6 therefore gave the Federal Legislature special jurisdiction over
the land used as the seat of the Federal Government, so that
the African members of parliament could move in an unsegre-

gated environment at least while attending parliament and visiting government offices. Here, too, a series of petty compromises did more to alienate than to reassure the participants. Southern Rhodesian whites gained the federal capital, but segregationists among them resented the "special privileges"—i.e., normal treatment—to be accorded to Africans who were elected or appointed to the federal parliament in their hitherto segregated Southern Rhodesian capital city. Africans gained nothing for Northern Rhodesia, and the few African MP's were hardly assuaged by their exceptional admission to white parliamentary company (including the dining room and bar in the parliament building) precisely because of its very obviously, indeed, ostentatiously exceptional nature.[10]

The federal constitution brought into being another device designed to reassure the African population that federation would not increase racial discrimination. Article 67 provided for an African Affairs Board, consisting of the three European members responsible for African interests and three of the African members. According to Article 71,

> It shall be the particular function of the Board to draw attention to any Bill introduced in the Federal Assembly and any instrument which has the force of law and is made in the exercise of a power conferred by a law of the Federal Legislature if that Bill or instrument is in their opinion a differentiating measure; and for that purpose they shall have the powers conferred by the subsequent provisions of this Chapter of the Constitution.

These powers enabled the Board at least to delay the final coming into effect of a bill, by having the governor-general "reserve" it "for the signification of Her Majesty's pleasure on the ground that it is a differentiating measure." This meant that the governor-general could not himself sign the bill before securing the approval of the appropriate member of the British Cabinet in London. Twice in 1957, the African Affairs Board

raised objections to bills—a constitutional amendment and a
change in the election law. The Secretary of State nevertheless assented to both. Thereafter, the African Affairs Board
was no longer considered adequate protection against discriminatory federal legislation by those Africans who had
entertained some hope about its possible effectiveness.

The Constitution of the Federation was put into operation, as it had been created, without popular participation,
except for the referendum held among Southern Rhodesia's
almost exclusively white electorate. We have seen how a series
of conferences, some of them private, others involving civil
servants, the final two held in London and attended by British
and Rhodesian politicians, led to the hammering out of the
constitutional text itself. The Constitution, after additional debate in the British Parliament, was given effect by a British
Order in Council. This genesis of the Constitution lent even
greater interest than usual to provisions for constitutional
amendment. According to Article 97, the Federal Assembly
could pass amending bills by a majority of two-thirds of all
its members, whereupon it required the assent of the Queen.
Moreover, the Legislative House of any of the three territories
or the African Affairs Board could object to amending bills, in
which case they again had to be reserved for the signification
of Her Majesty's pleasure, to be given only in the highly formal manner of another Order in Council, which was ruled out
in case either House of the British Parliament resolved against
the amending bill. Although this amending procedure seems
highly complex and cumbersome and seemed to some to provide adequate safeguards against constitutional amendments
detrimental to African interests, it was in fact invoked successfully for purposes of the Constitution Amendment Act of
1957, referred to above, removing what little confidence
Africans had retained in constitutional safeguards provided
for them under the Federation.

Once more, petty compromises failed to achieve their
overt purpose. White advocates of federation were given the
possibility of reshaping the constitution to their desires, cir-
cumscribed by the safeguards just described. They were,
therefore, very definitely denied full sovereignty even with

respect to purely "internal" matters. They never received the equivalent of external sovereignty under international law. The first item on the Federal Legislative List of the Second Schedule annexed to the Constitution dealt with

1. External affairs, that is to say—
   (a) such external relations as may from time to time be entrusted to the Federation by Her Majesty's Government in the United Kingdom; and
   (b) the implementation of treaties, conventions and agreements with, and other obligations towards, countries and organisations outside the Federation affecting the Federation as a whole or any one or more of the Territories . . . but not including relations between the United Kingdom and any of the Territories.

In other words, the Federal government could engage in the conduct of foreign relations only by explicit delegation from the British government. This meant, among other things, that it could not accredit diplomats to other states, that the highest-ranking foreign diplomats in Salisbury were not ambassadors but consuls-general (with the rank of minister), and that it could not be considered for membership in the United Nations. However, this rather bitter pill was sugared for the protagonists of federation by two provisions, contained in the Preamble to, and the last paragraph of, the Constitution. The fifth paragraph of the Preamble read as follows:

And whereas the association of the Colonies and territories aforesaid in a Federation under her Majesty's sovereignty, enjoying responsible government in accordance with this Constitution, would conduce to the security, advancement and welfare of all their inhabitants, and in particular would foster partnership and co-operation between their inhabitants and enable the Federation,

> when those inhabitants so desire, to go forward with
> confidence towards the *attainment of full membership of
> the Commonwealth.* . . . [Italics supplied.]

This implied—and was meant to imply—that the Federation
would eventually achieve so-called "dominion status," i.e., the
independence enjoyed by Canada and Australia since adoption
of the Statute of Westminster in 1931. Once dominion status
had been gained, the British government would presumably
lose much, though not necessarily all, of the restraining power
it exercised under the Constitution, e.g., with respect to the
amending process. (It would not necessarily surrender all in
keeping with the Canadian precedent, since amendments to
the British North America Act still require passage by the
British Parliament.)

How soon could dominion status be achieved? This question, according to some interpretations, was answered by Article 99:

> Not less than seven nor more than nine years from
> the date of the coming into force of this Constitution,
> there shall be convened a conference consisting of dele-
> gations from the Federation, from each of the three
> Territories and from the United Kingdom, chosen by
> their respective Governments, for the purpose of review-
> ing this Constitution.

On the insistence of the federal government headed by
Sir Roy Welensky, this conference was convened at almost
the earliest possible time. Instead of leading the Federation
toward dominion status, it marked the beginning of its end.

The Constitution, unlike some others in the Commonwealth, contained no bill of rights. Nor were the qualifications
of voters anchored in the constitutional document, which only
provided, in Article 10, that the Federal Assembly "may by
law make provision with respect to the election of elected
members," including qualifications of voters. In other words,

the Central African Federation did not follow the example of the United States Constitution, which left the qualification of voters essentially to be determined by the state legislatures. As a result, the franchise continued throughout the life of the Federation to be a hotly contested and divisive *federal* issue, in addition to being an issue in each of the three member states. Four different electoral laws, with differing and highly complex sets of qualifications of voters, were in effect within the Federation at any one time: the federal voting law and the three territorial laws. The qualifications—principally levels of income, of property owned, and of education—were such that virtually all adult whites could vote in both federal and territorial elections. For Africans, however, the situation could arise in which they were qualified to vote in territorial elections, but not in federal elections.[11]

Negligible numbers and proportions of African voters registered for or participated in the elections held under the federal and Southern Rhodesian electoral laws, which the African political leaders condemned as too obviously discriminatory against their people. A Northern Rhodesian election held on March 20, 1959, achieved a registration of 23,358 general voters, including 769 Africans, and 6,846 special voters, despite a boycott of the registration by one of the two African independence movements led by Kenneth Kaunda, who was later to become President of the Republic of Zambia. Voters' qualifications for this election were basically the same as under the federal act. By contrast, under the Nyasaland Election Law, 106,000 voters registered on the lower roll and only 4,401 on the upper roll, with the result that Dr. Banda's Malawi Congress Party won all 20 lower-roll seats.

All of these election laws were again the outcome of petty compromises. The white settlers thought that they had won protection against being "flooded" by an "illiterate and irresponsible electorate." The Colonial Office and the British government thought they had won more participation and representation than Africans had ever before enjoyed in any of the three territories—Southern Rhodesia's Legislative Assembly of thirty members, for example, had never included any non-white members before the Constitution of 1961 came

into effect. Politically conscious Africans, however, regarded
the concessions contained in these compromises as so inadequate, that they succeeded in imposing boycotts upon federal
elections and began to participate in Northern Rhodesia's and
Nyasaland's elections only after the British government had
clearly indicated that these two Protectorates would soon be
granted independence and that, therefore, the Federation
would have to be broken up.

Controversies about election law, like most other controversies during federation, basically involved the central issue
of race, stated, as usual, in constitutional terms. These debates
sometimes brought out the real intentions of the original
protagonists of federation more clearly than the statements
made by them before 1953. The whites—always with some
notable "non-racial" or pro-African exceptions—wanted to
reduce British and especially Colonial Office control as rapidly
as possible and were willing, for that purpose, to make token
concessions to African political demands as slowly as possible
without encouraging violent resistance. The British government wanted to consolidate its Central African holdings
against the increasing white racialist threat of South Africa
and the quickening movements toward full independence in
its East African territories, by promoting the differentiation
of Southern Rhodesia's race policy from South Africa's
through Southern Rhodesia's inclusion in one federal system
with the Protectorates of Northern Rhodesia and Nyasaland,
next-door neighbors of the constitutionally more advanced
British United Nations Trusteeship Territory of Tanganyika.
The great commercial and industrial companies wanted to
make more money and be subjected to fewer government con-
trols, goals which they might achieve by substituting federal
government supervision for British Colonial Office supervision
of their operations in the northern territories—most of the
companies moved their headquarters from London to Salisbury—and by consolidating and integrating these operations
for the whole of British Central Africa. The Africans in
Northern Rhodesia and Nyasaland wanted continued protection from the British government against the white settlers of
Southern Rhodesia and independence as soon as possible, and

they worked toward and eventually achieved independence largely by using antifederation agitation to stimulate nationalist consciousness among their peoples. The Africans of Southern Rhodesia, whose politics was always less militant and less well organized than in the north, were more ambivalent about their intentions, because federation might bring improvements for them. For the federal elections of November, 1958, 635 Africans registered as special voters in Southern Rhodesia, while only 53 and 11 registered in Northern Rhodesia and Nyasaland, respectively.

How strongly committed to their stated intentions were the various participants in the federal scheme? This is an important question—and one hard to answer—in any situation which, like this one, is not wholly or even mainly dependent upon the relative "power" of the groups involved. In terms of power (in the sense of organized means of physical compulsion), the white settlers of the two Rhodesias, after federation, possessed an undisputed monopoly of it and had the African populations at the mercy of the government in Salisbury. But, with few exceptions, the federal government always kept its use of that power within the restraints imposed by the Constitution and, through it, the British government. The white electorate of Southern Rhodesia was by no means wholly behind the federal experiment, as indicated by a 40 per cent opposition to it expressed in the referendum that accepted Federation in 1953. Much, if not most, of their opposition to federation was based upon fear of "racial flooding," not so much by Southern Rhodesia's own relatively well-controlled and docile Africans, as from Northern Rhodesia and Nyasaland, whose territorial governments would soon be in the hands of Africans and which would, under any constitutional arrangements politically feasible within a few years, outweigh Southern Rhodesia within the Federation. Reflecting these uncertainties, white politicians in the Southern Rhodesian, Northern Rhodesian and federal governments were unwilling to commit themselves definitely on behalf of any clear course of action. They remained unwilling to use the language of the American Revolution, which the rebellious regime of Ian Smith tried to paraphrase during 1965, to commit their lives, their fortunes, not to speak of their sacred honor. The British government, too, wanted to keep open as many future alternatives as possible and to procrastinate on any truly definitive decisions for as long as possible. In 1953, no one could be sure whether South Africa would continue on its steadfast course toward increased *apartheid* and out of the Commonwealth, or whether Tanganyika and Uganda would achieve independence within the quarter of a century then projected for that goal, or whether the Mau Mau uprising in Kenya would be successfully suppressed, or what would be Britain's strategic needs in Central Africa in the future evolution of the Cold War.

Moreover, it was becoming apparent that constitutional "entrenchment" was, in any case, not an efficient method of ensuring political permanence or stability or even of communicating one's desire to achieve these goals. (Entrenchment is that process of seeking to guarantee fundamental rights by embedding them in a constitution in such a way as to make them more difficult to amend a repeal than is the case with ordinary legislation.) At the time of the founding of the Federation, the Union of South Africa was passing through a constitutional crisis which revolved around the ultimately successful efforts of the Nationalist government to amend certain articles of the South Africa Act of 1909, which required a special amending procedure precisely in order to safeguard the parliamentary representation of certain Coloured (racially mixed) people.[12] Through elaborate legal and political maneuvering, the South African government had disentrenched these provisions with the unintended result of bringing home to both the British government and Africans in the Rhodesias and Nyasaland how impermanent and brittle even the most firmly laid constitutional foundations of even the most grossly unequal racial cooperation may be—and at that within the tradition of British constitutional practices. Even if the British government had wanted to make absolutely clear its utter determination to protect the existing political rights of, and to promote future political participation by, Africans in the federation, it could not have done so with optimum effectiveness through constitutional policy. On the other hand, in view of the South African example which was just then receiving much publicity in Southern Africa, Africans were not to be satisfied in either their fears of further white discrimination, or their demands for a firm table of advancement, by promises of constitutional safeguards. Consequently, neither white-settler proponents of federation nor the British government were ever able to muster or to manifest as much purpose behind their position, as were African opponents of the scheme able to muster against it.[13]

None of this is meant to imply that the Federation might not nevertheless have succeeded if various participating groups, especially the British government, had pursued more imaginative constitutional policies. For example, the very wording of the constitutional document itself could have been designed to contribute significantly to the success of the Federation. Instead, by its complexity, prolixity, and occasional apparent hypocrisy, the Constitution probably contributed to its own failure. We know from the experience of the United States that the nobility, purity, and elegance of the language of a constitution can make it a genuinely popular charter and thereby help greatly to popularize the goals, the institutions, and the procedures embodied in it. Both the Preamble to the Constitution of the United States of America and parts of its Bill of Rights, have performed such functions. The American Constitution, moreover, was—for its time—a product of democratic process drafted by elected politicians and ratified in the several states through a process involving popular participation. This was not true of the Constitution of the Federation of Rhodesia and Nyasaland, so that it stood much more in need of subsequent popularization. However, its language was not such that there was the slightest chance of promoting any popular understanding of the Constitution, especially among the poorly educated African population, and much less promoting and liking for it. It was simply too long, too legalistic, too all inclusive, and too substantive in its content to achieve popularity. For example, it included six articles of "Provisions as to procedure in Assembly," some of which could more appropriately have been left to nonconstitutional arrangements. An entire Chapter VII, running to nineteen articles, deals with Finance, and includes not only definitions of words ("For purposes of this article 'property' includes goods, animals and any other form of property other than moneys"), but also the proportion in which loans raised outside the Federation should be allocated between the Federation and the Territories (Article 90):

    (*a*) to the Federation, sixty-four [amended in 1958 to sixty-one] per cent.;

    (*b*) to Southern Rhodesia, thirteen [amended in 1958 to sixteen] per cent.;

    (*c*) to Northern Rhodesia, seventeen per cent.;

    (*d*) to Nyasaland, six per cent.

Substantive provisions like this are better left out of a constitution, because they are of insufficient importance for the fundamental functioning of the political system. They need to be adjusted to allow for economic and financial changes that have nothing to do with this basic functioning, and this then leads to changes in the constitution itself with the result that it will no longer be regarded as the enduring framework of government.

As late as 1960, suggestions were made to revamp the federal constitution thoroughly in an effort to make it, and through it a renovated Federation, more acceptable to its peoples, especially the Africans. Among these suggestions, some insisted upon the inclusion of a bill of rights. It seems doubtful in retrospect, however, whether the British government and its constitutional advisers at that time would have been capable of drafting or accepting a bill of rights or, as for that matter, an entire constitution, sufficiently succinct to elicit the support of ordinary people with strong suspicions. This inability is suggested by the Southern Rhodesian Constitution of 1961, and especially its Chapter VI, "The Declaration of Rights,"[14] and also by other British-designed constitutions in the Commonwealth of this period, including that of the Federation of Nigeria. The Declaration of Rights run to sixteen articles and about a quarter of the total length of the constitutional document. All of the rights declared there are surrounded with immensely detailed conditions, qualifications, and description.[15] Perhaps the complexity of the contemporary world as compared with that of the world known to the American founding fathers in 1788 made it difficult or inadvisable to say simply, "No one shall be deprived of life, liberty, or property without due process of law." Probably the drafters of the Southern Rhodesian Constitution feared that Africans would exploit such a simple formulation in order to prevent the passage of emergency legislation of a type frequently used for the control of nationalist agitation, or to challenge the constitutionality of such legislation after it had been passed. Conceivably the authors of this constitution were really concerned that adherents of certain religious sects, like Jehovah's Witnesses, would avail themselves of the simple formulation in order to resist public health efforts to prevent the spread of infectious diseases. In any case, they tried to anticipate all eventualities in this Declaration of Rights, as in other bills of rights in constitutions of this period and it seems doubtful, therefore, that they were capable of the bold, simple, and purposeful type of constitutionalism at the federal level which might have helped to hold the Rhodesias and Nyasaland together.[16]

ACHIEVEMENTS OF FEDERATION

Of the four Federations compared in this book, the Central African one lasted the longest. Ten years is a considerable period of time in the politics of an area and a continent that has been variously described as "in motion," "in transition," or "exploding." Even a political system with a more poorly designed constitutional framework could have been expected to bring about some noticeable and fairly enduring changes both internally and in external relations of the territories with each other and with the outside world. The Federation of Rhodesia and Nyasaland in fact brought about considerable changes of this type, the aftereffects of which are still visible

today, when Zambia and Malawi have their full independence
and Southern Rhodesia is in a state of rebellion which means
that it has *de facto* independence. Some of these long-run effects appear to have little to do with the overt intentions of
the participants in the founding of the Federation, while others
should be credited as their intended achievements. Still another
set of consequences of the decade of the Federation's existence
suggests the need for a reappraisal of the actual, partly covert
intentions of the founding parties when they agreed, and dis-
agreed, to the federal experiment.

The most tangible achievements, in the view of "federalists" who tried to save the links among the three countries
in the last few years of Federation, were the economic gains
attributed to it. Early protagonists of the scheme has usually
put economic gains forward as one of the principal "respectable" causes to be served by creating one large economy out
of the three smaller ones. Moreover, they usually advanced
the argument that the three economies complemented one
another, and that by creating an integrated common market
all three would gain substantially. The complementarity of
the economies could be demonstrated, certainly by comparison
with the Federation of the British West Indies. Northern
Rhodesia earned most of its income from copper, but it had
to import electric power in large part from the Congo, and
secondary and consumer goods from the outside world, including Southern Rhodesia. Southern Rhodesia's economy was
already at the time of Federation the most highly diversified
of the three. Most of its foreign earnings came from the export of tobacco, some from the export of a variety of minerals,
including coal to Northern Rhodesia. The beginnings of secondary industry existed, and some consumer goods were being
exported. However, the northern part of Northern Rhodesia
and all of Nyasaland were part of a free trade area under the
terms of the Congo Basin Treaty, so that lower-priced goods
from other parts of the world frequently kept Southern Rhodesian products out. For example, second-hand clothing and
household utensils were imported from Hong Kong. Southern
Rhodesia also employed more African workers from outside
than from inside its borders. The majority of these came from

Nyasaland and Northern Rhodesia, a minority from Mozambique and other colonies. Nyasaland's economy was the most backward of the three and its principal export consisted of manpower, to Southern and Northern Rhodesia.

Federation brought about considerable economic changes. Southern Rhodesia experienced an extraordinary boom, and the Federation as a whole for several years showed the highest annual rate of growth in the gross national product in the world. Salisbury as the dual capital became the headquarters of both major mining companies, Anglo-American and Rhodesian Selection Trust, and of the British South Africa Company. Secondary industry expanded by leaps and bounds in order to produce for the enlarged, and now protected, market. The Federation was able to raise foreign loans, especially for purposes of economic development, that probably by far exceeded what three separate colonial territories could have raised, even if the two Rhodesias had joined together for the restricted, purely functional purpose of, e.g., building Kariba Dam. This hydroelectric project quite literally forged a concrete link between the two Rhodesias. The World Bank advanced it the largest single loan it had made up to that time, and it is virtually certain that this American-controlled institution for international development would not have done so but for the existence and the promise of Federation. The federating of backward but developing countries for purposes of their economic and political advancement fitted neatly into contemporary projections of the American Dream onto the rest of the world. Other money for the dam came from the British government and, again, the great commercial companies who had a stake in the generation of more power for their mines, the resultant rise in land values, and the like. Federation also was followed by increases in the rate of white immigration, most of it from Great Britain and South Africa. This in turn acted as a further economic stimulus. More Africans became members of the cash economy, at least in the two Rhodesias where a high proportion of the newly employed Africans came from Nyasaland.

Although these economic arguments on behalf of maintaining the Federation appeared to be the most persuasive ones

to whites, both inside and outside Central Africa, they hardly
ever succeeded in persuading African opponents of the federal
scheme. Frequently, African politicians rejected the economic
argument on political grounds by saying, in effect, that they
would be opposed to prevailing political arrangements even if
these had brought about a tenfold improvement in the economic position of the Africans (which, of course, was not at all
the case). Dr. Banda once stated that his people were not like
pigs who worried only about their food—they wanted freedom
more than food. While the political rejection of the economic
argument was the most popular, there were also black and
white opponents of Federation, as well as disinterested outside economists, who rejected the economic argument on its
own economic grounds. Sometimes they denied that what
economic advance had occurred since 1953 was due to Federation. In other words, this advance would, in their judgment,
have occurred even without federation. Since history is ir-
reversible, one can never prove or disprove such arguments
about what might have been or what would have happened
anyway. But would trade and traffic between the two Rhodesias have increased as much as it did if the two had not been
linked together? Or, looking toward the future rather than
the past, would trade and traffic continue at the same expanding rate after dissolution of the Federation? At the time when
these controversies were raging, the answer could not be
given, but by now we know that Northern Rhodesia continued
to import most of its goods—not only power from Kariba and
coal from Wankie—from Southern Rhodesia even *after* the
Unilateral Declaration of Independence of November 11, 1965.

Another refutation of the economic case on behalf of
federation was highly critical of the type of economy that was
being brought into being in British Central Africa. One distinguished American economists used the Federation for a
"Case Study of Economic Development in a Dualistic Society,"
the subtitle of a book.[17] Greatly simplified, Professor Barber's
thesis was that the modern or cash sector of the economy was
developing at a much higher rate than the traditional or sub-
sistence sector, and that most of the benefits of development
redounded to the white population which both dominated, and

constituted by far the larger segment of, the modern sector. As a result, the development that might result from federation could well increase rather than decrease inequalities between whites and blacks.

A similar answer to the economic argument in favor of federation was made from the territorial as distinguished from the racial point of view. For example, the claim was put forward that economic development under federation favored Southern Rhodesia to the detriment of the other two territories, in general and in connection with specific projects like Kariba Dam. Damming the Zambezi River at Kariba Gorge was one development scheme among several competing for approval by the governments involved and the Federal Loan Council. The principal competition for the Kariba project, which came from the Kafue River project, and which would have involved only Northern Rhodesia, would have offered irrigation development for African and European agriculture in addition to hydroelectric power, and would have cost much less, thereby presumably leaving funds for other projects in Southern Rhodesia and especially in Nyasaland, which needed development most. The Kariba project won out, for reasons already alluded to, and the new dam firmly linked the two federal member states across the Zambezi River, their common frontier. Even at the time of construction, however, some antifederalists and some federalists, who were worried about Southern Rhodesia's excessive influence, thought it significant that the generating facilities were installed on the southern side of the dam and the boundary. After Southern Rhodesia's unilateral declaration of independence, this fact did indeed take on considerable importance, since it enabled the break-away regime of Ian Smith to threaten the Republic of Zambia with cutting off the power supply from Kariba on which the Copperbelt had become heavily dependent in the intervening years. This led some Africans to assert retrospectively that the dam, along with the Federation that had facilitated its construction, had from the beginning been designed to give the white settlers of Southern Rhodesia control over the rich Copperbelt. On the face of it, this was hardly a reasonable claim, because there was relatively little overlap between the personnel of the

break-away regime and the men who worked for the founding
of the Federation, and very few people could have had sufficient foresight in 1953 to anticipate the situation of 1965.
However, since federation had been imposed upon the Africans
despite their strong suspicions of the motives of its principal
protagonists, and because results always appear in a clearer
light and are more accessible to analysis than motives, this
kind of retroactive condemnation of the Federation only led to
the confirmation of an earlier political judgment as "historical."

Something similar happened with respect to changes in
the transportation and communications networks that took
place during Federation. Road connections between the two
Rhodesias were considerably improved, on the main highway
between Salisbury and Lusaka. Very little was done to improve
the road between Lusaka and Blantyre, the largest town in
Nyasaland, and virtually nothing to improve the road between
Salisbury and Blantyre, a large stretch of which passes
through Portuguese Mozambique. The Rhodesian Railways
were able to raise some private outside loans during federation and to modernize, especially through acquisition of additional rolling stock used for the export of Northern Rhodesian
copper. In retrospect, however, all this appeared to have been
designed from the outset to make Northern Rhodesia more
dependent upon Southern Rhodesia. The argument ran along
the following lines: Without Federation, transportation improvements—if they had taken place at all—might have invested more in links between Zambia and Malawi and especially
between Zambia and Tanganyika. Shortly after Zambia gained
independence, its President Kaunda and President Nyerere of
the United Republic of Tanzania approached Western governments and the World Bank to survey the feasibility of a railroad from the Copperbelt to the port of Dar es Salaam or
another port in Tanganyika, mainly for the political purpose
of making Zambia less dependent upon Southern Rhodesia.
The World Bank rejected the project as *economically* not
feasible without first conducting the survey, whereupon Tanzania invited a Chinese team to make it. Subsequently, a
Canadian group undertook another part of the study. After

the Unilateral Declaration of Independence, airlifts of copper
out of and gasoline into Zambia were organized under British,
United States, and Canadian auspices, from Leopoldville and
Dar-es-Salaam, and the roads between Dar-es-Salaam and the
Copperbelt were used for truck convoys of petroleum products.
Here again it could be argued that Zambia might have been
better prepared to deal with the economic consequences of
UDI had it not spent ten years in the Federation dominated
from Southern Rhodesia. Since radio broadcasting and televi-
sion came under federal control, it also seemed plausible that
Zambia and Malawi would have started sooner than they were
in fact able to do, with the organization of their own broadcasting systems, geared to achievement of their own "national
goals," in the order of priority that their leaders assigned to
these goals. The economic benefits of federation, to conclude,
were either rejected as irrelevant by those who were "seeking
the political kingdom first," or were simply denied, or were
looked upon as part and parcel of a sort of conspiracy on the
part of the white settlers to maintain themselves in control
of as much of Central Africa, and for as long, as possible.

If we take at face value the most discussed phrase of the
Preamble to the federal constitution, about partnership, as
signifying the founders' intention to improve relations between
the two major races and, for this purpose, moving toward
elimination of the grosser forms of discrimination against
Africans, then the achievements of the Federation in this area
would have to be considered greater than in the field of economic progress. In all three territories, but especially in
Southern Rhodesia, a large number of discriminatory laws
and regulations were eliminated, and discriminatory practices
based more on custom than on law were reduced, in some instances by being outlawed.

Since the federal constitution provided for African members of parliament from all three territories, Southern Rhodesian Africans gained a kind of representation they had
never before enjoyed. The federal civil service admitted
Africans to higher positions than they had previously occu-
pied in either the Southern Rhodesian civil service or the
Colonial Service which administered the two northern terri-

tories. Since postal service was a federal function under the constitution, discrimination in post offices, previously practiced especially in Southern Rhodesia, was abolished. The University College of Rhodesia and Nyasaland, established in Salisbury, was multiracial from the outset, partly as a token of good intentions, partly because all higher education was a federal function. The Southern Rhodesian Legislative Assembly passed a bill exempting the site of the University College from the provisions of territorial legislation for residential segregation. Similar Southern Rhodesian legislation made it possible for an African barrister to have his office in the white business district of the federal capital city. Toward the end of federation, the Federal Supreme Court decided that racial segregation in the municipal swimming pools of Salisbury was illegal, and this decision was accepted by the white population without violence or other demonstrations. (The high standard of living among whites in Southern Rhodesia made possible construction of a large number of private swimming pools, so that they could perhaps "afford" this relative indifference to desegregation.)

Discrimination against Africans in retail establishments, like butcher shops, was fought in Northern Rhodesia by a boycott and had been virtually eliminated in all three territories some time before the end of federation. Private firms began to employ Africans in the middle and, rarely, the higher levels of the industrial hierarchy in the last two years before December, 1963. Meanwhile, Africans were making considerable political and constitutional progress in Northern Rhodesia and Nyasaland. The number of Africans appointed and then elected members of their Legislative Councils steadily increased. Half-way in the decade of federation, Africans were appointed ministers in the two territorial governments. At times, the Colonial Service appeared to be giving encouragement to the organization of the African National Congresses in the northern territories, even though their opposition to federation had been made perfectly clear before its founding, and steadily grew after 1953. In retrospect, it seems that without federation neither of the two independence movements would have been able to increase its following as quickly and organize it as efficiently as was in fact the case. For example, Dr. Banda was still in England, and later in Ghana, when the Federation was established. He did not return home to Nyasaland until 1958, after he had been invited to come back for the specific purpose of taking over leadership of the African National Congress (ANC) in its fight against federation.

Similar developments took place in Southern Rhodesia, especially after its African National Congress was outlawed, and many of its leaders arrested, during the "emergency" of 1959. The emergency was declared by the governments of Southern Rhodesia and Nyasaland, which believed themselves to be in possession of information indicating that the two ANCs were about to use violence—to assassinate the Governor of Nyasaland. In the course of security operations incidental to declaration of the emergency, about sixty Africans were killed in Nyasaland, but no whites. In Northern Rhodesia at the same time, the movement which Kenneth Kaunda had led out of the African National Congress of that territory was also placed under severe restrictions and Kaunda along with other leaders was arrested, though no formal emergency was declared. The activities of all three movements gained considerable impetus from this experience of 1959. African politicians became more self-confident than might have been the case if the several governments involved had not given them the recognition implied in arresting them and outlawing their organizations.

Since one of the main charges made by African opponents of federation was the continuation of racial discrimination, the federal government and federalist politicians tried harder than they otherwise might have, to disprove this charge. They opened the highest professional positions in the civil service to Africans (few of whom had the required qualifications), they eliminated racially-discriminatory salary scales in the federal civil service, and they tried to recruit African politicians for the ranks of their own political movement, the United Federal Party (UFP). These Africans were generally condemned as "stooges" by the leadership of the independence movements, but the presence of Africans at the public political meetings and private parliamentary caucuses of the UFP brought about a degree of integration which most Rhodesians and outside observers would have considered impossible in the years before 1953. Even the federal opposition, the Dominion Party (forerunner of the Rhodesian Front which held all fifty upper roll seats in the Southern Rhodesian Parliament at the time of the Unilateral Declaration of Independence), had an African member of parliament in its federal caucus, most of whose members were usually described as white supremacists.

Discrimination in education was also reduced in the period of federation, both in the sense that Africans were admitted on equal terms to the University College, and through the allocation of more funds than before to African primary and secondary education by the three territorial governments. The Southern Rhodesian government claimed that it was spending a higher proportion of its revenues on African education and had a higher proportion of the primary-school-age African population in school, than any territory to the north of it in all Africa. A kind of competition was conducted in this respect among the three territories, especially between the two Rhodesias. Of course, much of this *might* also have happened without federation, but it seems reasonable to suggest that the constitutional division of powers over education on a racial basis and the allocation of large funds for European primary and secondary education pushed the governments involved into justifying these arrangements by highly publicized efforts to upgrade African education.

This last suggestion explains the response of African leaders to the reduction of racial discrimination, which resembled their responses to the economic argument on behalf of federation. They could not deny that some improvements had occurred. But they did reject the improvements either as merely "token," and designed to take the political wind out of the sails of their movements, or as generally insufficient because they failed to keep "proportional" pace with the general improvement of living conditions in the Federation and the elimination of politically relevant racial discrimination all over the world. The token argument would stigmatize Africans who became federal politicians (one even became a junior minister in the federal government) as "stooges." It would point to the very high entrance requirements of the University College, which made admission hurdles so high for the small number of Africans who could obtain a secondary education in the Federation, that only about one-third of the students in the University College were Africans even by the end of federation. This rejection of desegregation also emphasized the very slow pace of the process. For example, Southern Rhodesian land law had been changed to enable African barristers to have chambers in the city of Salisbury—but only one Southern Rhodesian African had qualified for the bar by 1963, so that they considered this mere token integration. Similarly, even if it was true that the three territories were spending much more money on African primary and secondary education in 1960 than in 1950, it was equally true—according to the "proportional" argument—that expenditures for European education had also risen, though European primary and secondary schools were of such quality in 1950 that they did not require much improvement, if any. African schools, on the other hand, were in such deplorable condition and in such short supply in 1950, that the Africans claimed their tenfold expansion and improvement by right. Similar claims were advanced in connection with the general reduction in discrimination, because the African leaders were very much aware of developments in the rest of the world during this period—including the desegregation decisions of the United States Supreme Court of 1954. They therefore argued that these improvements amounted to too little, too late—after all, Africans made up a majority of more than 95 per cent of the total population of the Federation, whereas Negroes made up a minority of only 10 per cent in the United States.

The African response to measures tending to reduce legal discrimination demonstrated what we might call the "anti-Hollywood effect." Hollywood movies about revolutions used to be based on the thesis that revolutions are made by utterly disenfranchised, down-trodden, starving, practically imprisoned people. In fact, most revolutions, like the French and the Russian, have been made by people whose condition was improving considerably during the preceding period, so that they became aware of the possibilities of further marked improvements through political action. In the Federation of Rhodesia and Nyasaland, both token desegregation and real improvements in the legal and social position of Africans, rather than satisfying their desire for equality, whetted their appetite for full democracy, that is, self-government by the African majority.

The legal position of Africans probably also improved as a result of federation, but again the improvements were minor, as seen by the leaders, and the connection between the improvements and federation was too obscure to impress ordinary people. Africans in Northern Rhodesia and Nyasaland retained their status as British-protected persons, while persons born in Southern Rhodesia, whether black or white, became federal citizens by birth. Protected persons could acquire federal citizenship by applying on a form, stacks of which could be found lying around federal post offices, but few availed themselves of this opportunity.[18] Appeals from the high courts of the three territories, which before federation went to the Judicial Committee of the Privy Council in London, went to the Federal Supreme Court provided for by the federal constitution. Although neither the federal nor the territorial constitutions contained bills of rights, it was possible to appeal civil rights cases to the Federal Supreme Court on "constitutional" grounds, but this did not in fact happen to any politically significant extent. One important reason for this failure to convert political controversy into constitutional litigation (on the model, for instance, of the National Association for the Advancement of Colored People in the United States) must have been the unpopular character of the federal constitution noted above. Another was the fact that there were only two or three African lawyers who could have represented African clients and who would have been likely to take the initiative in popularizing the political possibilities of constitutional litigation among their people. Moreover, the legal systems of Southern Rhodesia and the two northern Protectorates differed, the former being based on the Dutch Roman Law in effect in South Africa, while the latter used the English Common Law and a version of the Indian Penal Code (imported from colonial India). To the extent that Africans in the northern territories gave much thought to changes in their legal status at all, they probably noticed a deterioration in it, because their top leaders were jailed or detained in Southern Rhodesia after the emergency of 1959—Kenneth Kaunda, after a trial, in Salisbury, and Dr. Hastings K. Banda, without even having charges preferred against him, in Gwelo. Again it appeared as though federation had resulted in the extension of anti-African Southern Rhodesian practices to the north.

Paradoxically, Africans made the most tangible political progress during federation as a result of measures which they won from the British government, against the federal government, in their eventually successful efforts to destroy the Federation and to gain independence for the northern territories. Since the British government had undertaken, in the constitutional Preamble, to let Northern Rhodesia and Nyasaland continue, "under the special protection of Her Majesty, to enjoy separate governments for so long as their respective peoples so desire," constitutional advancement and the broadening of the franchise for these two territories was subject to direct bargaining between their politicians, both white and black, and the British government. Every time the qualifications for the territorial franchise were lowered or greater participation in territorial government was extended to elected African members of the Legislative Councils in Lusaka and Zomba, federal politicians predicted terrible consequences. At one point, the federal government even appeared to be threatening the British government with armed intervention in Northern Rhodesia, in case the next step in constitutional advancement there should be taken over protests from Salisbury. The British government nevertheless went steadily ahead in Nyasaland and Northern Rhodesia, within the framework of its general progress towards the liquidation of its African holdings. The surprising thing was that not only Nyasaland and Northern Rhodesia progressed constitutionally towards greater African participation in government and politics, but Southern Rhodesia did so, too, when it accepted the new constitution of 1961, in a referendum.

In order to persuade the white settlers to accept successive steps of constitutional reform, the British government employed a variety of techniques. It dangled the possibility of achieving full dominion status in front the federal government, but pointed to the preambular phrase, "when those inhabitants so desire." In other words, the inhabitants of all three territories, and especially those enjoying Her Majesty's special protection, would first have to be provided with means of expressing their desires, whatever these might turn out to be. This meant that dominion status for the Federation required at the very least that the northern territorial governments should clearly enjoy the consent of the bulk of their populations. When sixty Africans were killed during the emergency operations in Nyasaland, in 1959, the British government appointed a commission of inquiry, headed by Mr. Justice Devlin. The Devlin Commission concluded that federal security forces had exceeded the limits of force reasonably required by the apparent threat from Dr. Banda's African National Congress. His *Report* suggested that more adequate legitimate channels for the expression and representation of popular African political sentiments might prevent recurrence of a similar situation. In response to the Devlin Commission, the Southern Rhodesian government appointed one of its High Court judges, Mr. Justice Beadle, to inquire into the emergency in Southern Rhodesia, which his *Report* found to have been reasonably responsive to the allegedly grave threat to security raised by its ANC.

The British government advanced loans to all three territories and the Federation, for development purposes, which at least seemed to be conditioned upon political or constitutional concessions to African demands, especially in Southern Rhodesia, over whose native policy the British government no longer had a direct control. In 1959, Prime Minister Harold Macmillan appointed another commission, headed by Lord Monckton, to advise on the review of the Constitution of Rhodesia and Nyasaland, in preparation for a constitutional review conference provided for by Article 99 of the Constitution. The terms of reference for the Monckton Commission did not clearly state that it could recommend the dissolution of the Federation, a fact used by the opposition Labour Party to refuse to participate in it, and by African political movements to refuse to give testimony before it during the Commission's extensive travels in all three territories. The four governments in Central Africa also nominated members to the Monckton Commission. Nevertheless, and despite its apparently restrictive terms of reference, its *Report* recommended that the two northern territories be given opportunities to decide the question of secession after their electorates had become more broadly representative.[19] The British government accepted these recommendations, while the federal government rejected them—but there was little it could do to prevent their implementation. Subsequently, the British government moved to make the two northern governments more broadly representative, with the result that African majorities in their Legislative Councils brought into office African ministries unequivocally committed to withdrawing their territories from the Federation. The British government, at least, must have foreseen these developments starting, at the latest, in 1960, when it was moving Tanganyika rapidly toward its independence. Voting qualifications in Nyasaland and Northern Rhodesia could not for long be kept higher than voting qualifications in Tanganyika, whose African population was considered far behind that of Northern Rhodesia, especially in terms of education. Therefore—so the British government urged—federation could be preserved only if the federal and Rhodesian governments and their white electorates were to make sufficient concessions to the two northern territories, on the federal plane, and to African demands in Southern Rhodesia, to refute the allegation that Federation was a facade for the preservation of white minority rule in Southern Rhodesia and its extension to the north.

Such arguments helped persuade the Southern Rhodesian government, the electorate in a referendum, and, for a short while, the leaders of its African political movement to accept the new Constitution of 1961. This provided for the expansion of the Legislative Assembly from thirty to sixty-five members, of whom fifteen would be elected by lower-roll voters and would therefore presumably be Africans. The Declaration of Rights contained in this Constitution has already been men-

tioned. The major African political movements again boycotted the elections that were held under this Constitution, in
1962 and 1964, and they condemned as stooges those Africans
who let themselves be elected members of parliament by
ridiculously small numbers of African voters. Nevertheless,
the African MP's were able to voice African opposition to
such repressive measures as the series of "Law and Order
Maintenance" Acts and, eventually, to the Unilateral Declaration of Independence. In other words, even though the overwhelming majority of qualified Africans did not avail themselves of their right to vote in Southern Rhodesian elections,
the Constitution of 1961, which was negotiated two years
before the dissolution of the Federation, gave Africans un-
precedented opportunities for having their political views
stated in public—opportunities which continued to exist after
UDI.

The Southern Rhodesian Constitution was negotiated during a recess of the conference to review the federal Constitution. By the time that this conference began, in London, in
the winter of 1960–61, i.e., seven years after the founding of
the Federation, the British government had already brought
about a situation which made the inclusion of the leaders of
the African independence movements of the two northern
territories in the delegations led by their Governors plausible
and indeed indispensable. The conference occasioned several
walk-outs and proceeded by fits and starts. It was recessed in
order to give the political dust in the three territories a chance
to settle, so that their negotiators could speak from positions
of clear legitimacy. The Nyasaland election of 1961, in which
Dr. Banda's renamed Malawi Congress Party won an overwhelming victory, showed in which direction things were moving. After Northern Rhodesian elections in 1962, Kenneth
Kaunda's renamed United National Independence Party and
the minority African National Congress formed a coalition
government, on December 13, 1962. In Southern Rhodesian
parliamentary elections on the next day, the United Federal
Party lost control of the Legislative Assembly to the Rhodesian
Front, which formed a new government. Finally, on March
29, 1963, R. A. Butler, British Deputy Prime Minister and

Minister responsible for Central African Affairs, recognized Northern Rhodesia's right to secede from the Federation, a concession made to Nyasaland some time before. After this, all that remained to be done before the official dissolution and death of the Federation was to make arrangements for the orderly division of its institutional and financial assets and liabilities. Appropriately, much of this was taken care of at another conference held at Victoria Falls, and again the preparations for the conference involved an intensive bargaining process, in the course of which the Southern Rhodesian government threatened nonparticipation unless it were guaranteed a time table for its independence by the British government.[20] Two and a half years later, the content of these preparatory discussions still provided material for recriminations. For example, Mr. J. H. Howman, who in 1966 served as Minister of Information, Immigration and Tourism in the cabinet of Ian Smith, wrote a letter to the editor of the London weekly, *East Africa and Rhodesia,* after the Unilateral Declaration of Independence, which read in part:

> I then turned to the question of Rhodesia's independence, for we had asked Mr. Butler to have two days of discussion with us on this subject before the Victoria Falls Conference started. I confess that after a while I became somewhat nettled by my inability to draw anything concise out of Mr. Butler, who was of course a master of diplomacy, whilst I was very much a new boy in this field.
>
> Ultimately, I well remember turning to him with that sense of exasperation that lawyers get when they deal with an evasive witness and saying: "Mr. Secretary of State, I come to the conclusion that you have no intention of granting independence to Rhodesia under any circumstances whatsoever."
>
> His response was startling. He jerked up with obvious concern—he was sitting back in an easy chair—threw up his hands, and said words to this effect: "Please, I beg of you not to think that. The immediate problem facing us is the dissolution of the Federation. Immediately that is behind us the question of the independence of

Rhodesia can follow, and I have no doubt that we shall
be able to overcome the difficulties."[21]

As things turned out, they were unable to overcome *these* difficulties, though they were able to surmount with relative ease
those of dissolution. The Royal Rhodesian Air Force, a formidable instrument of power in terms of any conceivable defense
needs of either the Federation or Southern Rhodesia, was
taken over virtually intact by Southern Rhodesia, and of the
Army, the two northern countries retained only relatively
small contingents, partly because of Southern Rhodesia's insistence, mentioned in Mr. Howman's letter, partly because
Malawi and Zambia could not have afforded to maintain major
military establishments and did not, in any case, want to do
so. This division of the federal military establishment was
undertaken despite warnings and protests from African states
at the United Nations, which predicted that Southern Rhodesia
would use the disproportionately large means of force it thus
acquired in order to resist British efforts to move it toward
majority rule and ultimately in order to escape from British
control. In the opinion of these African states, the events
surrounding the Unilateral Declaration of Independence
(UDI) fully bore out their warnings. The British government
refused to heed resolutions concerning Rhodesia that were
passed by the General Assembly of the United Nations, beginning in 1962, because it considered relations between itself
and the Federation or Southern Rhodesia an "internal affair."
    The financial assets and liabilities of the Federation were
divided among the three successor states, with the United
Kingdom undertaking to contribute funds to smooth the transitional process. The Federal Broadcasting Corporation, whose
headquarters had been in Salisbury, gave up its northern operations. In Nyasaland, territorial broadcasting was begun
already before dissolution of the Federation, over protests from
the federal government. Malawi and Zambia began to issue
their own currency and postage stamps, and the Central Bank
of the Federation restricted its activities to Southern Rhodesia.
The Rhodesia Railways, Kariba Dam, and the Central African

Airways were placed under the control of joint boards, controlled by the Southern Rhodesian and Zambian governments in the case of the first two, and by all three governments in the case of CAA. In all three cases, these jointly controlled boards continued to operate for some time after UDI, though not always without friction. For the Rhodesia Railways, quarrels arose over alleged retention of excess rolling stock by Zambia just before UDI, and out of threats of work stoppages by white employees in Zambia who felt insecure after UDI. The difficulties caused by the location of the generating equipment on the Southern Rhodesian side of Kariba Dam have already been mentioned. The Zambian government requested in vain that the British government station troops to protect this equipment against Southern Rhodesian transmission stoppages or sabotage.

The Anglo-American Corporation and Rhodesian Selection Trust moved their headquarters from Salisbury, where both had only recently completed new skyscrapers for themselves, to Lusaka—even before the final dissolution of the Federation had been announced by the British government. However, despite these and similar moves by business firms, and to the surprise of many observers, much of the trade pattern developed during the decade of Federation persisted at least until Rhodesia's Unilateral Declaration of Independence in November 1965. By this time, Zambia had become heavily dependent upon Rhodesian supplies, not only of power and coal, but also of secondary and consumers goods produced in Southern Rhodesia. Malawi, too, continued to import supplies from Rhodesia, and to export its manpower to Rhodesia at about the same rate as during federation and before. Even the sanctions imposed after UDI upon Rhodesia by the British government, with United Nations support, did not affect this trade pattern very drastically until June, 1966, except for petroleum products, since these used to reach Zambia through Rhodesia, which the United Kingdom placed under an embargo. The interdependence between Rhodesia and Zambia worked in both directions. Immediately after announcement of the oil embargo, the Rhodesian government slapped a huge surtax on coal exported from the Wankie fields to Zambia.

The surtax would have made the cost of Rhodesian coal pro-
hibitive for Zambia's copper mining industry, and it might
have started to import coal from extra-African sources or tried
to return, as an emergency measure, to the previous practice
of using firewood cut in the Zambian bush. In any case, the
Rhodesian government revoked the surcharge before it became effective. On the other hand, the Zambian government
repeatedly postponed a complete cut in trade relations with
Rhodesia which was being planned with British cooperation,
initially to go into effect in February, 1966. It proved too difficult to find alternate sources of supply or, at any rate, to
find routes and means of transport that did not have to pass
through Rhodesian territory on their way to Zambia. In this
respect, ten years of federation had so strengthened the economic integration begun much earlier, that neither the formal
dissolution of Federation nor the abrupt though nonviolent rebellion of the white settlers, combined with the purposeful application of British power and the authority of the United
Nations, was able immediately to untie these bonds entirely.

Equally surprising for most observers was the extent to
which certain types of political ties were retained among the
three territories after dissolution. Of course, Southern Rhodesia no longer had means for exercising control over Malawi
and Zambia. In fact, its constitutional status fell behind that
of the two African states when these achieved full independence—and this particularly irked the white settlers, because
their colony had, after all, enjoyed responsible government
since 1923, while Malawi and Zambia had achieved that status
only little more than a year prior to independence. Nor did
the three countries exchange diplomatic representation which,
since all were members of the Commonwealth, would have
been provided by high commissioners or commissioners. But
informal contacts were maintained, not only through the
power, railway and airways boards, on which ministers
periodically met one another, but also through other exchanges,
including correspondence between the Zambian and Rhodesian
heads of government. There were also opportunities to use
London and the British government for purposes of political
communication, since all three countries remained members of

the Commonwealth and were represented in Britain by high commissioners.

At the Commonwealth Prime Ministers Conference of 1964, only Dr. Banda participated, as Prime Minister of Malawi, which had just become independent. Dr. Kaunda of Zambia could not attend, because he became President of the Republic with Zambia's achievement of independence three months too late. And the Prime Minister of Rhodesia was not permitted to attend, largely as a result of opposition from other African and Asian members of the Commonwealth, because of his government's refusal to grant its African population equal political rights. African Commonwealth members other than Zambia and Malawi apparently played a stronger role than these two former fellows of Rhodesia in urging the British government to apply increasing pressure to Rhodesia for African political advancement. Partly in response to this African pressure from within the Commonwealth, the Rhodesian government finally, after prolonged backing and filling, declared its independence from the United Kingdom. After this and following a call from the Organization of African Unity (OAU) that all its members break diplomatic relations with Great Britain unless it put an end to the rebellion by force of arms if necessary, only Tanzania and Ghana (until the overthrow of President Nkrumah) of all the Commonwealth members did in fact break relations. Zambia called for and received some military assistance and economic aid, including the British, United States, and Canadian supplied airlift. For Malawi, Prime Minister Banda urged caution in proceeding against Rhodesia, whose army and air force he considered so strong that they would immediately route any forces that the OAU could possibly marshal against them.

The process of dissolving the Federation had taken considerable time and, even after UDI, had not completely disrupted the patterns of relationships brought into being, or confirmed, by the decade of federation. Equally remarkable was the fact that the formal process of dissolution had proceeded as smoothly as it had, despite the threats to resort to violence made by both the federal government, white settlers, and spokesmen for the independence movements during the years leading up to December 31, 1963. Though occasional outbursts of violence within each of the three territories took place, starting with the emergency of 1959, no violence between them ever occurred.

THE REASON WHY

Why did the Federation of Rhodesia and Nyasaland fail? To this simple question, the simple answer is: because it never resolved the crucial issue of race relations in Southern Rhodesia. Measures taken in Northern Rhodesia and Nyasaland, mainly by the British government and in response to pressures from the African independence movements, demonstrated during the life of the Federation that it was entirely possible and within the power of the Southern Rhodesian government to resolve its central issue, by moving in the direction of equal political rights for its African majority. Some such moves were made, as in the Constitution of 1961 and through beginning steps towards eventual abolition of the Land Apportionment Act that provided the main foundation of discrimination. But all of these moves evidenced so much reluctance on the part of the ruling whites in Southern Rhodesia, that their reflection on the federal level clearly suggested to Africans in the northern territories that no Southern Rhodesian government in the foreseeable future was likely to show true commitment to those goals of federation which mattered most to the Africans themselves. After the United Federal Party lost the Southern Rhodesian election of December, 1962, to the Rhodesian Front, headed by the former leader of the Federal opposition party, Mr. Winston Field, the Southern Rhodesian government was no longer committed to continuing the Federation. When Prime Minister Field led his delegation to the dissolution conference at Victoria Falls in June, 1963, all three territorial governments and Great Britain were committed to ending federation, and even Sir Roy Welensky's lame-duck federal government had reconciled itself to the inevitable, concentrating its efforts upon retaining a maximum of the spoils of break-up for Southern Rhodesia.

Could Southern Rhodesia's racial problem have been solved? Because of the irreversibility of history, we cannot answer this question with assurance, but it does seems that stronger commitment to "genuine partnership" *and* more intelligently designed constitutional arrangements could have been used to absorb the Southern Rhodesian problem within the wider arena of the three territories. Unfortunately, both commitment and constitutional devices, instead of being strengthened during the last half of the Federation, were being weakened. Black Africa's rapid advance toward full independence, and especially the series of crises that began in the neighboring Congo in 1960, led even many Europeans in Rhodesia who had originally been hopeful about the possibility of building a truly multiracial Federation to surrender this hope. The majority of white settlers had probably never shared it, and Africans in all three territories sensed this and the decline in positive commitment to the ideal of partnership, at the very same time that they too became aware of apparently inexorable progress in the decolonization of Africa. Every time that a Southern Rhodesian government seemed willing to make the concessions that Africans had demanded three and five years earlier, African demands had already been doubled, so that everything they gained came too little, too late.

If stronger commitment to genuine partnership in Southern Rhodesia might have solved its racial problem, then the question about the reasons for the failure of the Federation becomes more complicated, and the answer to it also revolves around the fulcrum of commitment. From this point of view, we could say that the Federation failed, because no one who mattered was sufficiently committed to its success. In fact, most of those whose support was indispensable for the success of the Federation were committed to its failure. In retrospect, this seems true not only in the sense that various participants were pursuing contradictory and even mutually incompatible goals—that, after all, has often been true also in the more direct sense of commitment to the failure of the Federation itself, regardless of *its* goals, failure, i.e., of efforts to bring about some enduring political cohesion among the territories of Southern and Northern Rhodesia and Nyasaland.

Contradictions in the goals of the participants in and con-

tributors to the federal scheme have already become evident
and can be demonstrated more clearly than outright commitment to failure. The white settlers, the Colonial Office and
other branches of the British government, the commercial
companies, and the involuntarily included Africans were all
pursuing different sets of goals. Their various *overt* attitudes
were incorporated, to varying degrees, in the federal Constitution. The Constitution, as a result, became a series of petty
little compromises that were bound over the longer run to
alienate even those whose demands had been temporarily satisfied by the compromises. This was true, for example, of the
inconsistent division of functions, and of the very definition of
the "long run" for the Federation, in the provision of constitutional review after seven and before nine years had elapsed.

Covert commitment to failure of the Federation is harder
to demonstrate, especially if we wish to avoid the fallacy of
arguing *post hoc, ergo propter hoc*. In order to illustrate the
possibility of such covert commitment, and *only* for that purpose, we might paint a picture of the extreme cynicism and
hypocrisy by which some contributors to Central African federalism might have been motivated in the years before 1953:

(1) *The British government* realized that they would
have to grant independence to both Nyasaland and Northern
Rhodesia within the next decade or two, because of developments in East Africa. Neither of the two territories had well-
organized independence movements at the time. Federation,
by focusing African opposition upon itself, would stimulate
African political consciousness and, through federal institutions, would provide more Africans with parliamentary experience than existing territorial institutions could. Moreover,
Southern Rhodesia's white settlers might learn to live with
less segregation and less exploitation than they had grown accustomed to, partly as a result of the racial lessons of economic
expansion. And even if the white settlers would not accept
"genuine partnership"—whatever that might mean—after ten
years, they would by then nevertheless be less likely to opt for
joining South Africa.

(2) *The white settlers* were willing to make some insig-
nificant concessions to Africans on racial policy, so long as

they secured a monopoly of organized force in the three territories, because, after all, the only thing that mattered was
possession of military and police strength. Certainly strength
was the only thing the Africans understood.

(3) *The great companies* expected that their investments
in the promotion of federation would repay in the form of
higher royalties and land values, and in lower government
regulation from governments owing them some political obligations.

In this "cynical" interpretation, none of the principals
was primarily committed to the success of the Federation.
Each was more or less committed to primary goals that were
incompatible with at least some of the avowed, constitutionally
stated goals of the Federation: The British government was
really opposed to full dominion status for the Federation as
it was then constituted. The white settlers were *really* opposed
to racial partnership in territorial and federal politics. The
commercial companies were *really* at best merely uninterested
in anything political, hoping that minor "concessions" would
keep their profits rising regardless of constitutional arrangements in Central Africa.

This picture of cynicism and hypocrisy is not meant as
a realistic or a fair description. None of the parties ever conducted himself in a manner that would warrant the attri-
bution of so much cunning, cleverness, or foresight. The
point of this hypothetical reconstruction is simply to suggest
that, in addition to overt commitments, covert commitments
also may have made their contribution, and that, in addition
to conscious and stated motives, subconscious and unstated
ones also may have played a role.

All of this, if it is at all accurate and if we put it together
with the history of the other federal failures, points to an important difference between federations brought into existence
since World War II, and the older, "conventional" federations
—the United States, Canada, Australia, Switzerland, Germany—which have often been used as models. The contemporary federations should not be viewed by analogy to the
older, classical federal systems, which *were* meant to last, to
endure, or which were in the words of Chief Justice Marshall,

"designed to be permanent." The contemporary federations were not meant to be permanent—otherwise their constitutions would not have contained provisions for their own review after a stated period of time. This was true of all four federations considered in this book, and also of some other contemporary federal or proto-federal arrangements, like Western European Union. Our federations were meant essentially as makeshift arrangements designed to facilitate the transition from colonialism to independence (or, in the western European case, from full national sovereignty to whatever it is that inter"national" politics may be moving toward). By "federating" several colonies at different stages of constitutional advancement toward full independence, the British government was able to affect the average elapsed time before independence, to reduce the overall incidence of violence, and to shape constitutional forms and international alignments of the post-independence period. This pre-manipulation was made all the more effective precisely through employment of all the symbolism of federalism and action based on the false analogy to the older, conventional, "true" federations.

If our estimate of the intentions of the British government (muddling through as perceptively as usual) is reasonably accurate, then the Federation of Rhodesia and Nyasaland was in that particular sense, not a failure—regardless of what happens in Southern Rhodesia in 1966 and thereafter.

NOTES

1. Accord, Ronald Watts, *New Federations* (London: Oxford University Press, 1966), pp. 108–109.

2. Quoted by Sir Stewart Gore-Brown, "Note for Monckton Commission," (Shiwa Ng'andu, March 8, 1960, mimeographed).

3. *Memorandum on Native Policy in East Africa*, Cmd. 3573, H.M.S.O., (June, 1930).

4. *Rhodesia-Nyasaland Royal Commission Report*, Cmd. 5949, H.M.S.O. (1939).

5. Lord Hailey, *Note on the Bearing of Native Policy on the Proposed Amalgamation of the Rhodesias and Nyasaland* (confidential; London: H.S.M.O., 1941).

6. *Central African Territories: Report of the Conference on*

Closer Association, Cmd. 8233, H.M.S.O. (1951).

7. Robert I. Rotberg, *The Rise of Nationalism in Central Africa: The Making of Malawi and Zambia 1873–1964* (Cambridge: Harvard University Press, 1965), p. 227, n. 29.

8. *Statutory Instruments 1953 No. 1199, Rhodesia and Nyasaland Federation, The Federation of Rhodesia and Nyasaland (Constitution) Order in Council, 1953.* London, Aug. 1, 1953.

9. Constitution Amendment Act. 1957, Article 2.

10. See R. L. Watts, p. 163.

11. For details of the election laws, see Spiro, "The Rhodesias and Nyasaland," in *Five African States: Responses to Diversity,* Gwendolen M. Carter, ed. (Ithaca: Cornell University Press, 1963), pp. 432–39.

12. See Chapter 4, "Constitutional Crisis," in Gwendolen M. Carter, *The Politics of Inequality: South Africa since 1948* (2nd ed.; New York: Praeger, 1959).

13. "The reason for the failure of the Central African federation was that, like Pakistan, it was too centralized for the society on which it was imposed. The federal constitution, worked out as a bargain between the settlers and the British Government, failed to give sufficient expression to the realities of the African anxieties." R. L. Watts, p. 350.

14. Statutory Instruments 1961 No. 2314, Rhodesia and Nyasaland Federation, "The Southern Rhodesia (Construction) Order in Council, 1961."

15. For instance, Section 58:
(1) No person shall be deprived of his personal liberty save in the following cases, that is to say—
(a) in consequence of his unfit-

ness to plead to a criminal charge:
(b) in execution of the sentence or the order of a court, whether in Southern Rhodesia or elsewhere, in respect of a criminal offence of which he has been convicted; . . .
(h) for the purpose of preventing the spread of an infectious or contagious disease; . . .
(k) to such an extent as may be necessary for the execution of a lawful order requiring that person to remain within Southern Rhodesia or prohibiting him from being within such an area, or to such an extent as may be reasonably justifiable—
(i) for the taking of proceedings against that person relating to the making of such an order; or
(ii) for restraining that person during any visit which he is permitted to make to any part of Southern Rhodesia in which, in consequence of such an order, his presence would otherwise be unlawful.

16. Frederick A. O. Schwarz, in his study of the Federation of Nigeria, comments upon the same phenomenon and provides plausible explanations of it:

"But though the rights guaranteed are many, the exceptions to the guarantees, concise and prolix, specific and vague, could well render them symbolic rather than real protections and at the same time deprive them of much of their effect as symbols. What is given with one breath is taken away with the next as broad right is followed with broad exception." *Nigeria: The Tribes, the Nation, or the Race— The Politics of Independence* (Cambridge: M.I.T. Press, 1965), p. 180.

"Spelling out the exceptions in copious fashion makes the constitutional guarantees much less useful as an educative tool with which to imbue the people with the spirit of liberty. Laws can change attitudes, and none more than constitutions. But to do so they should be simply expressed. The school child who is taught that free speech is guaranteed with no ifs, ands, or buts is bound to develop a different instinctive reaction toward restrictions of free speech than the school child who is told that free speech is guaranteed except in several enumerated situations. Perhaps the greatest drawback to the way in which Nigeria's Bill of Rights is written is that it is dull. With all its carefully elaborated exclusions and the prolix and complicated exceptions, it becomes just another law. Lacking majesty, it is written for lawyers, not for the people." *Ibid.*, p. 182. A footnote continues:

"The precise, legalistic way in which judges and lawyers trained in the British tradition have usually interpreted constitutions is likely to make it difficult for them to tie the constitution to life and history, as is necessary to make it meaningful. Dean Griswold of the Harvard Law School has proposed the theory that the prolixity of the Nigerian Bill of Rights stems from the British tradition of statutory interpretation and legislative drafting. Statutes are interpreted literally as if they have a 'plain meaning' and constitutions, since they are regarded as statutes though they are written for the ages, cannot therefore be left with broad and sweeping language. He also points out that because of the nature of a constitution the attempt to be precise and certain would inevitably fail, as in fact it did. What exactly does 'reasonably justifiable in a democratic society' mean?"

"The British tradition can be influential in other ways. It tends to reinforce the fundamental rights provisions that deal with a fair criminal procedure because the tradition of fair trials and fair police practices have developed without a written constitution in British traditions and Judges' Rules. In this regard, it is perhaps significant that the only Supreme Court decisions holding that the fundamental rights provisions had been violated . . . involved the fair procedure provisions of the Constitution. On the other hand, Britain has a preventive detention law, and in the free speech field it has, despite general restraint in their use, extremely strict and repressive laws. The concept of restraints upon the supremacy of parliament is, moreover, alien to one trained in the British tradition.

"The British tradition which prohibits the courts from relying upon cases or materials other than those cited by the litigants is particularly undesirable with respect to constitutional law (where interests far wider than those of the litigants are at stake) and in countries where the experience with respect to constitutional issues is minimal. Perhaps it was that tradition that led Justice Brett . . . to quote a remark that the legislatures guard liberty and welfare to quite as great a degree as the courts (a comment which had been made by Justice Holmes in an economic regulation case) instead of referring to Justice Holmes' opinions in defense of free speech." *Ibid.*, pp. 182–83.

17. William J. Barber, *The Economy of British Central Africa* (London: Oxford University Press, 1961).

18. See S. Weinberg, *An Out-*

line of the Constitution of the Federation of Rhodesia and Nyasaland (Salisbury: Federal Government Printing, 1959), pp. 121–26.

19. *Report of the Advisory Commission on the Review of the Constitution of Rhodesia and Ny-* asaland, Cmnd. 1148 (London: H.M.S.O., October, 1960).

20. *Report of the Central Africa Conference, 1963,* Cmnd, 2093, H.M.S.O., July, 1963.

21. *East Africa and Rhodesia,* Vol. 42, No. 2155 (January 27, 1966), p. 409.

CHAPTER 3

West Indian Federation

by G. H. Flanz

INTRODUCTION

Many attempts have been made to explain the failure of the Federation of the West Indies. The subject was discussed at length in the British House of Commons, in the West Indies House of Representatives as well as in the legislatures of the component islands. In these debates, and in material in the major West Indies newspapers and in the statements made by leading politicians following the Federation's collapse, the variety of conflicting points of view may render it difficult for students unfamiliar with the Federation's history to discern the causes of the Federation's failure. Fortunately, a number of valuable articles were published within two years of the secession of Jamaica. These contributions have been supplemented by later analyses.[1]

Anyone trying to explain the reasons for the failure of the Federation of the West Indies finds himself in difficulty comparable to that of an analyst trying to explain the reasons for the failure of a marriage which began promisingly but which failed just the same. The analogy is not far-fetched. The Federation was, in the words of Premier Norman Manley of Jamaica, in the nature of a polygamous "trial marriage."

It is not difficult to identify the immediate causes of the break-up. What is difficult, however, is an assessment of the weight of various factors and issues which tended to tear the Federation apart. This assessment will begin with an inquiry into certain stages in the development of the Federation, and will be followed by an examination of the factors underlying these developments.

THE SEARCH FOR A SUITABLE FEDERAL PATTERN

In 1947 the British colonies of Jamaica, Trinidad and Barbados, together with the Windward and Leeward Islands, met at Montego Bay and agreed in principle to the establishment of a federal relationship. Four constitutional conferences were held between 1947 and 1957, supplemented by standing and *ad hoc* commissions appointed to examine various aspects of the proposed federal scheme. The Federation came into being in 1958, and in 1961 sought to revise its constitution preparatory to independence. In that year, however, Jamaica withdrew from the Federation after a local referendum had indicated popular discontent over continued membership. Following the later withdrawal of Trinidad and Tobago, the experiment came to an end.

The Federation began under the West Indian Constitution of 1957. It is generally accepted that this Constitution failed to provide for a strong central authority. Nevertheless, the system was not necessarily self-defeating, except for the important fact that most major revenue sources were left with the territories. Most of the critics of the Constitution who blame it for the failure of the federal system seem to be unaware that it was not this (1957) federal design that failed, but rather the more emasculated version that had finally emerged from the London Conference of May–June, 1961.

What came out of that Conference could be more appropriately called a confederation rather than a weak federation.

In draftsmanship, the original (1957) Constitution, which ran to fifty-eight pages, compared not unfavorably with other Commonwealth Constitutions.[2] But it could hardly be claimed that it had been carefully designed to serve as a provisional instrument to meet the specific requirements of the West Indies. Indeed, it could have been a federal blueprint for almost any other Commonwealth country. As far as the distribution of powers between territories and central government was concerned, only eighteen functions were put under the latter's exclusive jurisdiction, particularly matters of defense, exchange control, migration and emigration, the public service and the University College of the West Indies. The concurrent list, in which authority was shared, was much longer, consisting of thirty-nine specific powers, including industrial development. The severe restrictions imposed upon the Federal Government were most apparent in the prohibition of a federal income tax during the first five years.

It must be borne in mind, however, that provision was made for a mandatory review within five years. A mechanism was thus provided to redress the federal arrangement of power. But by the same token, impermanence was officially built into the federal structure. Moreover, to anyone favoring a strong federal government, the Constitution was most disappointing, being an amalgam of weaknesses and narrow-visioned compromises. "It must be recognized," J. H. Proctor, Jr. observed recently, "that these defects reflected the underlying geographic, demographic, economic and political reality. . . . The context was such that agreement could be reached only on the basis of numerous compromises which satisfied no one entirely. The alternative to federation on these admittedly imperfect terms, as the framers saw it, was not a better constitution but none at all; and they were convinced that it was of overriding importance to launch the Federation as soon as possible, since the task would only become more difficult the longer they delayed."[3]

Thus in 1956 Trinidad's centralization-minded Prime

Minister, Dr. Williams, asserted that "any federation is better that no federation,"[4] but once the Federation began operating, Dr. Williams told his Legislative Council that he had found only one federal constitution, that of the troubled Rhodesia and Nyasaland, which paralleled "this weak and anaemic Federation."[5] In vigorous and colorful language he criticized the system's financial straitjacket, and proposed an increase in federal revenue from 9 to 143 million West Indian dollars.[6] "Since 1947," he continued, "we have been able to see the same pedestrian approach which characterized the attitude to the problem of Federation in the previous century, all the previous weaknesses that I have emphasized, the absence of a comprehensive conception, the lack of clear economic perspectives; the inability of anyone to grapple with this problem of inter-territorial jealousies. All have dominated this ten- or twelve-year period since the Montego Bay Conference."[7]

Consequently, the first Inter-Governmental Conference, convened on September 28, 1959, established two ministerial committees to investigate some of the controversial issues. Committee I was concerned with constitutional and political issues, including the difficult problems of representation and freedom of movement. Committee II was to concern itself with the economic aspects of the Federation, especially the ways and means of creating a customs union. These committees set up "Working Parties" composed of officials from different parts of the West Indies to make necessary studies and to draft recommendations. Both committees, henceforth known as Alpha and Orion, got off to a promising start. On November 20, 1959, the Working Party of Alpha held its first meetings followed by a second series beginning on January 25 and 29, 1960. Official instructions and terms of reference were set out by the Chairman of Ministerial Committee I, the Federal Finance Minister, the Honorable Robert Bradshaw. The first matter taken up by Alpha was the formulation of the "essential attributes of sovereignty," i.e., a statement of the minimum powers which would render the Federation qualified for independent membership in the Commonwealth.

In the meetings of the Working Party, representatives from Trinidad and Tobago, under instructions from Dr. Williams, recorded their dissent from the official statement of "minimum criteria of sovereignty." They insisted that no sovereign state could guarantee freedom of movement to its citizens without accepting the responsibility for central economic planning and development in order to increase productivity and incomes in territories which are the source of emigration and alleviate the social and economic problems resulting in the territory of immigration. Thus even at the outset it became clear that the parties were divided on basic issues, with Barbados and some of the smaller islands immediately in opposition to Trinidad's initiative.

In the spring of 1961, as the Ministerial Committees were completing their work, it was still widely expected that the federal government would assume broader responsibilities in the fields of education, social security, labor legislation, price control, economic and social planning, and agricultural research and marketing. Nevertheless, Jamaican pressure defeated a proposal to increase the federal share of taxes on income and profits necessary to implement these powers, so that alternative revenue sources had to be considered. Jamaican influence was amply reflected in the Federal Government's *White Paper* of April 4, 1961, which set out a draft-blueprint for constitutional reform.

In reference to Committee I's proposals, the *White Paper* contained the following specific recommendations:[8]

(iv) Unit powers over matters on Exclusive List
That the Constitution should provide, as in the present Article 43 (2), for the Territorial Legislatures to legislate on matters on the Exclusive Legislative List until the Governor-General, by Proclamation, declares otherwise.

(v) Reserve List
The proposal agreed on by Committee I of the Inter-Governmental Conference, that the Federal Constitution should provide for a Reserve List, in addition to the Exclusive and Concurrent Legislative Lists, on which the subjects of Income Tax and Development of Industries would be placed for a period to be agreed.

It was agreed that while Income Tax and Industrial Development were fields in which the Federal Government should have a direct interest it was not at present proposed that the Federal Government should enter these fields, in view of the possibility that the economy of one or more Territories might be hampered or endangered should these subjects be brought under Federal control during the early years of independence.

The Procedure for transferring items from the Reserve List was referred to ALPHA, and the proposals submitted are as follows:

(a) If there is a prohibition against any such transfer for 10 years then at the end of that period the proposed amending law must be passed by each House of the Federal Legislature by an absolute majority and must then be approved by absolute majority of the representative Houses of the Legislatures of the Territories representing a majority of the electors in the Federation qualified to vote as electors at Federal elections.

(b) If there is no prohibition for any given period, the proposed amending law must be passed by each House of the Federal Legislature by a two-thirds majority and must then be approved by absolute majorities in a majority of the representative Houses of the Territorial Legislatures representing not less than two-thirds of the population of the Federation.

(vi) Residual Powers

That the power to legislate on matters which are not included in either the Exclusive or Concurrent Lists should, as at present, remain with Unit Governments.[9]

Soon after April 4, 1961, the debate began in earnest. Mr. Gomes, the veteran federationist from Trinidad, sharply attacked the *White Paper* in the Federal House of Representatives:

What these proposals suggest is a Federal Government, a national government—I emphasize that fact—that would be a prisoner of the whims of the Territories . . .

the Territories have gone too far in the effort to accommodate the chauvinistic and separatist views so rigidly and uncompromisingly asserted by Jamaica.[10]

Regarding the representation formula, Mr. Gomes reminded his colleagues that "We agreed that the larger units, while rightly receiving greater representation than the smaller, should not do so in the strict proportion to their populations but in a diminishing proportion."[11] There was no doubt in his mind that the proposed amendments constituted backward rather than forward steps and that Alpha had gone much too far in accommodating Jamaica and her Prime Minister Manley:

Jamaica seems to want everything out of the Federation, and wants to give nothing to it, and that's a plain fact. She wants maximum representation that will put her in a position where she will virtually supplant Whitehall. All it would mean is that Whitehall could cease to be, and Kingston would take over.[12]

Despite the obvious rifts separating its members, the Federal Government decided to go ahead with the planned Intergovernmental Conference (IGC) in Port of Spain and the London Conference of May–June, 1961. Sir Grantley Adams, Prime Minister of the Federation told his people in a broadcast that "If we miss this train, there may not be another one coming along in our time." The *Trinidad Guardian* summarized Sir Grantley's position in this way: "To develop the West Indies as a whole, to strive for the economic development of each Unit, not with a fragmentary approach but looking forward to the economic growth of the whole Federation— this in Sir Grantley's eyes is the ideal towards which our endeavours should be directed."[13] Yet the *Guardian* conceded that the ideal might not be immediately attainable and that concessions and compromises might be necessary to hold the parley together.

On May 21, 1961, ninety-three delegates and advisors assembled in Port of Spain to seek basic agreements that were to pave the way toward full independence.[14] Predictably, the Conference failed to resolve the heated issue of interterritorial freedom of movement which had become intertwined with the dispute over central economic planning. The proposals presented by the Chairman of the Conference proved unacceptable to the Federal Government, Barbados, Dominica, St. Kitts and St. Lucia. The other delegations were prepared to accept the following recommendations:

(1) Freedom of movement should be proclaimed in the Constitution as a fundamental objective of the Federation.

(2) Such a declaration would not invalidate legislation (territorial or federal) designed to protect the public order.

(3) Control over the movement of persons would be a federal responsibility and thus appear on the Exclusive List.

(4) However, these powers would not become operative for a period of nine years after independence except with the concurrence of all unit governments.

(5) There was to be a review after four years by the Federal Government and the unit territories to determine whether the waiting period should be shortened.

(6) No further restrictions were to be imposed upon freedom of movement by any unit territory without the consent of the Federal Government.

(7) After a stipulated period, each territory would have the right to enact, with the consent of the Federal Government, legislation and measures designed to protect itself against economic disruptions resulting from interterritorial migration.

(8) In cooperation with the territorial governments, the Federal Government was to work out an interim development plan whose primary aim would be to increase employment opportunities.[15]

The last stipulation was obviously quite unrealistic and was later rejected at the London Conference. The remaining "yes-but" proposals were merely an affirmation of the principle of the freedom of movement as an objective to be pursued in the years to come.[16]

Notwithstanding the failure at Port of Spain, Mr. Manley

on June 1, 1961, told the London Conference that there were "sharp differences of opinion about the form of federation we are to start with. These are differences about important details. But there can be no difference about the question that Federation for us is historically inevitable, nor can we doubt that shape it how we may today, it will grow and develop as necessity and advantage will dictate."[17] Mr. Manley failed to add, however, that it was becoming increasingly obvious that "necessity and advantage" for Trinidad would probably be considered unnecessary and disadvantageous for Jamaica.[18]

The London Conference made very few final decisions.[19] The issues of customs union, the Reserve List, freedom of movement, and even the date for independence were not finally settled. As for financial support for the Federation, the Conference reluctantly accepted the Jamaican contention that the Federal Government should draw its revenue from customs duties with the understanding that this formula ought to be reviewed after three years. Even so, Barbados, St. Kitts and St. Lucia voted against the recommendation. The *West Indian Economist* commented:

> The Federation has now been pared down to what Jamaica says she wants. It is up to Jamaica to accept it. If anything is wrong with the Federation now, Jamaica is to blame. . . . There is no point in continuing to talk about "independence" in isolation when the economy may at any time need external support, and the present political system makes heavy demands on the available ability and financial resources.[20]

THE JAMAICAN REFERENDUM AND ITS AFTERMATH

But Jamaica did not accept "it."

Shortly after the Inter-Governmental Conference, Premier Manley of Jamaica went forward with plans for a referendum on the issue of Jamaica's continued membership in the Federation. On July 18, 1961, The Federal House of Representatives approved the regulations which were to govern the referendum and subsequently passed the Federal Referendum Bill. On August 3, Mr. Manley announced that the referendum would take place on September 19, 1961. In June, 1961, the People's National Party (PNP) under Manley's direction published two pamphlets containing the most specific kind of information ever presented to the people of Jamaica concerning the whole issue of "federation."[21] The PNP argued that continued membership in the Federation was not only practical but indispensable. In contradiction to those who had insisted that "federation" would be costly and therefore would require increased taxation, the PNP pamphlets put great emphasis upon the savings that it expected to result from continued federal association:

> The true costs caused by Federation will only amount to about half a million pounds [$1,400,000], just a little over 1% of what we spend a year. The costs of independence are much greater. In about five years they may well amount to 3 million pounds [$8,400,00]. It is much cheaper to share the cost of Independence with other Islands than to try to go it alone.[22]

In his presentation, Mr. Manley pointed out that Jamaica was currently paying 43 per cent of the total federal expenditures and that this would increase to about 146 per cent during the next decade.[23] In a highly detailed accounting, he noted that none of the federal services made available to Jamaica since the beginning of the Federation had involved increased expenses to Jamaica over pre-Federation *ad hoc* provision of these services. Summing up, Mr. Manley balanced the savings to be derived and the added expenses to be incurred if federation were to end: "It will cost us nearly £1 million [$2,800,000] more going it alone than sharing . . . in Federation. It comes to this then: by leaving Federation we save £400,000 [$1,120,000] and we spend about £1 million more [$2,800,000]."[24]

The premier's figures were not accepted by the opposition

Jamaica Labour Party (JLP) led by Sir Alexander Bustamante. During the referendum campaign they insisted that an independent Jamaica would cost its taxpayers £200,000 ($560,000) less than Jamaica in the Federation.[25] The two estimates faced the voters with a dilemma. There had been much very general discussion about the advantages and disadvantages of Jamaica's membership in the Federation but comparatively little specific data had been disseminated concerning the economic aspects. The PNP's detailed presentation was an attempt at something better. It was suitable for the Jamaican intelligentsia, which formed the nucleus of the PNP's strength. Unfortunately, not nearly enough was done to make this information digestible by the masses. In June, 1961, after Manley returned from his triumphs at the InterGovernmental Conference in Port of Spain and the London Conference, he was in the best possible position to exploit his extraordinary popular appeal. Although he campaigned vigorously and with full coverage from the press, the issues could have been stated in simpler language and the opposition arguments more fully taken into account. There should have been many more broadcasts during the crucial weeks of July. The less intellectual, more popular appeals of the Jamaican Labour Party, headed by Sir Alexander Bustamante, the veteran politician, as well as the antifederation campaign of the People's Political Party (PPP), which purported to speak for Black Jamaicans, proved too much for Mr. Manley's forces.[26] On September 19, with only 60 per cent of the electorate participating, 55 per cent voted against remaining in the Federation.[27]

Widely differing opinions are still being expressed as to how different the results might have been had there been a larger participation. While it is by no means obvious that a larger vote would have resulted in more "yes" votes, few people would question that the vote could easily have gone the other way. Nevertheless, had the percentages been reversed, it would still not have constituted the kind of mandate which would have ensured Jamaica's becoming a permanent foundation on which to build a federation.

In October, 1961, the *West Indian Economist* noted in an editorial that

Voting was fairly closely on party lines and if the electorate did not grasp the real issue, it was because both
parties failed to put the important political concepts of
Federation and separatism before it. But the incapacity
of the parties to deal with ideas is part of the general
political situation. It is certainly related to the curious
eremitical conception of life, so widespread in Jamaica,
which now condemns it to isolation. While parties are to
blame for not dealing with ideas, it is only fair to say
that no one wants them to do so, and that a country which
shrinks from ideas cannot wish for union with others,
since the object of such a union is, very largely, to give
greater freedom to the play of ideas.

In any case, Mr. Manley was quick to accept this "mandate of the people" and proceeded to take the necessary steps
that would bring independence to Jamaica at the earliest possible date.[28] For a time, some of the smaller islands nourished
the hope of establishing a federation along more centralized
lines without Jamaica. An unduly optimistic note was struck
in an editorial which appeared on September 30, 1961, in *The
Voice of St. Lucia*:

We do not mourn the demise of the London plan of June
this year. We never entertained a high opinion of the Constitution which emerged from these and preceding talks
and we recognize that its weaknesses were forced upon
the rest of the territories by Jamaica.
While the departure of Jamaica from our group is to be
regretted, on purely nationalistic grounds, if Jamaica's
absence will permit us to plan a smaller Federation, less
ambitious in scope but sounder in structure, then it may
well be that we shall be left with something capable of
surviving, capable of being constructive and able to grow.
The opportunity for leadership which this situation offers
to Trinidad and Tobago is one which that territory, in
sober mood, can hardly afford to throw away.

After the Jamaican Referendum, the center of attention

shifted to Trinidad and particularly to its leader, Dr. Eric Williams. To some it seemed reasonable to assume that Dr. Williams could now seize upon this opportunity to rebuild the Federation along the lines that he had always advocated. On the other hand, Dr. Williams had repeatedly stated, especially in May and June, 1961, that if Jamaica were to withdraw, Trinidad and Tobago could not carry the entire burden.

During the fall of 1961, Dr. Williams kept everybody guessing. The opposition party, the Democratic Labour Party (DLP), pledged itself to support Trinidad's continued membership in the Federation. But Dr. Williams declared that continued membership or withdrawal from the Federation was not an election issue and that his government would make its decision after the elections.

In the December elections Williams' People's National Movement (PNM) scored an impressive but bitterly contested victory, increasing its majority in the House of Representatives to twenty seats against ten for the DLP.

With this impressive popular mandate behind them the PNM was ready to make its decision concerning the future of the Federation. On January 27, 1962, in a long and well-reasoned statement, the PNM announced Trinidad and Tobago's withdrawal from the Federation.

Dr. Williams presented the withdrawal of Trinidad and Tobago and the dissolution of the Federation as inevitable consequences of Jamaica's secession: "Thereupon, the Government of Trinidad and Tobago took the stand that the secession of one territory meant the abandonment of the 1956 compact for the Federation of ten territories. The Trinidad and Tobago slogan was '1 from 10 leaves 0.' "[29]

WHY DID THE WEST INDIES FEDERATION FAIL?

The more one delves into the background of the Federation and studies its transformation during the first three and a half years, the more one becomes convinced that there were a number of important factors which made the failure almost

inescapable. The basic problems of the Federation were caused
by geographical and historical factors, which were aggravated
by deep-rooted attitudes of insularism and petty nationalism.
These divisive forces were reinforced by economic factors, and
particularly by the uneven economic development of the different territories before and during federation. (This was
especially true in the case of Jamaica and Trinidad, where
the significant progress made in certain key industries
prompted some influential individuals to assert that these
islands would be better off unburdened with the responsibility
for the improvement of the much poorer small islands.) These
major difficulties were further compounded by defects in
political institutions and in leadership, and tangentally by the
lack of a credible external threat—even Fidel Castro was not
taken very seriously as such by Jamaicans—which might have
fostered West Indian unity.[30]

We shall examine briefly the more constant and relatively
clear geographic and historical factors which led to the Federation's failure, and then treat in detail the more sophisticated
economic and political conflicts.

GEOGRAPHICAL AND HISTORICAL FACTORS

The geographic factors require little elaboration. A look
at the map suggests that the distance between Jamaica and
Trinidad is too great to be bridged effectively by inter-territorial associations. Even in our age, a distance of 1,250 miles
represents a tremendous obstacle for political union. Much
progress has been made in improving inter-island air transportation and communications. But for most West Indians, jet
transportation is still too expensive and inter-island sea transport is too slow. The result is that the inhabitants of Jamaica
are unacquainted with those in Trinidad and the eastern
Caribbean.

However, when some people speak of the "geographical
absurdity" of the West Indian Federation, they should remem-
ber that the original plan of the Federation included not only
British Guiana but also British Honduras. Had these terri-

tories joined, it would have made a great deal of difference from an economic point of view. It would also have placed Jamaica in a more central position, economically, geographically, and politically.[31]

Prominent historians of the West Indies, such as Eric Williams, have concluded that isolationism, rather than centralism, is part of a historic Caribbean tradition.[32] The failure of the British Colonial Office during the first half of the twentieth century to move more emphatically to establish common institutions among the islands no doubt tolerated and encouraged this insular tendency. As late as 1940, the officials concerned with the administration of Colonial Development and Welfare funds were admonished that there was to be "no derogation from the rights and privileges of local legislatures, upon whom rests a large measure of responsibility for the improvement of conditions in their several territories. . . ."[33] The creation of the Caribbean Commission in 1940 failed to result in a drastic reorganization of the inter-island administrative machinery because the Commission cooperated closely with the existing Colonial Development and Welfare bureaucracy which did not alter its *modus operandi*. In any event, the Commission's role was only advisory and consultative. Definite encouragement for regional planning was not given until after World War II. In noting Britain's late and sporadic interest in moving toward some type of federation in the West Indies, Thomas G. Matthews has pointed out that "At first this interest was motivated almost solely by anticipated economies in a more centralized colonial administration."[34]

On the other hand, as for the West Indians themselves, it has been observed that "There has always been some truth in the view that federation and West Indian nationhood were born in Toronto and London rather than in the Caribbean. It was the West Indian abroad who felt the common bond of history, it was the West Indian who stayed at home who objected to any wider union."[35] For the most part, these West Indians, as they came to know each other in English universities, developed interpersonal and interterritorial loyalties to which they remained strongly committed after their return, although some of them who entered politics found it necessary or expedient to express more nationalistic views. Others, moreover, turned this factor around to claim that federation was essentially a British (and Canadian) product, serving not the interests of the West Indies but of the Empire.

The people in the small islands of the East Caribbean must also be seen to have developed a different outlook from that prevalent in Jamaica. They tended to feel a closer kinship with the people of Trinidad. Indeed, many prominent Trinidadians came from Barbados, Grenada or St. Vincent. Dr. Williams, whose ancestors came from Barbados, had as his ideal not so much a federation composed of the British West Indies but rather a multilingual, Caribbean Pan-Antillean federation.

But even Eric Williams has reluctantly asserted that isolationism, rather than cooperation, is part of the traditional Caribbean outlook.

In 1947, at the Montego Bay Conference, the Colonial Office obtained West Indian assent for a "trial" federation which would be granted independence if it proved successful. Almost at once, the geographic problem arose in the form of a confrontation.

Even before the Federation came into existence in 1958, the traditional nationalistic attitudes of each of the West Indian territories had come into conflict regarding the location of the federal capital. The decision to locate the capital in Port of Spain, Trinidad, was made in 1957. It disregarded recommendations made by a Special Site Commission composed entirely of British members, which had recommended Barbados and Jamaica ahead of Trinidad. The Commission, unhappily, had also made some insensitive remarks concerning alleged political instability of Trinidad, and stressed that Barbados was the most "British" of all the islands.[36] These statements resulted in the rejection of Barbados to the annoyance of many Jamaicans who for political and geographic reasons would have preferred either Barbados or centrally located Antigua to Port of Spain which was the farthest removed from Jamaica—certainly geographically and perhaps politically.[37] From the very outset, then, factors of history and geography of the West Indies worked to divide the new Federation.

ECONOMIC FACTORS AND CONFLICTS

There are some well-informed observers who feel that of all the factors, the economic one deserves primary attention. I am inclined to agree with this provided that one is referring to the final stages of the Federation. In the early stages of the indigenous West Indian Federal movement, i.e., during the 1920's and 1930's, the economic factor received, perhaps mistakenly, very little attention. To those who advocated it, federation was an ideal and an ideology which could not afford to be weakened by adverse economic calculations. A few months after the failure of the Federation, Dr. Williams gave a political summary of the basic economic differences between Jamaica and Trinidad:

> Jamaica wanted a loose confederation with limited revenues and limited powers, based on a customs union among the territories which excluded significant products of its own. Jamaica advocated a federal government whose revenues were derived from import duties and which had no powers whatsoever over income tax and industrial development. Trinidad and Tobago, on the other hand, led the fight for a strong central government with adequate revenues to carry out the inescapable responsibilities of a new independent state. The government of Trinidad and Tobago advocated customs union, freedom of movement of labour and capital throughout the Federation, a single West Indian currency, a Central Bank, and federal powers over income tax and industrial development.[38]

CONFLICTS IN THE INDUSTRIAL SECTOR

All the islands have certain common economic characteristics. They are all predominantly agricultural and the standard of living is relatively low. It should be noted, however, that in Jamaica and Trinidad, the relative importance of agriculture had already begun to decline significantly even before the Federation was formed. In the initial years of the Federation, both islands made further impressive advances in their industrial development. In Jamaica progress was due largely to the thriving bauxite industry. In Trinidad it was primarily a matter of oil revenues. Effective use was also made of income from the growing tourist industry. However, this economic development program did not bring about a sufficient reduction of unemployment and the seriousness of this problem in Jamaica was of general concern.[39] In Trinidad the unemployment problem was not as serious and the standard of living there was rising more rapidly than in Jamaica. But Trinidadians were worried about the increasing number of immigrants who came to Port of Spain, especially from Granada and St. Vincent. On the basis of figures compiled by the government of Trinidad and Tobago, the number rose from 4,020 in 1958 to 6,115 in 1959. Labor leaders, therefore, exerted pressure on the government of Trinidad and Tobago to curb this flow from the neighboring islands. Dr. Williams responded by making it plain that there could be no freedom of movement of persons within a federation unless there were also a corresponding freedom in the movement of goods. This Jamaica would not accept without seriously aggravating its own unemployment problem and this "double bind" was a primary cause of the federation's troubles.

Aside from Jamaica and Trinidad, only Barbados showed significant growth potential. The smaller islands continued to have trade deficits and there was no significant improvement in their very low per capita incomes. They depended heavily upon grants-in-aid from the United Kingdom. Indeed, about 20 per cent of their expenditures were derived from that source.

It was widely assumed that in the future Jamaica and Trinidad would be expected to assume a greater part of this burden of subsidizing the small colonies formerly carried by the United Kingdom. It was this kind of projection of future obligation which tended to increase the suspicion that federation was a British invention designed to help Britain rather than the West Indies and this belief swelled the ranks of the antifederationists in the two largest territories.

Between 1958 and 1961, influential groups of business people in Jamaica became convinced that their economic interests and the economic development of their islands would be facilitated by cutting existing federal ties. This was particularly true of the Jamaican cement interests, but there were others, like the banana growers, who feared competition from the Windward Islands. Some industrialists, like Mr. James F. Gore, stated openly that Jamaica should seek an association with the United States or Canada and thus benefit economically as Puerto Rico has done. Others pointed out that lower labor costs favored Trinidad in competitive trade. They pointed out that in most commodities, from shirts to corrugated aluminum sheeting, Trinidad was able to offer better prices to the small islands.

There were, of course, counter-arguments. At about the same time that the Federation came into being, the government of Jamaica, headed by Mr. Manley, issued a *National Plan for Jamaica, 1957–1967,* a public document of seventy pages. Among its stated assumptions it held that "Federation of the West Indies will not materially affect the size and direction of Jamaican foreign trade in the near future." It was also assumed, "(4) that neither Federation of the West Indies and a Customs Union nor any other foreseeable cause will seriously change the present pace and pattern of Jamaican industrial development including hotel construction, and the effect of incentive legislation." But the plan did not sufficiently explain how it had arrived at these assumptions or whether and how it would be possible for Jamaica to contribute to the development of the resources of the Federation and at the same time continue to push ahead with its own development plan.

A case in point is Jamaica's bauxite and alumina industry. In the "Report on Jamaica 1961," published by the Jamaica Information Service, it was stated (p. 6) that "The production of bauxite and alumina increased substantially and the mining sector's contribution to the island's domestic product, to the Government's revenue and to export earnings rose accordingly. The steady growth and diversification of the manufacturing sector continued and this sector now appears to have established its position as the largest contributor to total domestic product." Such statements tended to support inflated estimates that some Jamaicans had of their potential prosperity and when this failed to materialize, there was a tendency by labor, management and the public to blame federation. Yet the rosy projections and expectations were, in fact, not supported by official statistics even at the time they were made. The same publication gave the following figures:[40]

Year	Bauxite Exported (tons)	Alumina Exported (tons)
1958	4,799,037	373,108
1959	4,196,793	399,210
1960	4,147,555	665,361
1961	4,974,802	603,466

These statistics hardly indicate a base for predicting or reporting "steady growth" in bauxite exports.[41] In 1962 bauxite exports increased by some 20 per cent to some 6 million tons. However, alumina exports declined below the 1961 and 1960 levels.[42] In 1963 bauxite export dropped considerably to 5,162,000 tons but alumina exports rose substantially (15.6 per cent) to 726 thousand tons. However, it was officially acknowledged that "The decrease in the value of bauxite exports exceeded the increase in alumina export earnings so that for these products combined there was a fall in total earnings of some £700,000 [$1,960,000] between 1962 and 1963, from £30.2 [$84,560,000] million in 1962 to £29.4 [$82,320,000] million in 1963. The 1963 earnings represented 41.8 per cent of the value to total domestic exports as against 48.06 per cent in 1962."[43]

Trinidad, on the other hand, had made significant advances. Some of the key resources, especially oil, had been discovered much earlier and by 1958 a marked improvement in the standard of living had taken place. She was able to employ most of her people who were willing to work and could absorb substantial numbers of immigrants from the neighboring small islands such as Grenada and St. Vincent. Her prosperity was further enhanced by a low-tariff policy and by a wage differential favorable in relation to Jamaica. Dr. Williams had vigorously pursued a policy of extending Trinidad's trading area. Trinidad's lower prices coupled with much lower shipping rates put her in a highly favored position as far as the East Caribbean area was concerned. Jamaica could hardly expect to compete effectively in view of her higher basic prices and the inevitably higher shipping charges.

These basic facts produced a situation in which the economic interests of Jamaica and Trinidad appeared diametrically opposed to each other. Even insofar as research could alter this appearance, it was insufficiently and ineffectively employed. In principle, Jamaica agreed to a customs union but she wanted to proceed slowly and by stages. By the spring of 1961 the patient and competent efforts of federal, Jamaican and Trinidadian economists had resulted in blueprints for such gradual accommodation of their conflicting interests. Unfortunately, all this work had been carried out in almost complete secrecy and their documentation, research and studies remained confidential. Under these circumstances, people of goodwill were denied access to important information supporting the economic case for federation while antifederationists made sweeping and unfounded statements which, standing unchallenged, influenced not only the less educated but also some intelligent business people in Jamaica. The failure of these people to support Mr. Manley at the time of the referendum very largely determined the fate of the Federation.[44]

PROBLEMS IN AGRICULTURAL MARKETING SERVICES

There were fewer conflicts among the agricultural producers of the various islands, so that the absence of a customs union proved a disappointment to those expecting a unified approach to agricultural marketing. Moreover, the lack of a unitary agricultural authority necessitated the institution of cumbersome *ad hoc* arrangements to stabilize prices for citrus fruits, sugar, bananas, and cotton, which were marketed primarily abroad.

In 1959 the Federal Minister of Trade and Industry led a citrus mission to the United Kingdom and obtained renewal of the previous British commitment to purchase citrus concentrates from the West Indies. The five-year plan which emerged from the conference depended for its financing about one-half on Colonial Development and Welfare allocations, without which the territorial governments would be unwilling to continue research and improvement in agricultural techniques. But competition from the United States remained a serious threat, and although prices remained fairly steady there were occasional significant fluctuations. With its limited jurisdiction, the Federal Government was unable to give long-range assurances to the West Indian citrus growers.

Sugar, on the other hand, was one of the commodities that had long been under firm federal control and the Federal Government was undoubtedly in a better position to negotiate for the entire industry. This was demonstrated in 1960 when the United States agreed to purchase additional quantities of sugar from the West Indies and British Guiana.

With regard to the banana industry, the situation was somewhat comparable to the citrus industry in that it was necessary to send frequent and sizeable missions to the United Kingdom to negotiate new agreements. The situation was further complicated by the keen competition which the Jamaican banana growers had to face from the Windward Islands. As a matter of fact, in the first two weeks of February, 1961, the Windward Islands exported more bananas to the United Kingdom than Jamaica and Trinidad combined.[45] It had long been recognized by the Federal and Territorial Governments that there was a real need for systematic long-range arrangements among the various territories in the marketing of bananas. However, little progress was made in that direction.[46] It need hardly be pointed out that these periodic missions were expensive and the failure to speak with one voice tended to create a poor impression abroad. The Federal Ministry of Trade and Industry could do little more than provide good offices and make suggestions to the territorial representatives. A federal statutory board for the marketing of bananas, as well as similar boards for the marketing of sugar and citrus, might have provided more suitable results.[47]

With respect to the marketing of rice, the role of the Federal Government was considerably extended. The government of British Guiana had long ago expressed the desire for a simpler marketing arrangement in which the Federal Government would negotiate on behalf of the Territorial Governments. Through this scheme, British Guiana was assured a definite market and the territories were guaranteed a fixed amount of rice at fixed prices. This plan came into effect on October 1, 1959, and was scheduled to remain in effect until the end of 1962.

The powers of the Federal Government were even greater with respect to the marketing of oils and fats. During World War II, in the face of severe shortages of oils and fats, the Regional Economic Committee established a regulatory system which included fixed prices. In 1957 it was decided to put these arrangements on a more permanent basis.[48]

In sum, in the industrial sector, and in some important parts of the agricultural sector of the Federation's economy, the existence of a central government created at worst hostility and at best apathy; it was seldom able to produce the kind of concrete advantages which could have engendered support for the Federation.

DEFECTS IN LEADERSHIP AND IN POLITICAL INSTITUTIONS

Prominent and well-informed observers have cited erratic and arbitrary actions of certain political leaders as contributing to the downfall of the Federation. For example, on September 22, 1961, an editorial appeared in *The Torchlight*, a Grenada newspaper, which noted that "No factor or combination of factors has been as effective in bringing about the debacle as Sir Alexander Bustamente's catatonic insistence that the Federation should be destroyed. And there was no better way of meeting his demands than to sound the opinion

of his countrymen by means of the referendum." Speaking in
the House of Commons, Mr. Donald Chapman, M.P., concluded
that ". . . instead of fighting the issue on its own merits, [Sir
Alexander Bustamente] wrapped it up in a fight on the frustration of the Jamaican people because economic advance was
not fast enough; he wrapped the whole thing up with a vote
of confidence in the Government, as opposed to the issues about
the actual Federation itself."[49]

Although one may agree with these analyses, the conduct
of the other politicians should also be noted. Norman Manley,
Sir Alexander's eminent cousin, may be criticized for excessive
idealism or lack of political realism. Long before the referendum, many prominent Jamaicans who had great respect and
affection for Mr. Manley confided that they regarded his decision to hold a referendum as a serious political misjudge-
ment. Similarly, Dr. Williams has been accused of achieving
alienation through arrogance. No one who is familiar with the
political history of the Federation is likely to ignore some of
the blunders of Sir Grantley Adams. He had an unfortunate
way of making improvised statements which provoked vigorous rebuttals and often required lengthy revisions and explanations from the Prime Minister,[50] a circumstance leaving him
open to accusations of lack of leadership.

Finally, in considering defects in the political institutions
of the West Indies which contributed to the Federation's weaknesses, it is important to note the point made by Mr. Ede
(South Shields) in the British House of Commons:

When I was in the West Indies I was told that members
of an Island Parliament, that is to say, the Trinidad or
the Jamaican Parliament, or any other Island Parliament, were not available to become members of the
Federation Parliament. I think that some of the trouble
may be traced to that fact. The names of Norman Manley
and Alexander Bustamante have been referred to in this
debate. Both of these very astute politicians believe in
making the "base" secure before they wander off on some
procession towards higher things elsewhere. Had they
been able to sit in the Federal Parliament with Sir Grant-

ley Adams, some of the troubles which arose might not have occurred.[51]

There can be no doubt about the correctness of this assessment. It should be noted, however, that originally this incompatibility had not been part of the general federal design. The Standing Closer Association Committee had recommended that for a period of five years members of unit legislatures should also be eligible for membership in the House of Representatives or in the Senate. Undoubtedly, the inclusion of such experienced parliamentarians as Norman Manley or Eric Williams in either body would have tended to raise the general level of debate in the two federal bodies.

EPILOGUE

Abott has pointed out that since the break-up of the Federation, the movement has been away from regional economic cooperation not only in the field of sugar but with respect to several other commodities.[52] In addition, one of the most unfortunate negative aspects of the break-up was the dispersal of a remarkable staff of dedicated civil servants who had served the Federation so well during its final period, much of which, unfortunately, remains shrouded in secrecy. The absence of any comparable kind of permanent secretariat or administrative machinery has greatly hampered the work of the "summit" meetings of the Prime Ministers and Premiers of Jamaica, Trinidad and Tobago, Barbados and Guyana.

Looking back at the whole experiment, it may be concluded that, with the exception of Dr. Williams, most of the leading personalities of the West Indies Federation in the course of the decade prior to its break-up never came sufficiently to grips with the economic realities.[53] Their entire approach was excessively petty-political. Well-preserved insularity and economic self-interest, rather than a broad, enlightened federalist ideology were the stuff of which the

Federal Constitution was made, and in this it correctly fore-
told its own failure.

It is unlikely that a new political design of federalism will
be attractive to the West Indies. What may be needed is a
more pragmatic, more widely regional approach to the development of common services. Out of these efforts a more
workable pattern of association and cooperation may yet
emerge.

NOTES

1. Charles H. Archibald, "Fail-
ure of a Federation," *Round Table*,
Vol. 52 (1961–62), pp. 273–78; and
"The Failure of the West Indies
Federation," *World Today*, Vol. 18
(1962), pp. 233–42. Amitai Etzioni,
in *Political Unification: A Compar-
ative Study of Leaders and Forces*
(New York: Holt, Rinehart and
Winston, Inc., 1965). J. B. Kelly,
"The End of the Federation: Some
Constitutional Implications," *The
West Indian Economist*, Vol. 4
(1962), pp. 11–26. Hugh W.
Springer, *Reflections on the Fail-
ure of the First West Indian Fed-
eration*, Harvard University Center
for International Affairs, "Occasional Papers in International Affairs," Number 4 (July, 1962).
Elizabeth Wallace, "West Indies
Federation: Decline and Fall," *In-
ternational Journal*, Vol. 17 (1962),
pp. 269–88. See generally, R. L.
Watts, *New Federations* (London:
Oxford University Press, 1966).

2. J. C. McPetrie, "The Constitution of the West Indies," *Public Law* (Autumn 1959), pp. 293–
309.

3. J. H. Proctor, Jr., "Constitutional Defects and Collapse of
the West Indian Federation," *Public Law* (Summer, 1964), p. 150.

4. Eric Williams, *Federation,
Two Public Lectures*, (Trinidad,
1956), p. 12.

5. Legislative Council of Trini-
dad and Tobago, *Revision of the
Federal Constitution* (Port of
Spain, 1959), p. 19.

6. *Ibid.*, p. 36.

7. *Ibid.*, p. 37.

8. Federation of the West Indies, The West Indies Review of the
Federal Constitution, 4 April 1961,
pp. 8, 9.

9. The West Indies, *Review of
the Federal Constitution: Summary
of matters and recommendations
for consideration by the Inter-
Governmental Conference* on 2nd
May 1961, p. 6.

10. *The Parliamentary Debate*,
54th Sitting, 4th April 1961, Col.
644. Mr. Gomes also added: "It is
quite obvious that what is contemplated is not a federation but a
confederation, which is a weak,
watered down version of federation, and in my humble submission
will never serve the needs of a
West Indian Nation as distinct

from a West Indian Federation, holding relatively subordinate status, which is what the position is at the moment." *Ibid.* at Col. 643.

11. *Ibid.* at Cols. 664–65.

12. *Ibid.* at Col. 663.

13. *Trinidad Guardian,* April 24, 1961.

14. The proceedings are discussed here in some detail because no full account and appraisal has yet been provided. A. Etzioni has attempted a summary in his *"The West Indian Federation: A Constitution Against Reality,* Sixth World Congress, International Political Science Association, Geneva, September 21-25, 1964, pp. 17–18.

15. This was to be agreed upon at the London Conference a few weeks later and put into operation on January 1, 1962.

16. The Barbados delegation was unanimous in its insistence to reopen the question of freedom of movement at the London Conference. Dr. Cummins, the Premier of Barbados, told this writer upon returning from the Inter-Governmental Conference (May, 1961) that he did not accept Dr. Williams' stand which would defer freedom of movement for nine years after independence.

17. *The Daily Gleaner,* June 2, 1961, p. 10.

18. In his opening speech in London on May 31, 1961, Sir Grantley stressed the importance of freedom of movement from the West Indies to the United Kingdom: "At the moment of independence we need a period of time in which to deal successfully with the grave responsibilities of nationhood without having to suffer the indignity of having a door that has traditionally and generously been kept open, now slammed in our

faces . . . . We do not think that migration is the solution of our economic difficulties but we want at least time to show that the other remedies which we are preparing can make our people want to stay at home because home is able to give them the opportunities which they now seek here." In 1961, Dr. R. B. Davison made an interesting study of "West Indian Migration to Britain 1955–1961." On the basis of his sample survey and his analysis, he did not hesitate to state that "People are flocking from the West Indies to Britain to seek an improvement in their economic situation." *The West Indian Economist,* Vol. 4, No. 3 (September, 1961), p. 14. He also concluded on the basis of his analysis of economic data of the individual territories that "The higher the national income per head, the lower the migration pressure" (p. 19).

19. Mr. Robert Bradshaw is reported to have expressed the view that more time should have elapsed between the IGC and the London Conference. This, the "Political Reporter" observed, would have given "the Unit Governments and the unit peoples more time to sort out their disagreements before coming to London only to wrangle all over again on points which should have been decided in the West Indies." *Sunday Gleaner,* June 4, 1961.

20. *The West Indian Economist,* June, 1961, p. 5.

21. PNP., *Federation Facts,* Kingston, Jamaica, 1961; N. Manley: *Federation: What it Will Really Cost,* Kingston, Jamaica, 1961.

22. PNP., *Federation Facts,* p. 5.

23. Manley, *Federation: What it Will Really Cost,* p. 5. The Premier noted that there were

four different kinds of expenditure
that had to be taken into account:

I.   Administrative Costs
II. Regional Services
III. Cost of Independence
IV. Cost of Transferred Services.

With respect to the first category
the cost amounted to £352,611
($987,300) and covered the follow-
ing items: the Governor General
and his staff, the Supreme Court
and law officers, the Ministries and
Departments, the Federal Parliament, Advisors, etc. The maintenance of the regional services requires an expenditure of £500,000
($1,400,000) and concerned the fol-
lowing items: The University Col-
ege, The West Indies Shipping
Service, The Meteorological Services, Regional Research, other Regional Services.

Mr. Manley noted that none of
these services had involved an additional expense to Jamaica since
the beginning of the Federation.

In Category III, the following two items required realistic
assessment: (1) Defense, and (2)
Overseas Representation. With respect to the cost of defense, Mr.
Manley noted that in 1961 Jamaica had contributed £252,410
($706,748) to the total cost of
the £587,000 ($1,643,000) for the
maintenance of the West Indian
Regiment. He expected the total
cost to increase considerably because of the removal of British
soldiers. Jamaica's cost would, of
course, be increased in the event
that the West Indies were to be
dissolved along with the Federation.

In Category IV one would
have to calculate the cost of fed-
eralizing the postal and telegraphic
services as well as the joint operation of civil aviation. No specific figures could be readily presented but Mr. Manley expressed
this opinion: "If the Federal Gov-

ernment is in a position to take
over the Post and Telegraph Services early, Jamaica will save
about £400,000 ($1,120,000) be-
cause this is a loss we are not
meeting out of own revenues."
Ibid., p. 9. Mr. Manley also noted
that after nine years, as agreed at
the London Conference in June,
1961, the customs services would
also come under federal control.

In addition to these four categories, one would also have to calculate the cost of advisory services.
"A part of the increase in administrative costs relates to the costs
of certain advisory services which
is now being paid for by special
grants made to the West Indies
under the United Kingdom Colonial
Development and Welfare Act.
These amount to £155,000 ($434,-
000) yearly and include the salaries
for civil aviation, medical, education, building, banking, marketing
and agricultural advisors, etc."
Ibid. at p. 11. Obviously when the
West Indies cease to be colonies,
"they will have to pay for these
important services out of their
own pockets." *Ibid.*

On the basis of these calculations Mr. Manley estimated that if
Jamaica were to leave the Federation, the savings on administrative
expenditures would amount to
about £400,000 ($1,120,000) dur-
ing the first year. In his opinion
nothing could be saved on regional
services and the costs might increase considerably if Jamaica
should have to carry alone the cost
of the University College of the
West Indies. The costs of representation abroad would increase from
£828,000 ($2,318,400) to £1,800,000
($5,040,000). *Ibid.* at p. 12.

24. *Ibid.* at p. 13.

25. *Spotlight,* August, 1961,
p. 12.

26. In addition to these forces,
prominent Jamaicans in New York

City, headed by W. Adophe Roberts and W. A. Domingo played leading roles in the antifederation campaign. Later the Federation Committee of the Jamaica Progressive League of New York tried to counteract the effect of this propaganda. A statement by this group appeared in *The Daily Gleaner* of September 2, 1961, asking that the voters, "Stay in the Federation— Vote Yes." It was signed by Fred L. Reid, Chairman of the Committee. Toward the end of the campaign, Abe Issa, the leading figure in Jamaica's tourist industry and widely known as "Mr. Jamaica," presented some cogent arguments in favor of continued federal association. *The Daily Gleaner*, August 26, 1961: Hon. Abe Issa: "Referendum—The Need for our own Decision."

Among the Jamaican industrialists, James F. Gore appeared to be the most outspoken antifederationist. *The Daily Gleaner*, August 7, 1961: James F. Gore: "Independence for Jamaica."

27. Eight days before the referendum a public opinion poll had been conducted by Radio Jamaica in which 18,000 people were interviewed. An American expert, who directed the poll, reported that 86 per cent of the persons who were interviewed expected to vote. Of these 46 per cent in favor of Federation, 27 per cent were opposed and 9 per cent said they were undecided. Several antifederationists questioned the validity of this poll. Mr. Edward Seaga observed that Jamaicans were not accustomed to disclose their political preferences to strangers. For another comment, see Mr. Seaga's letter in *The Daily Gleaner*, September 25, 1961.

28. Dr. Gordon Cummins, the Premier of Barbados, was quoted in *The Daily Gleaner* of September 21, 1961 as saying: "As far as the Federation is concerned, it is a positive setback, for another twenty-five or thirty years. I think the rest of us can still make a try, but the outlook will not be as rosey as before."

Mr. George Charles, St. Lucia's Chief Minister, thought it "unlikely that Trinidad would remain in the federation, and any union of the other remaining territories would surely break down." *The Daily Gleaner*, September 22, 1961.

On the other hand, Mr. Albert Gomes, the Trinidad MP, was able to see some redeeming features in the referendum debacle. He was glad to see "the odious Lancaster House blueprint consigned to the rubbish heap of history where it always belonged. . . ."

"There can be no doubt," said Mr. Gomes, "that the remaining territories excluding Jamaica can come together and work out a true and viable Federation and if they can do that, Trinidad and Tobago might well come to realize that this is the best sort of union for her." *The Daily Gleaner*, September 21, 1961.

On this issue Mr. Gore was joined by Mr. Millard Johnson, the leader of the Peoples Political Party and self-appointed spokesman of black Jamaicans, who argued that the campaign between Mr. Manley and Sir Alexander was a mere sham. *The Daily Gleaner*, September 6, 1961: "Serving Interest of Privileged Few by Millard Johnson of PPP."

On the day of the referendum *The Daily Gleaner* carried two full-page advertisements by the leading spokesmen of Jamaica's industrial community. Abe Issa's statement was entitled "We Cannot Go Back and Cannot Stand Still." He asserted that "Federation is the only solution—the only real solution—

for the problems of Jamaica."
Among the "troubles that could be
solved only within the federation,"
he listed (1) the country's poverty
and its need of foreign capital;
(2) Jamaica's economic vulnerabil-
ity which could only be solved by
greater industrial diversification;
(3) unemployment and the cost of
living which could both be remedied
only by providing "a larger and
more varied economic unit"; (4)
lack of political experience which
required a larger brain reserve
of first class ability; (5) and the
need for a viable defense force.

Mr. Gore's statement had the
following caption: "Jamaicans Today is the Day to Vote No for
Federation Because . . ." He then
listed twenty somewhat repetitive
arguments. At the outset he asserted that Jamaica with its thirty
votes against the thirty-four votes
of the other islands "will always
be out-voted. Federation will take
us down to the level of the small
islands. We want instead to rise
and become a wealthy nation but
we cannot do this if we join the
Federation with eight poor islands."

Mr. Gore made it clear, as he
had done on many previous occa-
sions, that Jamaica's economic future depended on closer ties with
the United States:

"The American people and
Government started the Banana industry of Jamaica, then our big
Bauxite industry, then our Tourist
industry and several small industries. . . . America will buy and
can buy every single item now being produced in Jamaica. America
can also buy and will buy twice
the quantity of sugar now being
produced in Jamaica and we can
get a sugar bonus as part of the
rent for the American bases in Jamaica. . . ."

"The United Nations now have
99 members, large and small nations. When Mr. Manley gets
Freedom for Jamaica, from England this year, we will also become the 100th member of the
United Nations. Therefore, vote
NO for Federation."

In contrast to Sir Alexander's
statements and comments, Mr.
Gore referred to Mr. Manley with
great respect and he stated that
"we would like Mr. Manley to become the first Governor-General of
the Commonwealth of Jamaica for
the rest of his natural life. . . ."

29. Williams, *History*, p. 257.

30. An excellent summary of
the inter-relationship of various
factors has recently been provided
by Sir Jock Campbell:

"The whole of the Caribbean
has been a corridor for Europe and
North America, though rarely a
meeting place for those who live in
it. The economics of many of the
islands have been geared to a colonial relationship—the production
of primary products (sugar, bananas, bauxite, oil) in exchange for
manufactured goods. The Caribbean sea is criss-crossed by these
multitudinous umbilical cords."

"The West Indies: Can They
Stand Alone?" *International Af-
fairs*, Vol. 39 (July, 1963), p. 336.
See also R. L. Watts, *New Federa-
tions* (London: Oxford University
Press, 1966), p. 91.

31. Jamaicans troubled by
problems of overpopulation were
impressed that British Honduras
had a population of less than
100,000 living on an area of 8,600
square miles. Their territory,
roughly half that size, had to ac-
comodate a population of about
1,600,000.

32. Gordon Merill, "The Survival of the Past," in *The West Indies Federation*, ed. David Lowenthal, (New York: Columbia Uni-

versity Press, 1961), pp. 20 f. A century ago Barbados demonstrated its own kind of separatism and its unresponsiveness to certain federal schemes. In 1876 it was proposed to enlarge the existing Leeward Federation by adding the Windward Islands and Barbados to it. But the Barbadian planters would have nothing to do with it. Even then the argument was made that the well-to-do Barbadians had much to lose and nothing to gain by associating with the much poorer islands. However, this was a class attitude rather than an expression of popular sentiment. In more recent times, especially during the period under study, Barbadians manifested a very positive attitude toward federation.

33. *Statement of Policy on Colonial Development and Welfare,* London, H.M.S.O., 1940, CMD 6175, p. 8.

34. "Jamaica, Trinidad and the British West Indies," in *Politics and Economics in the Caribbean,* Institute of Caribbean Studies (Rio Piedras: University of Puerto Rico, 1966), p. 184.

35. Brian Chapman, "Jamaica's Future in Doubt," *Manchester Guardian Weekly,* September 28, 1961, p. 4.

36. David Lowenthal, "The West Indies Chooses a Capital," *The Geographical Review,* XLVIII (1958), 336–64.

37. Between 1948 and 1961 the question of relocating the capital was raised many times. Chaguaramas and Antigua were the most frequently mentioned alternatives. But the choice of Chaguaramas would have involved a three-way dispute between the government of Trinidad, the federal government and the government of the United States.

38. Eric Williams, *History of the People of Trinidad and Tobago,* (Port of Spain: PNM Publishing Co., 1962), p. 256.

39. The Migrant Service Division of the British Government reported in 1959 that 19,663 West Indians had emigrated to the United Kingdom. Of these 12,573 came from Jamaica as contrasted with 1,073 from Trinidad. In 1960 the total rose to 20,110, of which 13,577 came from Jamaica and 953 from Trinidad.

40. Jamaica Information Service, *Report on Jamaica 1961,* p. 334.

41. See also: *Economic Survey of Jamaica 1961,* Government of Jamaica (Central Planning Unit), 1962, pp. 43–45.

42. *Economic Survey of Jamaica 1962,* 1963, p. 43.

43. *Economic Survey of Jamaica 1963,* 1964, pp. 44–45.

44. This writer deplores the fact that he was not authorized to document the statements he has made relevant to the customs union. He greatly appreciates the access he was given to this information on Sir Grantley Adams' authority. At the present time, the Colonial Office does not appear willing to release these documents, although historians and students of West Indian affairs are certainly entitled to know the facts. It is to be hoped that Sir John Mordecai, the former Deputy Governor-General of the Federation, will refer to these facts on the basis of his unsurpassed familiarity in his forthcoming study concerning the formation and dissolution of the Federation.

45. The West Indies, *Trade and Industry,* February, 1961, p. 1.

46. A temporary scheme was agreed upon in March, 1961, between representatives of Jamaica

and the Windward Islands and another conference was held in June, 1961, under the chairmanship of the Federal Minister of Trade and Industry. In the spring of the following year a large mission was sent to the United Kingdom to negotiate a new agreement.

47. Such a proposal was made several months before the demise of the Federation with respect to the marketing of cotton, because of the disastrous situation in 1959. To a large extent, this was due to the general slump in the world cotton market and to the decline of the Lancashire textile industry. Keen competition by India prompted Antigua and St. Vincent to ask the Federal Government for help. In May, 1960, the Minister without Portfolio chaired a meeting of all interested parties which was assembled for this purpose. At this meeting the representatives of the cotton producing territories and the West Indies Sea Island Cotton Association accepted the proposals of the Federal Government for a Federal Statutory Board. Legislative implementation had to be abandoned with the demise of the Federation.

48. It was decided that a conference of unit territories and British Guiana should be called annually by the Federal Government to set the requirements for the following year. Such conferences were usually called at the beginning of each year. Some of the smaller territories, especially Antigua, found their interests (the cotton-seed oil industry) were given sympathetic attention. Export prices were steadily raised. Thus in the January, 1959, conference the F.O.B. price for a ton of copra was set at $320 (BWI). This constituted an increase of $20 over the previous year. In January, 1960, at the 13th annual conference, this price was raised another $20 to $340 (BWI). Similar upward adjustments were made in the export prices for raw oil.

49. T. G. Matthews, p. 191, has recently expressed this view: "Alexander Bustamante, the Prime Minister of Jamaica, shoulders more responsibility than any other single politician for the collapse of the Federation."

50. Nevertheless, the conduct of these men must be judged against their own political backgrounds. Those who accuse Manley or Sir Grantley of indecisiveness tend to ignore the difficult political predicament in which they found themselves. Valuable historical background can be found in Morley Ayearst, *The British West Indies, the Search for Self-Government* (London: Allen and Unwin, 1960; New York: New York University Press, 1960).

It should also be noted that Sir Grantley did make some positive contribution to the Federation. In the course of the debate in the House of Commons following the Federation's demise, Mr. Ede (South Shields) said: "I sincerely regret that the Colonial Secretary should have had today to stand at the Dispatch Box to apologize for some of the indignities which have been inflicted on Sir Grantley Adams in the last few months. Sir Grantley Adams, were he a member of this House, would be a distinguished and leading member of it, respected I am quite sure on both sides of the House as a man of infinite resource and a very wide mind." *Parliamentary Debates*, House of Commons, March 26, 1962, p. 923.

51. *Parliamentary Debates*, House of Commons, March 26, 1962, p. 922.

52. "While it is true that the

break-up of the Federation did not cause this move away from regional representation it is certain that the splitting up of the area into different political entities has widened the gap of basic economic interests. Can this widening gap be bridged by new commodity agreements in such crops as bananas, citrus, coffee, and cocoa? Is it possible for some form of economic cooperation to be worked out for these crops for the politically disparate groups into which the area is now divided? In specific terms can the banana growers in Jamaica? These are questions to economic cooperation with those in the Windward Islands? Will the coffee and cocoa growers in Trinidad and Grenada find identity of economic interests with those in Jamaica? These are questions to which only time can supply the correct answers but viewed against the background of present irreconcilable agricultural policies and interests in the different producing units the common ground for economic cooperation shrinks daily." George C. Abbott, "The Future of Economic Co-operation in the West Indies in the Light of the Break-Up of the Federation," *Social and Economic Studies*, Institute of Social and Economic Research, University of the West Indies, Jamaica, Vol. 12, No. 2 (June, 1963), 177.

53. In this connection, it should be briefly noted that the second federal experiment which sought to create an East Caribbean Federation was from the very outset characterized by primary emphasis upon basic economic factors. The experiment failed, largely because the United Kingdom was not prepared to provide the necessary funds that Barbados regarded as indispensable if she were to lead the little seven into a viable new federation. This was clearly restated in a recent editorial of the (Barbados) *Advocate*, April 20, 1966, p. 4:

"The quantum of aid which Britain was prepared to give the proposed East Caribbean Federation was one of the vital matters on which the British Government maintained a stubborn silence. It was one of the shoals which wrecked the Federation. . . .

"If Britain is prepared to discuss a new form of association, following the collapse of federal negotiations, then it is reasonable to assume, the territories can be told of the policy and quantum of financial assistance attached to the new association."

CHAPTER 4

The Federation of Malaysia: An Intermediate Failure?

by Frank N. Trager

THE EMERGENCE OF MALAYSIA

When World War II ended, the British returned to their Malayan and Borneo territories but it was fairly clear from 1946 on that their rule—direct and indirect—begun with the acquisition of the islands of Penang (1786) and Singapore (1819) and gradually extended throughout the nineteenth century over the mainland Malayan peninsula, would not last. Anticolonialism, nationalism and the demand for *merdeka* (freedom or independence) would not and could not be stilled. It came, as we shall see, in stages. The process was complicated because of the various political and related administrative patterns which, developed between 1874–1914, then obtained within these territories. Five of the nine States of Malaya proper, Johore, Kedah, Kelantan, Perlis, and Trengganu came, under British rule, to be known as the Unfederated States of Malaya. The remaining four, Negri Sembilan, Pahang, Perak and Selangor, were known as the Federated States. Each was bound to Britain by a treaty that made them

125

protectorates. All except Negri Sembilan were sultanates with
hereditary royal lines; while Negri Sembilan's coalition of
clans elected a paramount chief. The islands of Singapore,
Penang, and the Malacca area were crown colonies and were
known as the Straits Settlements. The three British Borneo
territories were governed, respectively, as a Protectorate-sul-
tanate (Brunei); a colony (Sarawak), ceded to the British
Crown in 1946 by the third Rajah whose family, Brooke, had
ruled it as a private domain since 1841; and the domain of a
chartered company, (North Borneo, or Sabah, as it came to
be known later). Over all this the British governor of the
Straits Settlements who also served as High Commissioner for
the Malay States, presided.

     After a false start—the ill-fated Malayan Union, 1946–
1948—the nine Malay States together with Penang and the
Malacca area, making 11 states in all, agreed on January 21,
1948, to form the Federation of Malaya, still under British rule.
Sabah, Sarawak and Singapore continued as Crown Colonies
(though the last named received an increased measure of
"home rule"), outside this Federation. Then the Malayan Communist Party launched its armed revolt, called the "Emergency." The Federation leaders and the British worked together for years to suppress this rebellion and eventually
succeeded. The "Emergency" was declared at an end in 1960.
It had both helped to insure but also to delay independence.
The Federation of Malaya achieved its *merdeka* on August 31,
1957. It became a rotating constitutional monarchy with its
chief of state [the *Yang di-Pertuan Agong*] elected for a five-
year term from among the Conference of Rulers [*Majlis Raja-
Raja*], the nine traditional sultans or chiefs and the governors
of states not having a ruler. The supreme head is addressed
as "Majesty." He appoints the prime minister from among the
elected political leadership (then, as now, *Tunku* [Prince]
or *Tengku Abdul Rahman Putra Al-Haj*), and also the remaining members of the Council of Ministers on the advice of the
prime minister. The Council of Ministers or Cabinet is responsible to the Parliament. The latter under the Federal
Constitution of 1957 was a bicameral, British-type Parliament
with the 104-member House of Representatives [*Dewan Ra'*

ayat] popularly elected by citizens and the 38-member Senate [*Dewan Negara*] twenty-two of whom were elected by the State Legislatures and sixteen were appointed by the *Yang di-Pertuan Agong*.

In an official copy of the 1957 Constitution (see bibliography) there is a footnote attached to its title. It reads:

> This Constitution may be classified as *federal*, in the sense that the powers conferred by it are divided between the Federal and State Governments, each government being legally independent within its own sphere; as *monarchical*, in the sense that it establishes the office of Supreme Head of the Federation, or Yang di-Pertuan Agong, as a constitutional monarch, parallel with the recognition and guarantee of the position of each of the Rulers; and *rigid*, in the sense that it requires special machinery for its amendment (*see* Article 159) and cannot be amended by the ordinary legislative process. [Italics in original.]

At independence the Federation of Malaya significantly omitted Singapore, although it included the other two former Straits Settlements. There was at the time a single overriding reason for this omission. Prime Minister Abdul Rahman and his colleagues rightly feared that the addition of Singapore, a Chinese-dominated island, to the Federation would jeopardize the delicate distribution of population and control *within* the Federation. The small and favored Malay majority would be politically, economically and otherwise overwhelmed if the Chinese of Singapore were to have been then added to the Chinese sector of the population within the Federation of Malaya. Hence the *Tunku* at that time refused to enter into any negotiation that would have brought Singapore within the 1957 arrangement. Under the terms of the 1957 Constitution, Islam became—as it has remained—the official religion although freedom for all other creeds was provided for; Malay was to become the official language within ten years (i.e., 1967) although English was also recognized as an official language; and Article 153 (Appendix 1) insured that a "special position" was to be accorded Malays in respect to the civil service and other government posts, education, and the issuances of business permits and licenses.

On the other hand merger with the Federation of Malaya had been favored by Singapore. The latter had become, as regards internal affairs, a constitutionally self-governing state in June, 1959, headed by Lee Kuan Yew whose Peoples Action Party (PAP) the previous month had captured 43 out of 51 seats in the elections for the Assembly (54 per cent of the popular vote). Prime Minister Lee Kuan Yew had campaigned on a program which called for "independence [of Singapore] through merger" with Malaya, but he was reported as having said that "merger" was at least ten years away.

To the surprise of most observers, *Tunku* Abdul Rahman on May 27, 1961, while casually—it appeared—addressing a luncheon meeting in Singapore of the Foreign Correspondents' Association of Southeast Asia, said:[1]

> Malaya today realises that she cannot stand alone and in isolation. Sooner or later she should have an understanding with Britain and the peoples of the territories of Singapore, Borneo, Brunei and Sarawak. It is premature for me to say now how this closer understanding can be brought about, but it is inevitable that we should look ahead to this objective and think of a plan whereby these territories can be brought closer together in political and economic co-operation.

On June 3, Prime Minister Lee Kuan Yew, speaking at the Singapore National Day rally, responded affirmatively:[2]

> . . . we welcome and support the declaration of the Prime Minister of the Federation of Malaya that it is inevitable that we should look ahead to this objective of close political and economic association between the Federation, Singapore, Brunei, Sarawak and North Borneo. This declaration should accelerate the speed of political progress towards complete independence for us.

From then, events proceeded swiftly, although not without both internal and external opposition. An agreement in principle between the Federation of Malaya and Singapore for merger was reached in August. Negotiation with London officially began in November. An investigating body, the Cobbold Commission, visiting the Borneo territories between February and April, 1962, found that "a federation of Malaysia is an attractive and workable project and is in the best interests of the Borneo territories."[3] Further meetings in London in July concluded that a formal agreement should be prepared "within six months," and would provide for[4]

(a) transfer of sovereignty in North Borneo, Sarawak and Singapore by 31st August, 1963;

(b) future relationship between Singapore and the new Federation;

(c) defence arrangements as set out in the Joint Statement by the British and Malayan Governments dated 22nd November, 1961; and

(d) detailed constitutional arrangements including safeguards for the special interests of North Borneo and Sarawak to be drawn up after consultation with the legislatures of the two territories.

A new intergovernmental constitutional committee for a Federation of Malaysia under the chairmanship of Lord Lansdowne, the British Minister of State for the Colonies, began its work. Revolt in the Sultanate of Brunei in December, 1962—speedily repressed—caused that Protectorate to withdraw from the proposed Federation; while both the Philippines and more particularly Indonesia registered opposition to it. The Lansdowne Committee published its constitutional report in February, 1963. The UN accepted an invitation to ascertain the wishes of the remaining Borneo territories and, after a whirlwind investigation in late August and early September, found their people favorably disposed to Federation.[5]

All of the constitutional and political arrangements were put together so that on September 16, 1963 the Federation of Malaysia was proclaimed "as a constitutional monarchy based upon parliamentary democracy" comprising the eleven states of the Federation of Malaya, Singapore, Sabah, and Sarawak. The whole was a federalized country under a strong, centralized constitution. The latter enlarged the parliamentary monarchical system previously applicable to the eleven states of the Federation of Malaya. Now there were fourteen states each having a constitution with residual authority for matters not specifically covered by the federal constitution.[6]

The Constitution protected the equality of citizens before the law though it gave extensive police powers to the Federal Government. It again made Islam the official religion of Malaysia but provided for the right to practice a creed of one's own choice. It took cognizance of the purported economic and educational handicaps of the Malays and indigenous peoples by providing special opportunities for them in the matter of education and vocational opportunity within the government (civil service). Its direction, however, was toward multiracial parity looking to a future of a common, equally advanced citizenship. The two federal houses were enlarged to 159 and 60 members respectively. But Singapore's electorate, several times more numerous than that of Sabah and Sarawak, was granted 15 seats in the more powerful House of Representatives in contrast to 16 and 24 respectively to the other two states. In addition, though there was to be a common federal citizenship, the rights of movement within and immigration into the several states were largely controlled by the several states—an obvious move to prevent the potentially overwhelming number of Chinese in Singapore from freely settling in the other states.

On the other hand, as a result of the recommendations of the Jacques Rueff World Bank Mission to Malaya and Singapore (1962–1963), economic measures of considerable benefit to the latter were made part of the agreements to bring Malaysia into existence. These covered the establishment—never completed—of a common market between Singapore and the rest of Malaysia; guarantees to Singapore for its existing entrepot trade (especially in Malayan rubber and tin) ; certain tariff and tax concessions and other plans for economic development in the new federation.[7]

Less than two years later—on August 9, 1965—the "Proclamation of Singapore" and the "Proclamation on Singapore" appeared respectively from the offices of Prime Ministers Lee Kuan Yew and Abdul Rahman.[8] The *Tunku* had "evicted" (the word comes from the Singapore account) Singapore from the Federation of Malaysia. The Proclamations more elegantly say that from this date forward "Singapore shall . . . cease to be a state of Malaysia and shall become an independent and sovereign state and nation. . . ." The separation agreement between the two parties provided for continued cooperation "on matters of defence, trade and commerce."

The Federation of Malaysia remained in being without Singapore, and consisted of the eleven states of Malaya, Sabah, and Sarawak. Will it continue? Singapore, shocked by the quick cut of Rahman's decision is an independent but troubled state uncertain of its future. As Seymour Topping wrote in an excellent account (*The New York Times Magazine*, October 31, 1965) : "Lee Kuan Yew, Prime Minister of Singapore, raised his clenched fists before his eyes swollen with tears and frustration and shouted, 'We have a right to survive.' "

What happened? And why did a merger so recently entered upon break up so quickly? Economic interdependence, the requirements of defense against the military aggressive and subversive role of Indonesia's "confrontation" policy, the latent threat of renewed Communist rebellion, the ordinary elapsed time factor required to gain experience with relatively new political institutions—all these and other reasons should have held the merger together. The fact is that they did not. "What happened" becomes intelligible primarily in terms of why events happened the way they did.

It is not an oversimplification to say that the factors contained in the word, "race" *as applied to Malaysia*, are the basic explanation for its present failure. Without the problem of "race" the merger may have been sorely tried by variations in socio-economic and political policies advocated respectively by Abdul Rahman and Lee Kuan Yew, and by the friction between their personalities, that is, between the older, more conservative builder of a successful political and "racial" coalition, and the young-man-in-a-hurry, pressed by a crypto-

Communist opposition largely composed of members of his own "race," to assume the posture of a "socialist" leader committed to the honorable view that "race" should be subordinated to progress. But these and related differences, while important in themselves most probably would have been insufficient to bring about the eviction of Singapore from the Federation of Malaysia.[9] Fundamentally, the Tunku's decision was taken because he feared the further consequences of Singapore's pressure—regarded by him and, even more so, by chauvinist Malay leaders as "Chinese" pressure from Singapore, designed to upset the "racial" balance *within* Malaya. There had already been two periods of "racial" riots in Singapore in the summer and early fall of 1964. Further strife seemed to be hovering in the wings, and as the Prime Minister said in his August 9, 1965 statement to the Parliament, "There is not one problem but many, and that which gives us the most concern is the communal issue. . . . Irresponsible utterances are made by both sides, which reading between the lines is tantamount to challenges, and if trouble were to break out the innocent . . . will be sacrificed at the altar of belligerent . . . troublemakers of the country."

THE ISSUE OF "RACE"

In a profound sense the issue of "race" in Malaysia is unique. If one uses the word "race" to name the three great divisions of mankind as caucasoid, negroid, and mongoloid, then, though there are different races in Malaysia, race in this sense is not the prime mover in the conflict. That is, the issue is not one of skin color or hair texture or anatomical variations in eyes, nose, etc.; it is not a conflict between "whites" and "blacks." Essentially, the many-sided "race" issue of Malaysia is basically inter-ethnic—between Malay and Chinese, both of who belong to the mongoloid race. The words "race" and "racial" in the Malaysian context almost invariably refer in the first instance to these two ethnic groups; and, as a minority reference they apply also to other indigenous groups related to the Malayo-Indonesian peoples, and to immigrants from the subcontinent of India, that is Indians, Pakistanis and Ceylonese.

The "race" problem for the earlier Federation of Malaya (1957) and for the Federation of Malaysia (1963) rested on an anomaly: a majority of its total population was made up from relatively recent immigrant groups. That is, the Chinese, Indians and Pakistani, and Europeans outnumbered the Malays and other indigenous peoples who are generally regarded as of Malayo-Indonesian origin. The Malays, as distinct from all other racial and ethnic groups, had become or were about to become a minority in their own land.

Based on the census of 1957 and 1960 the following are the relevant figures.[10]

	Total Population in Millions	Indigenous* Percentage	Chinese Percentage	Others** Percentage
Malaya	6.3	49.8	37.2	13
Singapore	1.45	13.4	73.9	12.7
Sabah	.45	67.4	23.1	9.5
Sarawak	.75	68.8	30.7	.5
Malaysia	8.95	46.8	41.4	11.8

To present these figures in this way is not to say that all "indigenous" people, including the Borneans, recognize themselves as "Malays": nor do all Chinese regard themselves as

* Malays and those classified as Indigenous by the Borneo Territories Census. (The word "native," usually pejorative, in this context is acceptable when applied to the Malay-related peoples of the Borneo states.) Some 27 groups, other than Malays, from Bukitans to Ukits are listed in Art. 161A (7) of the Malaysia Constitution.

** Others include Indians and Pakistani (chiefly), Europeans and other non-Indigenous, non-Chinese.

a unified ethnic group. Variations of language, religion and other aspects of culture within the non-Malay groups of Bornean natives present a rich and not infrequently conflictual texture. But the point is that they are non-Chinese and together with the predominantly Muslim Malays they make up a small plurality as against each other "race." In related fashion though Chinese represent different dialect-speaking immigrant groups: e.g., Hokkien (largely in the former Straits Settlements), Teochiu (concentrated in Kedah and Penang), Hakka (Borneo territories) and Cantonese, their "patterns of historical growth have to some extent masked these dialect differences by new class (and political) differences."[11] The Chinese did not appear in significant numbers until well after the British developed the Straits Settlements and the mining industry. Until the 1930's fewer than one-third of the Chinese in Malaya had been born there. The existing sex ratio was two Chinese males to every female. They came and planned to return to China. However, by 1947 two-thirds of the Chinese community was Malayan by birth.

But in both cases, there are marked occupational and status roles. The Chinese are largely "urban focussed if not actually urban-dwellers, usually involved in supplying goods and services,"[12] while the Malays and other indigenous people readily fall into the rural, agrarian and water-faring groups, the bureaucracy, and a small upper class of Malays who in fact rule. The Indians and Pakistanis are divided into two main occupational groups, the plantation workers and other rural forces (about 60 per cent of their total) and the urban commercial, and professional service groups.

This "plural society," to use J. S. Furnivall's phrase, throughout the colonial era, and mainly because of it, lived in separate communities, perpetuating their differences in language and culture in most ways: by adherence to their separate Muslim, Confucian-Buddhist, or Hindu religions; by their own vernacular schools in which the language of instruction would be Malay, Chinese (Mandarin), Tamil, Hindi; by economic and occupational stratification; and by leadership appeals which were based on the "interests" of each grouping.

"The plural society," wrote Furnivall, "arises where economic forces are exempt from control by social will."[13] Each community lives side by side "but separately." There is a division of labor "along racial lines"—a kind of "caste system but without the religious basis" as in India. Such a society as a whole comprises separate racial sections; each section is an aggregate of individuals rather than a corporate or organic whole; and as individuals their social life is incomplete."[14]

Historically, under the British, the pattern of development into the Malayan plural society occurred much as Furnivall has depicted it. The country, divided into states, was ruled by chiefs with little centralized power. Sub-chiefs, together with their families, tended to form a ruling class within a district of the state. The mass of peasants within that district fell under their near-absolute rule. After British dominance was established, these rulers were maintained under the guidance of English and subordinate Malay officers. The Malay peasantry, unaccustomed to work in the mines and plantations, remained in a backward state while Chinese and Indian labor were brought into the country to develop it. The old Malay aristocracy became part of the new administration while the peasantry remained little changed. There was minimal interaction between the indigenous and foreign elements of society. Each carried on as best it knew how in the Furnivallian manner. The Malays and other indigenes were economically subordinate to the Chinese, while at the same time maintaining through their special privileges and otherwise upper-ruling-class political and bureaucratic superiority.

This was the general condition, which a few farsighted Malay, Chinese, and Indian leaders sought to modify. The Malays formed the United Malays National Organization (UMNO), the Chinese, the Malayan Chinese Association (MCA) and the Indians, the Malayan Indian Congress (MIC).[15] Together these organizations formed the Alliance Party, first to contest municipal elections in February, 1952, and then to advance the slogan of *Merdeka* [Freedom] for the federal elections of 1955.

The Alliance Party won 51 out of the 52 seats it contested,

capturing 79.6 per cent of the total vote; and Tunku Abdul
Rahman became Chief Minister for Home Affairs.[16] Though
the Alliance was composed of the three communal parties, the
political strategy of the Tunku, by assigning 15 districts (35
per cent) to the MCA when the Chinese registered voters then
constituted only 10 per cent of the total electorate and a majority in only two of the 52 electoral districts, underlined his
firm determination to make the Alliance into something which
had *not* existed before–a multiracial political instrument for
the achievement of Merdeka and for a high degree of communal cooperation.

The Tunku contributed his vision and his ability to persuade the 80 per cent or more of the Malay electorate to vote
for, among others, the Chinese and Indian candidates of the
Alliance. Chinese MCA leaders helped to provide the funds
necessary for the campaign, and it was clear that they, too,
appreciated the possibility for a multiracial future.

This issue of a cooperative, multiracial society was cau-
tiously and carefully nurtured not only by the Tunku and his
chief assistant, now Deputy Prime Minister Tun Abdul Razak
(who may well be the next prime minister), but also by key
leaders in the Chinese community of Malaya. Together they
have held the Alliance as the parliamentary majority coalition or party since the 1950's.

The MCA was brought into existence by Tan Cheng Lock
whose son, Tan Siew Sin, Finance Minister since 1959, subsequently inherited his father's leadership in the organization.
These Chinese in Malaya have sought to dissociate the Chinese
community from the Malayan Communist Party (MCP)
(who membership is 95 per cent Chinese and who launched
and conducted the insurrection between 1948–1960). They
have also sought to maintain a balance between Malay and
Chinese citizens in the Peninsula States without sacrificing
Chinese interests. This they have been able to do with moderate but growing success. That is, their position in Malaya—
politically, economically, in the professions and in the University at Kuala Lumpur both as students and faculty—gave
evidence of a growing accommodation between the two main
groups. It was this racial alliance of Malays, Chinese and

Indians that brought Merdeka to the Federation in 1957 and brought about Malaysia in 1963. And it was this balance which Lee Kuan Yew sought to upset, chiefly by making the MCA a target for displacement by his party and by rather unsubtle attacks on the Alliance as such. As Tan Siew Sin said in a rebuttal speech in Parliament, June 2, 1965, Mr. Lee is fond of the "subject of percentages, and this is where, I think, the trouble started." He quotes Lee as having referred to the Chinese as having 42 per cent of the Malaysian population in contrast to 39 per cent for the Malays in all of Malaysia. And by inference suggests that such talk fanned the flames of racial discord and division.

The "racial" issue is aggravated by uneasiness *within* each of the major communities. The Chinese of Singapore, Sabah, Sarawak and Malaya itself are by no means a unified bloc operating always with a singleness of purpose and program—though on certain negative issues, for example "Chinese culture is in danger," a large majority can be welded into a political movement. Rather, the Chinese in Malaysia are susceptible to variant appeals stemming from Communist Peking, National Taipeh, and from "third-force" Chinese seeking Socialist or Liberal or Conservative political goals. Similarly, though the Malays and native peoples of the Borneo states broadly belong to one major ethnic group within mankind, they, too, are divided by religion, language and loyalties. Some are Malayo-oriented; others have reacted to the idea of a Greater Malayo-Indonesian people whose very numbers would provide security against the Chinese. And still others are Muslim theocrats or Bornean animists and tribalists who live on both sides of the Malaysian-Indonesian Borneo border.

Race, however, has furnished the base, whether wisely or otherwise, for assent or dissent. In the case of Malaya or Malaysia it has served some important positive purposes— and it has also been harmful. But it is not a lasting cement. Its bind washes away under the assault of values and goals, policies and programs which transcend race or which appeal to more incisive demands and interests men acquire. These latter include religion, nationalism, even chauvinism, and preferential economic and political advantage.

At this point the following propositions—all basically related to race—have validity in the Malaysia context:

1. Malay concern about the Chinese majority in Singapore helped to bring about the 1957 Malayan Federation without Singapore.
2. Malay antagonism to the Malayan Communist Party, which most people there knew to be a Chinese-membership party, helped to bring about the defeat of the MCP in long years of bitter warfare.
3. Malay fear of mainland Chinese Communist power and its rising influence in Singapore's politics helped to create the Malaysian Federation—thereby in effect diluting their concern over Chinese population and Chinese Communists in Singapore in the statistics of Malayo-Bornean ethnic demography.
4. Malay concern about the non-Communist Chinese, practicing Singapore's agressive brand of politics, now, after 1963, having access to Malaya proper caused Malay leadership to evict Singapore from the Federation of Malaysia.

RACE AND POLITICS: MALAYA

In preparation for Merdeka in 1957 the UMNO and the MCA—the leading organizations of the Alliance which won the 1955 elections—reached an agreement on the key issue of Malayan citizenship. All who were citizens before independence and all those born *within* the Federation *after* independence were automatically granted citizenship. Those who had been born in the Federation before the date of independence, and who had not yet acquired citizenship were eligible for citizenship at the age of eighteen or later provided they fulfilled two qualifications: a residence requirement of five of the preceding seven years; and an elementary knowledge of the Malay language. Aliens born outside the Federation were required to have been domiciled there for eight out of the preceding twelve years. A limited language concession was made to those who were over forty-five years old.[17] Thus the majority of the alien Chinese population could potentially be phased into Malayan citizenship. Malay ascendance for the time being was preserved. But the fact that citizenship was available satisfied moderate Chinese demands and influenced the course of the 1959 elections, as we shall see presently. In return for this the Chinese agreed to recognize the special privileges of the Malays in respect to their position in the civil service and the preservation of government posts, scholarships, and business permits.

An equally touchy problem was that of education. British governmental commissions had been turning out reports for years in order to solve the conflict between the Malay desire for a national Malayan school system and the desire of the Chinese and Indians to retain their own schooling system. The Alliance government's Minister of Education, Abdul Razak, was appointed the head of yet another commission which this time reached a satisfactory agreement—while Malay was to be retained as the national language and to be taught in all primary schools, the various communities could also retain their own schools with their "native" language the medium of instruction. Malay was also required for admission to all publicly supported secondary schools and for entry into government service. However, English (which the educated Chinese used) could also be employed for official and educational purposes.

Since elections under the new Federation of Malaya Constitution were not to be held prior to 1959, the Alliance coalition, led by Prime Minister Abdul Rahman, was in a position to demonstrate its ability to translate its terms into practical effects, and incidentally to strengthen its position among the several racial communities.

An important first step was a final offer of amnesty to those Communist guerrillas who surrendered before July, 1958. This led to the highest surrender rate of the entire emergency period and it was estimated that less than a thousand guerrillas remained. (Today, 1966, the number has declined to 500 to 600). The success of this program was also related to the changing tactics of the Malayan Communist Party. There were indications that the MCP now placed more emphasis on infiltrating into the political parties, trade unions, and educational institutions. "The largest actual or potential Communist support lies among the rural and working-class China-oriented Chinese many of whom probably are not eligible for citizenship. . . . The Communists may, however, ultimately widen their support among the Chinese by posing as champions of the actual or imagined grievances of the community. It is therefore important that the present . . . Chinese who . . . head the community be leaders in fact as well as in name. Their success or failure will partly be determined by the degree of political opportunity and political effectiveness they will have in a Malay-dominated electorate and government, and partly also by their ability to compromise and to counsel the Chinese community in moderation."[18]

The continuing Communist threat, primarily Chinese in membership, encouraged the more advantaged Chinese community leaders to support the UMNO, if for no other reason than fear of economic loss. It also encouraged them to endorse social and economic improvement necessary for the maintenance of the whole society and this made them somewhat more progressive than they might otherwise have been. The Malay community leaders were willing to make political concessions to the MCA lest a disgruntled Chinese community would respond to the new communist tactics.

The first Federal election since the gaining of independence in 1957, held on August 19, 1959, demonstrated the effectiveness of the Alliance. The electorate had grown from 1,280,000 in 1955 to 2,177,000 and more significantly there had been a dramatic shift in the racial composition of the registered voters, as the Chinese had put on a major registration drive. In 1955 the proportion of Malay voters to Chinese had been 7 to 1; in 1959 under the new citizenship rules and a Chinese electoral registration drive it became somewhere between 3 to 1 and 2 to 1.

The Alliance won the election handily but with a noticeable decrease in strength. It took only 74 of 104 seats as compared to 51 of 52 in 1955. It was opposed by the Pan Malayan Islamic Party (PMIP) which contested 58 seats, the Socialist Front (contesting 38 seats) which concentrated its strength in the southwest-central regions of the Federation, the People's Progressive Party (PPP), anti-Malay, pro-Chinese, with 13 of its 19 candidates concentrated in Perak and the Party Negara with nine or ten candidates. "The Pan-Malayan Islamic Party called for Malaya for the Malays in an Islamic-theocratic state . . . Party Negara, like the Pan-Malayan Islamic Party, took the stand that more should be done to preserve and safeguard Malay rights and privileges and argued that the Malays had been badly let down by the existing constitution."[19] Party Negara won one seat, but the PMIP, locally strong in the two east coast traditional Malay states of Trengganu and Kelantan won 13 seats. The PPP on the other hand, a Chinese party advocating equalitarian rights, multilingualism, a change in educational policy favorable to the Chinese, and nationalization of the tin and rubber industries, won four of the twenty seats in Perak, demonstrating some disenchantment with the MCA among the Chinese. The Socialist Front, which was composed of the Labor Party and the Party Ra'ayat, both of which had been infiltrated by crypto-Communists, had a class appeal with the traditional Marxist policies of a planned, nationalized economy, and sympathies for some kind of relationship with Indonesia. Its one noteworthy feature was that it was nonracial, or, more accurately, intercommunal. For the Labor Party was non-Malay and the Party Ra'ayat largely Malay. It won eight seats. Three independents who had resigned from the MCA also won.

Perhaps more significant than loss of seats primarily to communal opposition was the sharp drop in the Alliance's percentage of the poll, from 79.6 per cent in 1955 to 51.5 per cent in the 1959 federal elections. "In spite of the large increase in the size of the electorate, the total number of votes cast for the Alliance in the Parliamentary election of August, 1959 (with 100 seats out of 104 contested) was less than the votes cast for the party in the Federal elections of 1955 (with 51 seats out of 52 contested)—790,000 against 818,000."[20] Obviously both extreme communalism or "racial" chauvinism as well as extreme Marxism were threats to the leadership of the still-victorious Alliance. Its middle-of-the-road program required firm implementation to keep the Federation going on its balanced way. As one thoughtful scholar put it, "The compromise which has been worked out on the political plane between Malays, Chinese, and Indians within the Alliance puts a premium on caution in the manipulation of economic and social change. It encourages moderation and damps down an enthusiasm for radical politics. . . . The compromise of the Alliance will presumably go on working as long as it can keep within bounds the realization of the principle on which it is based; it could be destroyed by the logic of the communalism which it imperfectly enshrines."[21]

This was the background for the adoption by the Federal Government of the Second Five-Year Plan, launched in February, 1961, to raise standards of living for both the rural Malay peasant and the Chinese urban worker. (The First Plan, 1956–60 had allocated $M1,149 million (approx. $383 million) to public investment whereas the Second Plan almost doubled this amount). $M2,150 million (approx. $717 million) was to be invested in land development, roads, ports and transport, public works and utilities, industry, social services and rural development. The expressed objectives of the Plan were: "to improve the economic and social well-being of the rural population and to redress the imbalance between rural and urban areas; to provide employment . . . for the growing population; to raise the *per capita* output; . . . to diversify Malayan (agricultural and industrial) production; and to improve and expand . . . social services in such fields as education, medicine and health, and housing."[22] That these were not mere words has been attested to by competent investigators.[23] And Prime Minister Abdul Rahman could report in 1965 that "Malaysia has the second highest standard of living in the East, following only that of Japan. Its economy is sound and stable. Its foreign exchange and reserves (December, 1964) total $1 billion." New investment is "pouring in," trade "expands with every passing year. All these achievements are due to a healthy spirit of free enterprise and the successful working of our democracy owing to the tolerance, good will and efforts of our people of many racial origins."[24]

The reward for these efforts, including the proposal for merger with Singapore, Sabah and Sarawak, came to the Tunku's Alliance coalition in the elections of 1964. His multi-racial party triumphed over all opposition, winning 89 out of 104 seats in the House of Representatives, thereby gaining 15 seats more than it had won in 1959. The other 15 went to: the PMIP 9 (a loss of 4); the PPP 2, (a loss of 2;) Socialist Front 2, (a loss of 6); PAP (the People's Action Party—Lee Kuan Yew's Singapore party that entered for the first time nine candidates to test its ability against the MCA in the Peninsula States) 1; and the UDP (United Democratic Party) 1. The Alliance also won 240 out of the 282 Assembly seats in the eleven Peninsula States—a gain of 29.

The extent of victory for the Alliance was undoubtedly furthered by the determined opposition of its government to the fantastic and shameful aggression of Indonesia. The latter's "confrontation" policy against the Federation of Malaysia alienated Malay support for a Pan Malayo-Indonesia Islamic outlook; and the anti-Chinese riots in Indonesia during May, 1963 limited the appeal of the Marxist groups who typically sought Malayan Chinese support for their "non-Communal" policy and programs.

In the new 159-member Parliament of Malaysia, the Alliance together with its allies in Sabah and Sarawak held 125 seats. The opposition, extending from the PMIP (9) on the Right to the Barisan Socialists (3), Sarawak United People's Party (3) and Socialist Front (2) on the crypto-Communist Left, could make little headway against the overwhelming endorsement of Prime Minister Tunku Abdul Rahman's leadership and party. Lee Kuan Yew's People's Action Party held 13 seats in the Federation's Parliament, 12 of which were won in Singapore.

RACE AND POLITICS: SINGAPORE

Raffles' Island, twenty-six miles from east to west, and fourteen miles from north to south, is the fifth-ranking port in the world and still the headquarters site of British naval,

air and ground defense bases in the East. It is also composed
of nearly two million people, 75 per cent of whom are immigrants and their descendants from South China. The island is
linked by a short causeway to Malaya and by intimate and
intricate economic modes of interdependence. Malaya can live
with ease without Singapore. The city-state of Singapore, dependent upon its role as a trading and manufacturing center,
basically requiring food and other primary product imports
for survival, may have real difficulty in living, at the highest
standard of living in Asia, with a per capita income exceeding
even that of Japan, without Malaya. For Malaya has historically performed the role of hinterland supplier and
buyer.[25]

Negotiations begun in 1956 by Chief Minister David Marshall of Singapore for increased self-rule failed to reach an
agreement with the United Kingdom government. By 1959,
however, there was a constitution establishing an internally
self-governing State of Singapore which reserved to the British Crown the responsibility for foreign matters, external defense and certain aspects of foreign trade. In that same year
the People's Action Party won 43 out of 51 Assembly seats
and Lee Kuan Yew, as Prime Minister, formed the first government under this constitution.

The "great-Grandson of an emigrant Chinese peasant, a
Cambridge educated," forty-three-year-old lawyer, "one-time
ally of the Singapore Communists and now their most adroit
adversary," as Seymour Topping describes him, is by everyone's account an extraordinary young man. His leadership in
Singapore—even during the 1964 communal riots which I wit-
nessed—*was* extraordinary. So is his impatience. Friend and
foe alike have said he is a young man "too much in a hurry"
even to listen to himself. Once his appraisal held that a ten to
twenty year period was necessary to accomplish what he, in
fact, helped to bring about and to ruin in twenty-five months,
the merger between Singapore and Malaya into Malaysia.

As Prime Minister of the State of Singapore—British
style—he recognized early that Singapore's merger with the
Federation of Malaya—which in 1957 had rejected Singapore
for "racial" reasons set forth above—was a sure and early

route to true merdeka for Singapore. He knew that the idea of merger was not new; that it was feasible and probably acceptable in British quarters, provided Malay and British Defense interests could be accommodated. The idea for a United States of Malaysia had been proposed by one of the most popular and knowledgeable British servants, Commissioner-General, Sir Malcolm MacDonald, friendly to both the Malays and the Chinese. And MacDonald's proposal had been adumbrated as early as 1887 by Lord Brassey, a director of the North Borneo Company.[26] In 1960 Lee Kuan Yew's Party declared,

> To achieve freedom it is no longer just a simple question of fighting the British. We must also resolve the two fears which make the Malay majority in the Federation not want the Chinese majority in Singapore.

Thus the PAP determined on a campaign of Malayanization as one way to woo Kuala Lumpur: "Malay was adopted as Singapore's national language, Malay cultural pursuits were actively encouraged while a sympathetic Malay was installed as . . . Head of State. In terms of real impact in both Kuala Lumpur and Singapore, these measures were of little significance." But Lee persisted in proposing merger as the "best way to contain Communist subversion across the causeway which linked Singapore to Malaya."[27] As the *Economist* (London, December 17, 1960) put it, "seldom so rich a territorial gain has been so brusquely refused. Seldom can a socialist government (Singapore) have so ardently proposed marriage to a conservative government (Kuala Lumpur), and in vain" (quotation, D. P. Singhal, cited).

By mid-1961 Lee Kuan Yew's strength in the Singapore Assembly had declined to twenty-five—a bare majority—when fourteen left-wing and crypto-Communist PAP Assemblymen defected to form the Barisan Socialist Party. This may have been the catalytic agent in helping the Tunku finally to work for an inclusive Malaysian merger. For his address on May

27, 1961[28] to the Foreign Correspondents in Singapore (see
above) was followed by a July 25 invitation to Lee Kuan Yew
to meet with him for discussion on the issue. From that date
on, the action for merger proceeded swiftly on all sides as
indicated above. Lee had apparently convinced the Tunku that
he and his party would be "reasonable" Chinese, thereby allay-
ing the fears of Malays in Malaya, and at the same time would
be Chinese allies against the Malayan Communist Party which
had been and was still primarily Chinese in membership. Obviously, too, Lee and his party in Singapore was a preferable
Chinese partner to a Communist Chinese triumph in Singapore
which inevitably would rekindle the Chinese Communist
danger in Malaya.

That there were other factors, for example the economic
interdependence[29] and defense needs of the area as a whole,
is true, but in my view the basic issue was and is the so-called
racial one—how the Malay and Chinese communities, and their
several parts, relate to each other.

Lee Kuan Yew now proceeded to improve his position
within Singapore. He proposed to submit the merger proposal
to the people of Singapore, although constitutionally he was
not required to do this. Though the Legislative Assembly had
approved the merger on December 6, 1961, by the vote of 33
to 0, Lee's plan was to obtain popular support to answer the
Communist charges and dispel claims that the merger did not
have approval of the people. Issues such as citizenship, na-
tionality and inadequate representation were debated by the
parties. Students at Nanyang University demonstrated after
four of them were arrested for conducting a poll of the proposed referendum. The University had been a stronghold of
Communist influence, as well as a supporter of Chinese education. On July 6, 1962, Lee had the Singapore Legislature pass
a Referendum Bill which was to decide whether the people of
that city supported its inclusion into Malaysia.[30] The referendum was held on September 1, 1962, with almost 400,000 voting in favor of federation (70 per cent of the ballots).

It should be pointed out that there were certain extenuat-
ing factors which affected the voting. For one, Prime Minister
Abdul Rahman had earlier threatened to close the causeway

connecting Singapore with the mainland if Singapore voters rejected Malaysia, thus putting an economic stranglehold on the island.[31] For another, the referendum itself did not give the voters much of a choice. The voters were able to vote *for* the federation, but no provision was made on the ballots for *negative* votes. In addition, all blank ballots were to be counted as if they were in favor of Malaysia.[32] Thus it was that though the opposition in Singapore had valid criticisms of the Malaysia proposal, they were given little leverage to block it.[33] For all practical purposes the referendum ended any legal attempts to prevent the inclusion of Singapore in Malaysia. The already mentioned anti-Chinese riots in Indonesia during the spring of 1963 effectively solidified non-Communist Chinese support for the federation. After federation had been accomplished in September, 1963, Lee led the PAP to a 37-seat victory in the Singapore election held on September, 27. Since the Party had held only 25 seats previously, this appeared to be an effective demonstration of support.[34] However, Lee's internal troubles were not yet over. While he gained 47 per cent of all votes cast, his chief crypto-Communist opposition, the Barisan Socialist party, won 33 per cent of the vote, though their representation in the Singapore Assembly declined from 14 to 13 seats. The remaining seat was won by the United Peoples Party, again electing the popular, leftist former Mayor of Singapore, Ong Eng Guan.

However, the struggle for power within the majority Chinese community was to be transferred in 1964 to a struggle for power between the PAP, largely Chinese-supported, and the MCA, Chinese communal unit within the Alliance coalition of Malaya. This contest alarmed both the Malays of Malaya and those of Singapore (who number about 14 per cent of the population on the island). In the Malaysian federal elections of April 25, 1964, the PAP of Singapore entered nine candidates in Malaya constituencies regarded as generally safe for MCA-Alliance candidates. Lee campaigned for his Party candidates on the slogan of a "Malaysian Malaysia," a slogan designed to challenge the "racial balance" of the Alliance coalition. He fared badly; only one of his candidates defeated the MCA but his campaign, garnering 2 per cent of the total vote, was seen as "a vehicle for Lee Kuan Yew's ambition to become the first Chinese Prime Minister of Malaysia."[35] Even those who greatly admire Lee and are critical of his opponents in Kuala Lumpur indicate that "the decision to contest elections in Malaya may have been unwise and the tactics of the campaign may have been inappropriate."[36]

Shortly after this campaign, rioting between Malays and Chinese broke out in July (in Malaya and Singapore) and again in September of 1964 (in Singapore). Thirty-three deaths and some six hundred injuries resulted.[37]

The second session of the Malaysian Parliament opened on May 27, 1965. In his speech from the throne (prepared by the ruling Alliance Party) the Yang di Pertuan Agong referred to the external threats to Mayasia from Indonesia and to non-specified threats to the nation from within. He added, "If those concerned achieved their objective, it would mean chaos for us and an end to democracy." Lee Kuan Yew challenged the statement by moving an amendment to the speech expressing "regret" that the throne had not specified the internal threats. With this motion the parliamentary and public proverbial "fat" was in the fire. Lee wanted, he said, reassurance that Malaysia "would continue to progress with its democratic Constitution towards a Malaysian Malaysia." In response Tan Siew Sin, Minister of Finance (and leader of the MCA) insisted, in a rebuttal speech, June 2, House of Representatives, that "the concept of a Malaysian Malaysia was born on the day the Alliance was born," and that Lee Kuan Yew throughout his speech of "thirty or so pages" supplied no evidence that the government had failed "to project or to practice the policy of a Malaysian Malaysia." The following day Deputy Prime Minister Tun Abdul Razak took up the cudgels against Lee in the Parliament.[38]

As Parmer points out, "Lee left no one in doubt that [his proposal for] Malaysian Malaysia [Parmer calls it a near-brilliant phrase with which to attack the Alliance] meant he opposed Malay political predominance in the Peninsula. . . . Lee did not merely criticize the terms of 1957 in speech and in print; he took political action. In May 1965 [actually in April,

F. N. T.] the PAP led in organizing the Malaysian Solidarity Convention . . . composed of the PAP and the PPP, the United Democratic Party, the Sarawak United Peoples Party and . . . the Machinda Party of Sarawak."[39] This coalition, obviously more left than the Alliance, and Chinese-led, was designed to challenge the Alilance as well as to supplant the MCA—but whatever its multiracial goal and class orientation, there was no doubt as to how it was publicly regarded. It relied on the Chinese for support and expressed itself increasingly in racial terms.[40]

The uproar in Malaya and Singapore following these events grew in volume and virulence. The Tunku returned from a health visit to England and on August 9, in Parliament, he announced that he had the "unpleasant" duty to separate "Singapore from the rest of the Federation."[41]

And so he did.

Various authorities have suggested that though "race is an important factor in Malaysian politics . . . the real argument has been about the same kind of policy difference as separates parties in Britain."[42] Or, again, that the separation, though interpreted as a "clash of Malay and Chinese interests . . . is better attributed in the first instance to the inability or unwillingness of the central government to allow a major political figure an important role in national decision making and in the second to an unsuccessful challenge by the Singapore government of the formal and informal rules by which politics are conducted in Malaya."[43]

Such explanations either are tendentious (the Fabians) or put the cart before the horse (Parmer). A role in decision-making was not denied to Lee Kuan Yew. In a careful and reliable paragraph, Tun Abdul Razak in his June 3, 1965 speech specifies a number of important issues on which Lee and his deputies shared in the decision-making process with the central government, especially in matters of internal security (Communism) and defense. Despite the fact that Lee Kuan Yew's PAP was programmatically committed to some form of "democratic socialism" and that the Alliance was committed to "free enterprise," neither party advanced beyond supporting a wide spectrum of "New Dealish" welfare actions and a considerable amount of public sector investment by the Federal government.

What is true is that Lee Kuan Yew was and is a man very much in a political hurry. He had made what appears to have been a private proposal to the Tunku to have himself and his PAP displace the MCA as the Chinese sector of the Alliance —a proposal rejected by the Tunku; and he then either sincerely or cynically went out to capture that role by threatening and contesting the "racial" equilibrium in the delicately balanced political-demographic equation which makes up Malaysia. When this was finally perceived and accepted as his policy by the Alliance leadership and when Lee Kuan Yew repeatedly failed to accept the analogy offered by the Tunku—[since] "there can only be one Prime Minister for the nation. . . . I was hoping to make Singapore the New York of Malaysia and had begged the politicians in Singapore to give their thought for the fulfillment of this objective"—the end came. The Federation was not dissolved but Singapore was separated from the Federation so as, in the Tunku's words again "to allow Lee Kuan Yew to be the Prime Minister of Independent Singapore in the full sense of the word. . . ." In a private letter, subsequently published by its recipient, the Deputy Prime Minister of Singapore, Dr. Toh Chin Chye, the Tunku implied that emotion—racial emotion—had outrun reason: Since he could not "control" the situation, he sought an "amiable settlement of our differences" as "the only possible way out."[44]

PROSPECTS FOR THE FEDERATION OF MALAYSIA, SINGAPORE, MANQUÉ

The Federation of Sarawak, Sabah, Singapore with the Federation of Malaya institutionally and initially resolved a number of issues. Britain was able to divest herself of remaining colonies in Borneo (Brunei is still a quasi-independent sultanate which opts for its present status as a protectorate of sorts).[45] Singapore reacquired the productive raw materials base and market on which much of its economy is based (it takes about 20 per cent of Malaya's exports). Malaya found a solution to the issue of "race" as between Malaya and Singapore by becoming the leader of an enlarged federalized country. In theory the fourteen states were coequals; in practice the Federation of Malay States was first among equals.

Sarawak and Sabah have played both a less and more important role in Malaysia than had been expected. Less important because these erstwhile colonies were very much less advanced than the other two components of Malaysia. Malaya would have no difficulty in surviving as a federation without them; and they need Malaysia's central developmental support and the Anglo-Malayan Defence Agreement. North Borneo, renamed Sabah, never had held a local election until December, 1962 and that one was held under the intimidating influence of the quickly suppressed Brunei revolt led by A. M. Azahari and his People's Party (*Partai Rakyat*). In these elections the Sabah Alliance, composed as the Malaya Alliance, won 90 per cent of the vote. In Sarawak the Sarawak United People's Party (SUPP), led by troubled and troublesome Chinese and infiltrated by Communists, opposed the idea of Malaysia, as did a pro-Indonesia or separatist Malay group, Party Negara. Once again the Sarawak Alliance group made up of Malays, Chinese opposed to the SUPP, and native parties won the 1963 elections. Of the 36 seats in the State Assembly, the Alliance held 26 and the opposition 10.[46]

However, the irresponsible [but now terminated] confrontation policy of Indonesia toward Malaysia gave more than expected political cohesion to the new Federation. The armed attack across the Borneo borders sufficiently alarmed Malay, native, and some Chinese enough to cause them to look to Kuala Lumpur and London for protection. Bornean tribes whose members inhabit both sides of the arbitrarily defined borders may not have felt any initial Malaysian loyalty or patriotism, but under attack by Indonesian guerillas they drew closer to Malaya and supported the idea of the Malaysian Federation.

This is not the place to review the range of issues and documents related to the Indonesian confrontation policy. The bibliography has grown to considerable proportions since that

policy was officially enunciated on February 11, 1963.[47] But
it is necessary to cite its main chronological outlines if we are
to estimate the prospects of Malaysia since separation from
Singapore.

1. In May 1961 Abdul Rahman announced his interest in
a Malaysia Federation.
2. On November 13 Foreign Minister Subandrio of Indonesia wrote a letter to *The New York Times*: "As an
example of our honesty and lack of expansionist intent
. . . we wish the Malayan government well if it can succeed with this plan."
3. On November 20 he repeated the substance of this
letter to the General Assembly of the United Nations
before whom he explained the ethnological and geographical aspects of the whole island of Borneo. However, he
specifically called attention to the "three British Crown
Colonies" which were outside the juridical limits of the
"former Netherlands East Indies" and hence not a part
of Indonesia. Again he "wished them [Malaya] success
with this merger . . . based upon the will for freedom of
the peoples concerned."
4. At the end of December, the Indonesian Communist
Party (PKI) resolved that the efforts for the formation
of Malaysia were "an unacceptable colonial intrigue—
[which] meets with the resistance of all democratic and
progressive forces in Malaya, Singapore, Sarawak, Brunei
and North Borneo." Therefore the Central Committee of
the PKI called upon the Indonesian people and Government to struggle against the imperialists, "especially in
face . . . of Malaysia . . . a new concentration of colonial
forces on the very frontiers of our country." The government of Malaya-Malaysia was described as one which
suppressed "democratic . . . movements . . . in these five
countries which aim at . . . genuine national independence
and freedom from imperialism."
5. Indonesia was officially silent about Malaysia through
most of 1962,[48] silent mostly because there was no way in
which it could intervene without interfering directly in
the domestic affairs of the components of the new state,
and being open to a charge of aggression at the same

time. The continued pressure of the British and Malayans
for the formation of Malaysia, however, and the opposition to the proposal by various parties within North
Borneo gave the Indonesians the chance to make statements of "concern" for the popularity of Malaysia. With
the indication that Malaysia was not to be received with
unanimous support, Indonesia could come out in favor of
self-determination for the colonial peoples.[49] By September, 1962, therefore, Subandrio was saying that Indonesia "could not remain indifferent to Malaysia." If British or American bases were to remain, there might be
counteraction such as the setting up of a Soviet base "in
our part of Borneo."[50] After the outbreak of revolt in
Brunei in December, 1962, official opinion in Indonesia
supported the rebel group called Kalimantan Utara.
Sukarno provided training areas for the rebel troops in
Indonesian Borneo. He also provided the supplies and even
several hundred of his own troops to assist the guerrillas.[51] On February 11, 1963, Foreign Minister Subandrio announced at a press conference at his home the
official Indonesian policy of opposition to Malaysia. "Confrontation" in word and deed had begun.

Since Indonesia is not here my concern, suffice it to indicate that that country suffered as a consequence of its mis-
begotten policy. Malaysia not only invoked its Defence
Agreement with England, it was enabled also to arouse the
patriotism of a wider range of citizens—Malay, Chinese, and
native within the fourteen States of the New Federation.
British-Malayan battalions—strung out along the Borneo
borders of Sarawak and Sabah, contiguous with Indonesian
Borneo, a border about as long as the distance from London
to Warsaw—suffered casualties but little difficulty in punish-
ing the Indonesian invader. Since the aborted coup of the PKI
in September–October, 1965, they have had even less trouble
in stabilizing the border area. Between May 29, and June 1,
1966, Tun Abdul Razak for Malaysia and Adam Malik for
Indonesia—both Deputy Prime Ministers—met in Bangkok
for a "free and frank exchange of views," designed to end the
conflict. Though President Sukarno, even after shorn of most,

if not all of his domestic powers, has been able to hold off the ratification of what the Malayans call the "Bangkok Accord," at this writing (September, 1966) there seems to be little more to it than a formal ending. The shooting is over. The two governments have exchanged high-level meetings not only on the immediate issue of ending "confrontation" but also of reopening diplomatic and economic relations which include Singapore.

In the meantime, in early 1966, Malaysia renewed its interest in the Association of Southeast Asia (Malaysia, the Philippines and Thailand). A meeting of its Standing Committee took place in March, 1966—the first since 1963—to lay the groundwork for the holding in August of the third meeting of its Foreign Ministers. ASA may be the instrumentality for resolving a territorial dispute between Malaysia and the Philippines over the latter's claim to North Borneo territory as it has already provided the forum for renewing diplomatic relations between these neighbors.[52]

Thus under enlightened leadership the eleven states of Malaya—the 1957 Federation—will be likely to retain the Federation with at least the two Bornean states of Sarawak and Sabah. It is possible that Sarawak and Sabah will combine with Brunei whose economic well-being, especially its oil riches, might contribute viability to a tripartite Bornean State. Perhaps all three may unite in a Borneo Island State attached neither to Kuala Lumpur nor to Djakarta but maintaining various levels of friendly relations with both. Apparently the latter possibility is unlikely, while the former possibility, although economically viable, might lack the strong political-institutional base necessary for continuity and security. Conceivably, continuity and security for such a small state could be provided under the aegis of a UN trusteeship: but this, too, is a development which has heavy odds against it.

There are, it would appear, no wholly satisfying solutions to the conflicts underlying the relations between Malaya and the two Bornean states which, in so many senses, are distant from it. Although the existing Federation of Malaysia is potentially prosperous, it will need not merely economic and defense support, but external assistance to help it forge a nation by integrating its cultures. It will need this external benevolence for some time to come if it is to surmount some of the inherent and inherited difficulties of a state built on communities rather than a single people.

This brings us, as a conclusion, to the situation's center of gravity: the relationship of the approximately seven million persons in Malaya to the two million in Singapore—a relationship chiefly involving the indigenous Malays and the Chinese. It is probable that Malaya, alone, with its citizens who are Malays, Chinese and others, will survive without Singapore. Like Belgium or Canada, its task will be to find solutions for ethnic, religious, linguistic and cultural diversity. Although it has the resources and, at present, the leadership to do this, such "nation-building" is never an easy task.

Singapore is in another category. Since it is physically too small for its expanding, vigorous population, some portion of its people may have to emigrate. But where can they go? Peking? Taiwan? Third countries? This is not an easy question to answer. It is widely believed that the Chinese, who are the great majority of Singapore's population, like many other pockets of Chinese expatriates in Asia, maintain as a matter of cultural honor, the "Chineseness" of their community, and informed opinion about the Singapore Chinese now holds that Peking exerts a stronger pull than Taipeh because it is the homeland. We may reject generalization about Chinese group coherence insofar as it presumes a mystique about this one ethnology that we are usually unprepared to admit for others. (After all, certain national groups whose cultural identities are probably qualitatively as strong as the Chinese, give contradictory evidence on this point. The French have retained a separateness in Canada, and lost it in the U.S.A., as, indeed, have the Chinese in some Western countries.) But whatever reason may dictate, the fact is simply that opportunity for Singapore emigration in Asia, or elsewhere, is not readily available. The "overseas Chinese" issue in every country of South and Southeast Asia is one which each country's leadership has no desire to intensify by permitting immigration.

What then for Singapore? There are states, now members of the United Nations, with populations smaller than Singapore. But few of these are as small in land mass as Singapore.

Singaporeans have adopted a state anthem (in Malay) entitled, *Majulah Singapura,* "Singapore Marches On." Can
Singapore in fact march on, shouldering its responsibilities
and facing its adversities as a small, independent, highly in-
dustrialized and commercialized state—a "third China"? All
one can say is that it is possible: because of the varied skills,
energies, and life-affirming philosophies of its people. But
should they be put to this test? The answer is that it is not
necessary.

It appears that it would be beneficial for both Kuala
Lumpur and Singapore to recognize that their separation is
not a fluke—that it has deep roots in the psycho-cultural differences between Malay Muslims and Chinese "pork-eaters";
between a slow-paced tropical people (the Malays) and the
"twenty-four-hour" workers (the Chinese men, women and
children); between two groups each wishing to conserve its
own traditional values and tending to denigrate the value
system of the other. Recognition of the roots of the separation
problem could lead to steps to ameliorate its effects. Malaysia
was one such step, and its failure must not discourage other
imaginative attempts by responsible and patient Malay and
Chinese leaders to find an accommodation and a long-term
solution.

The view put forward here rests on a finding of two fundamental causes for past failure: long-standing racial or
ethnic suspicion, anxiety and fear; and impatient political
ambition which, for short-run gain, exploited racial or ethnic
self-interest and bias. The resultant conflict and rivalry pre-
cipitated the separation. In this connection the moves made to
surmount the conflict and the rivalry—the 1957 Malaya Constitution and the 1963 Malaysian Constitution—were useful
but not sufficient instruments. For in 1957 it was made quite
apparant by the Malays that the Singapore Chinese were not
wanted at all. Singapore was overtly and explicitly excluded
from the Federation of Malaya. And though it was joined to
the Malaysia Federation in 1963, the social compact with the
Malays was such that, under the Malaysian Constitution,
Singapore citizens had to accept certain unequal limitations

on their rights of citizenship which applied to them everywhere in the Federation outside of Singapore.

Nor were the institutions of the polity—the Parliament, the apparatus of parties, the public services, the communications media—sufficiently experienced to mend the deficiencies in the instruments *before* they were cast aside. To deny the Malay concern or fear or anxiety about the Chinese, to patch it over with democratic and socialist slogans, these are equivalent to deliberate delusion. The Malay will not become a second-class citizen in his own country. To ignore the legally and other imposed restraints on the Chinese is equivalent also to deliberate delusion. He, too, will not remain a second-class citizen in his adopted country. The "plural society" of colonial Asia helped to create this situation. But the pluralist society of a Switzerland or a United Kingdom or even a United States may suggest that, however difficult it is to achieve the goal of equal citizenship, irrespective of race or creed, it is nonetheless possible to work at building such a society by law and education, by induced (but not violent) cultural accommodation.

But without patience and disinterested good will, the centrifugal force of racialism, of mutual distrust, which shattered the federation between Kuala Lumpur and Singapore, will not be vitiated.

T. H. Silcock, a very knowledgeable student of Malayan affairs, has written that separation between Malaya and Singapore "is accepted and desired by most of the inhabitants of the Federation. . . . On the other hand the great majority of the inhabitants of Singapore regard the separation as . . . an accident of the end of colonial rule which in the long run cannot possibly prevail against the obvious facts of economics and geography."[53] I do believe this is the case. Malaya, I have said, can survive without Singapore because it can afford to pursue its own development, even if thereby ignoring the "obvious facts of economics and geography." Singapore can also survive, but only in the short run. Consequently, the first move for a new try at reconciliation must come from Singapore, from Lee Kuan Yew, who has been so impatient of his

Asian senior. He must renounce the political ambition which
in the past has made him disrespect Abdul Rahman's rightful
political interests and ask the latter for his help in rebuilding
a pragmatic multiracial society and federal state. Rebuilding
cannot come quickly; it cannot come by any other process than
the living together of disparate groups who in time accept
each other's intrinsic worth and who, in the political kingdom,
learn to act as equal citizens before the law.

APPENDIX

THE FEDERAL CONSTITUTION OF MALAYSIA

*153. (1) It shall be the responsibility of the Yang di-
Pertuna Agong to safeguard the special position of the
legitimate interests of other communities in accordance
with the provisions of this Article.

> Reservation of quotas in respect of services, permits, etc., for Malays.

(2) Notwithstanding anything in this Constitution, but
subject to the provisions of Article 40 and of this Article, the Yang di-Pertuan Agong shall exercise law in
functions under this Constitution and federal law in
such manner as may be necessary to safeguard the special position of the Malays and to ensure the reservation
for Malays of such proportion as he may deem reasonable of positions in the public service (other than the
public service of a State) and of scholarships, exhibitions and other similar educational or training privileges or special facilities given or accorded by the
Federal Government and, when any permit or licence
for the operation of any trade or business is required
by federal law, then, subject to the provisions of that
law and this Article, of such permits and licences.

(3) The Yang di-Pertuan Agong may, in order to ensure

* *See* Article 38 (5).

in accordance with Clause (2) the reservation to Malays of positions in the public service and of scholarships, exhibitions and other educational or training privileges or special facilities, give such general directions as may be required for that purpose to any Commission to which Part X applies or to any authority charged with responsibility for the grant of such scholarships, exhibitions or other educational or training privileges or special facilities; and the Commission or authority shall duly comply with the directions.

(4) In exercising his functions under this Constitution and federal law in accordance with Clauses (1) to (3) the Yang di-Pertuan Agong shall not deprive any person of any public office held by him or of the continuance of any scholarship, exhibition or other educational or training privileges or special facilities enjoyed by him.

(5) This Article does not derogate from the provisions of Article 136.

(6) Where by existing federal law a permit or licence is required for the operation of any trade or business the Yang di-Pertuna Agong may exercise his functions under that law in such manner, or give such general directions to any authority charged under that law with the grant of such permits or licences, as may be required to ensure the reservation of such proportion of such permits or licences for Malays as the Yang di-Pertuan Agong may deem reasonable; and the authority shall duly comply with the directions.

(7) Nothing in this Article shall operate to deprive or authorise the deprivation of any person of any right, privilege, permit or licence accrued to or enjoyed or held by him or to authorise a refusal to renew to any person any such permit or licence or a refusal to grant to the heirs, successors or assigns of a person any permit or licence when the renewal or grant might reasonably be expected in the ordinary course of events.

(8) Notwithstanding anything in this Constitution, where by any federal law any permit or licence is required for the operation of any trade or business, the law may provide for the reservation of a proportion of

such permits or licences for Malays; but no such law shall for the purpose of ensuring such a reservation—

(*a*)   deprive or authorise the deprivation of any person of any right, privilege, permit or licence accrued to or enjoyed or held by him. or

(*b*)   authorise a refusal to renew to any person any such permit or licence or a refusal to grant to the heirs, successors or assigns of any person any permit or licence when the renewal or grant might in accordance with the other provisions of the law reasonably be expected in the ordinary course of events, or prevent any person from transferring together with his business any transferable licence to operate that business; or

(*c*)   where no permit or licence was previously required for the operation of the trade or business, authorise a refusal to grant a permit or licence to any person for the operation of any trade or business which immediately before the coming into force of the law he had been *bona fide* carrying on, or authorise a refusal subsequently to renew to any such person any permit or licence, or a refusal to grant to the heirs, successors or assigns of any such person any such permit or licence when the renewal or grant might in accordance with the other provisions of that law reasonably be expected in the ordinary course of events.

(9)   Nothing in this Article shall empower Parliament to restrict business or trade solely for the purpose of reservations for Malays.

(10)   The Constitution of the State of any Ruler may make provision corresponding (with the necessary modifications) to the provisions of this Article. . . .*

* Such provision has been made in all the State Constitutions concerned: see *Johore Gazette* Notification (New Series) 43A of 1957; *Kedah* Legal Notification 27 of 1957; *Kelantan Gazette* Notification 241 of 1957; *Negri Sembilan Gazette* Notification 453 of 1957; *Pahang Gazette* Notification 270 of 1957; *Perak Gazette* Notification 1413 of 1957; *Perlis* Legal Notification 5 of 1957; *Selangor Gazette* Notification 403 of 1957; and *Trengganu Gazette* Notification 227 of 1957.

NOTES

1. These excerpts have been widely quoted. See, for example, *Malaysia Official Year Book, 1963* (Kuala Lumpur: Government Printer, 1964), p. 33; "Formation of Malaysia," *Current Notes on International Affairs* (Canberra: Department of External Affairs), Vol. 34, No. 10 (October, 1963) 5; Gordon P. Means, "Malaysia—A New Federation in Southeast Asia," *Pacific Affairs*, Vol. XXVI, No. 2 (Summer, 1963), 138.

2. "Formation of Malaysia," *Current Notes on Internal Affairs*, p. 7. *See also* D. P. Singhal, "The United States of Malaysia," *Asian Survey*, Vol. 1, No. 8 (October, 1961), 16.

3. Report of the Commission of Enquiry, North Borneo and Sarawak, Knebworth House Hertfordshire, June 21, 1962, Art. 237, p. 94.

4. "Formation of Malaysia," *Current Notes on International Affairs*, p. 13.

5. On August 8, 1963, U.N. Secretary-General U Thant, in response to requests from the Philippines, Indonesia and Malaya "agreed to ascertain, prior to the establishment of the Federation of Malaysia, the wishes of the people of Sabah (North Borneo and Sarawak). The U.N. teams arrived in the Borneo territories on August 16; U Thant announced his favorable "findings" on September 14. For full text, see *Malaysia Official Year Book 1963, op. cit.,* pp. 50–55.

6. The three necessary documents are:
a. Federation of Malaya, *Malayan Constitutional Documents* (2nd ed., 2 vols.; Kuala Lumpur:

Government Printer, 1962). Vol. 1 consists of ten sections, 414 pp. inclusive of an index. This contains various acts leading to independence in 1957, the Federal Constitution of 1957 and acts and amendments between 1957 and 1961 pertaining to the further development of the Constitution. Vol. II, 446 pp., contains the State Constitutions of the eleven States of the Federation of Malaya. Hereafter, *Malayan Constitutional Documents*. The already cited *Malaysia Official Yearbook 1963* contains a valuable descriptive summary of this Constitution and the governments (federal and states) which it created. See pp. 21–28, 51–120.

b. *Malaysia, Agreement concluded between the United Kingdom . . . the Federation of Malaya, North Borneo, Sarawak and Singapore* (London: H.M.S.O., 1963), Cmnd. 2094, 234 pp. This contains the Agreement, Bills relating to it, certain other Agreements (e.g., Defence, Compensation, Common Market, Communications, etc), and the State Constitutions of Sabah, Sarawak and Singapore. Hereafter, *Malaysia,* Cmnd. 2094.

c. *Malaysia, The Federal Constitution incorporating all amendments up to the 1st March, 1964. Together with Sections 73 to 96 of the Malaysia Act (No. 26 of 1963)* (Kuala Lumpur: Government Printer, 1964), 173 pp. Hereafter, *Malaysia, the Federal Constitution.*

7. *Report on the Economic Aspects of Malaysia By a Mission of*

the International Bank for Recon-struction and Development (Singapore: Government Printing Office, 1963).

8. "Malaysian Prime Minister's Statement [at the Malaysian Parliament], August 9, 1965." Released in the U.S. by the Malaysia Information Service, August 12, 1965, No. M 142, Washington, D. C. It has been called in Malaysia "Singapore Breakaway"; See R. S. Milne, "Singapore's Exit from Malaysia; The Consequences of Ambiguity," *Asian Survey*, Vol. VI, No. 3 (March, 1966), 175–84. The "Proclamations" with accompanying background material were published as a pamphlet by the Singapore Government, Ministry of Culture, 1965.

9. This analysis and the first draft of this chapter was prepared prior to the appearance of R. S. Milne's article, "Singapore's Exit," *op. cit.* Professor Milne, Head of the Department of Political Science at the University of British Columbia, served as a Visiting Professor in Singapore during the period of the Malaysia Federation. He examines a variety of data and arrives at a conclusion similar to mine: "The essence of the conflict had become more and more 'racial.'" (p. 177).

10. From T. G. McGee, "Population: A Preliminary Analysis," in *Malaysia, A Survey,* ed. by Wang Gungwu (New York: Frederick A. Praeger, 1964), pp. 68 and 73. See also Tom Harrisson, "The Peoples of North and West Borneo," *ibid.,* pp. 163–78.

11. *Ibid.,* p. 77.

12. R. O. Tilman, "The Sarawak Political Scene," *Pacific Affairs,* Vol. 37 (1964–65), 416–17.

13. *Colonial Policy and Practice, A Comparative Study of Burma and Netherlands India*

(Cambridge University Press, 1948), p. 306.

14. *Loc. cit.* But see full section, "The Plural Society," pp. 303–12, a concept that Furnivall began to develop in one of his first papers written in 1910.

15. *Journal Southeast Asian History* is one of the most useful sources for documentary articles on Malaya. See for the UMNO, founded in 1946, Ishak bin Tadin, "Dato Onn and Malay Nationalism. 1946–51," Vol. 1, No. 1 (March, 1960), 56–88. Dato Onn was its founder; Tunku Abdul Rahman became its leader on his resignation in 1951. In this same issue, pp. 34–61, see Soh Eng Lim, "Tan Cheng Lock—His Leadership of the Malayan Chinese." See also Vol. VI, No. 2 (September, 1965), for Margaret Roff, "The M.C.A. 1948–1965," pp. 40–53. Also, same issue, Michael Leifer, "Singapore in Malaysia. The Politics of Federation," pp. 54–70; R. S. Milne, "Political Parties in Sarawak and Sabah," pp. 104–17. K. J. Ratnam's doctoral dissertation (University of London) now amended and published as *Communalism and the Political Process in Malaya* (Kuala Lumpur: University of Malaya Press, 1965), 248 pp., is a valuable summary work roughly up to 1961. Dr. Ratnam holds that "most political parties are classifiable by the positions they occupy in the Malay versus non-Malay continuum," p. vi.

16. Abdul Rahman, "Malaysia: Key Area in Southeast Asia," *Foreign Affairs,* Vol. 43, No. 4 (July, 1965), 658–70. For a more complete treatment of this election, see K. J. Ratnam, *op. cit.,* Ch. VI.

17. L. A. Mills, *Malaysia: A Political and Economic Appraisal.* (Minneapolis: University of Minnesota Press, 1958), p. 102.

18. J. N. Parmer, "Malaya's First Year of Independence," *Far Eastern Survey* (November, 1958), p. 163.

19. T. E. Smith, "The Malayan Elections of 1959," *Pacific Affairs* (March, 1960), p. 43. No official breakdown of the electorate by communities is available. K. J. Ratnam, *op. cit.*, has a variant breakdown. He cites, pp. 200–201, a total of 2,144,000 voters with 1,217,000 million (56.8 per cent) Malays and 764,000 (35.6 per cent) Chinese.

20. T. E. Smith, p. 46. For a full description of racial and regional representation in the Cabinet, see R. L. Watts, *New Federations* (London: Oxford University Press, 1966), p. 276.

21. Maurice Freedman, "The Growth of a Plural Society in Malaya," *Pacific Affairs* (June, 1960), pp. 167–68.

22. *Malaysia, Official Year Book, 1963* (Kuala Lumpur: Government Press, 1964). The Supplement, p. 29.

23. See for example, G. D. Ness, "Economic Development and the Goals of Government in Malaya," in Wang Gungwu, *Malaysia*, cited, pp. 307–20, esp. p. 317. Also "The Malaysian Economy," *Current Notes on International Affairs*, Canberra, Vol. 36 (September, 1965), 572–80. The $M is equal to about 1/3 of $1 U.S. *The Economic Development of Malaya*, Report of a Mission of the International Bank for Reconstruction and Development (Singapore: Government Printer, 1955), is useful as a basic resource book on Malaya. See also for later developments, T. H. Silcock and E. K. Fisk, *The Political Economy of Independent Malaya, A Case-Study in Development* (Singapore: Eastern Universities Press, 1963).

24. *Foreign Affairs*, cited, p. 664.

25. Lee Kuan Yew, *The Battle for Merger* (Singapore: Government Printing Office, 1961), p. 4. "Without this (Malaya) economic base Singapore would not survive." This pamphlet of twelve radio talks by Singapore's Prime Minister is a necessary document on the merger.

26. For a perceptive article, see D. P. Singhal, "Imperial Defence, Communist Challenge and the Grand Design," *India Quarterly*, Vol. 18 (April-June, 1962), 134–53.

27. These quotations are from Michael Leifer, "Communal Violence in Singapore," *Asian Survey*, Vol. 4 (October, 1964), 1117. Mr. Leifer, like Mr. Singhal, is to be read carefully as one of the keen students of Malaysian affairs. Lee Kuan Yew devoted virtually every one of the twelve broadcasts (and all the documents in the published version) that make up *The Battle for Merger* to the Communist danger to Singapore and to the proposed merger. He did so, as he said, as a former member of a Communist United Front.

28. Though this was the first public reference to merger, there appears to be some evidence that the Earl of Selkirk, British Commissioner-General in Singapore, had been quietly engaging in "triangular diplomatic negotiations between Britain, Malaya and Singapore" to further merger. And the Tunku and Lee Kuan Yew had begun rather frequently to find time to play golf.

29. Lee had pointed out (*The Battle for Merger*, pp. 4–6) that merger means "one integrated economic development . . . that wasteful duplication of facilities in the two territories will come to an end."

He cited the duplication in building airport facilities, competitive rubber markets, oil refineries, etc. He also called attention to the need for "central government control" of security, i.e., the British defense agreements, located in Singapore. It is also significant that the separation of Singapore from Malaysia was accompanied by an Agreement to enter into a treaty for "External Defence and Mutual (Economic) Assistance" (see Malaysian Prime Minister's Statement of August 9, cited).

30. *The Economist* (London) July 14, 1962, p. 165.

31. Ibid., April 28, 1962, p. 354. The causeway is an important fact between the island of Singapore and the mainland states. Over it moves the raw materials to Singapore; and considerable human traffic-labor from Singapore. This threat was successfully repeated in December, 1965, after separation when Singapore contemplated a trade agreement with Indonesia during "confrontation." The agreement did not materialize.

32. *Ibid.*, September 8, 1962, p. 878. There were 144,000 blank votes responding to the call of the Barisan Socialist group which set up a united front Referendum Working Committee to win blank votes. The Referendum listed three plans of merger containing variations on the issues mentioned above. Plan 1 received the bulk votes. Plans 2 and 3 received approximately and respectively 9400 and 8000 votes. Plan 1 called for (a) Singapore to join the Federation, retaining local autonomy in labor and education; (b) all citizens of Singapore to automatically become citizens of Malaysia; (c) Singapore to be given 15 seats in Parliament; (d) multilingualism would be retained in Singapore.

33. *Ibid.*, November 25, 1962, p. 772. A key criticism revolved about representation in the Federal Parliament. On a population basis Singapore was entitled to 23 or 24 seats. However, on the basis of continuing special privileges for the Malay and indigenous non-Chinese population this was limited to 15 seats.

34. Ibid., October 5, 1963, p. 25.

35. Michael Leifer, "Communal Violence in Singapore," cited, p. 1119. See also Jean Grossholtz, "An Exploration of Malaysian Meanings," *Asian Survey*, Vol. 6, No. 4 (April, 1966), 228. The Alliance won 89 out of 104 seats with 58.7 per cent of the valid votes. The MCA in its part of the campaign received 18.5 per cent of the vote and elected 27 of its candidates.

36. J. Norman Parmer, "Malaysia 1965: Challenging the Terms of 1957," *Asian Survey*, Vol. VI (February, 1966), 114.

37. See articles by Leifer and Topping, cited.

38. These speeches have been made available in the United States by the Malaysian Information Service, Text Nos. 142 and 143, June 18, 1965. Also, *Malaysian Bulletin*, No. NB 18 (June, 1965).

39. J. Norman Parmer (February, 1966) cited, pp. 114–15.

40. R. S. Milne, "Singapore's Exit from Malaysia," *op. cit.*, pp. 180–81. See also Jean Grossholtz, "An Exploration of Malaysian Meanings," *op. cit.*, pp. 230–32. Professor Grossholtz indicates that Lee fanned the flames of racial tension by his actions and statements.

41. Malaysia Information Service, Text on "Separation of Singapore," August 10, 1965. This contains the terms of Separation to which both sides agreed. They cover

"an understanding that we shall cooperate closely on matters of defense, trade and commerce." When Lee subsequently threatened to barter with Indonesia while the confrontation was still a military matter, the Tunku countered by a threat to close the causeway and trade with Singapore. Lee thereupon backed down. Singapore *is* dependent on Malaya for the products which enter her entrepot trade and commerce.

42. Don Esslemont, "Malaysia: Politics Before the Split," *Venture.* Published by the Fabian Society, London (September, 1965), p. 18.

43. J. Norman Parmer (February, 1966), cited, p. 111.

44. *Far Eastern Economic Review* (August 19, 1965), p. 351; Also published in Jean Grossholtz, "An Explanation of Malaysian Meanings," *op. cit.*, p. 240.

45. The Brunei revolt began almost like a farce. Its leader was A. M. Azahari of the *Partai Rakyat* who spent the duration of the struggle in Manila turning out press releases. The revolt was proclaimed in the name of the Sultan, who may have been intrigued with the idea of regaining former Brunei-Borneo territory. But no one seems to have told him, for he managed to escape from the rebels, flee to the local police station, and there call for British aid to suppress the insurrection. The revolt was originally planned for the spring of 1963, but due to reports indicating that Kuala Lumpur knew what was going on, the rebels acted prematurely and it misfired. The revelations of captured rebels during subsequent investigations discredited anti-Malaysia leaders, in the Borneo territories. British troops were safely in control of the situation by April, 1963. See Hamilton Fish Armstrong, "The Troubled Birth of Malaysia," *Foreign Affairs*, Vol. 41 (July, 1963). Brunei with its 2,226 square miles and 84,000 population (1960) is a present anomaly. It is surrounded on the landward side entirely by Sarawak. Its crude oil exports, accounting for 94 per cent of its exports by value reaches the outside world through the Lutong refinery in Sarawak. It survives as an outmoded protectorate only with the United Kingdom's somewhat embarrassed involvement. Brunei is the Commonwealth's second-largest oil producer. Brunei's oil wealth—not too widely distributed—has been providing per capita average income of more than $450 per annum. Sooner rather than later—especially after the effects of the Indonesian confrontation policy abates—its Sultan will probably accede as one of the Borneo-Malaysian states; or as an integral part of Sarawak. See, T. E. Smith, *The Background to Malaysia*, Chatham House Memoranda (London: Oxford University Press, 1963), pp. 46–47.

46. See Robert O. Tilman, "Elections in Sarawak," *Asian Survey*, Vol. 3 (October, 1963), 507–18; "The Alliance Pattern in Malaysian Politics: Bornean Variations on a Theme," *South Atlantic Quarterly*, Vol. 63 (Winter, 1964), 60–74; and "The Sarawak Political Scene," *Pacific Affairs*, Vol. 37 (Winter 1964–65), 412–25. See also, Gordon P. Means, "Malaysia—A New Federation in Southeast Asia," *Pacific Affairs*, Vol. 36 (Summer, 1963), 138–59. In 1965 the three Alliance Parties (Malaya, Sarawak, and Sabah) formed the Malaysian Alliance Party Council (Singapore's Alliance group was a member until the separation). This Council may be the beginning of a *national* or federal Malaysian party. If so, it

will be the first one so formed on the principles which originally brought together and held in political embrace Malays and Chinese of Malaya.

47. Justus M. van der Kroef, "Indonesia, Malaysia and the North Borneo Crisis," *Asian Survey*, Vol. 3 (April, 1963), 173, gives the date as January 20.

48. The document for this and the foregoing points from, *Malaya/Indonesia Relations 31 August, 1957 to 15 September, 1963*, Kuala Lumpur, 1963.

49. Donald Hindley, "Indonesia's Confrontation With Malaysia: A Search for Motives," *Asian Survey*, Vol. 4 (June, 1964), 905.

50. Justus M. van der Kroef, cited, p. 175.

51. Richard Butwell, "Malaysia And Its Impact On The International Relations Of Southeast Asia," *Asian Survey*, Vol. 4 (July 1964), 942.

52. See Association of Southeast Asia *Newsletter*, Vol. 1. No. 2 (April 30, 1966). Normalization of relations between Malaysia and the Philippines was announced on June 3, 1966; see *Malaysian Bulletin*, No. NB 31, June, 1966, Embassy of Malaysia, Washington, D. C. See also, the King's Address at the opening of Parliament on June 14, in which he "hails" two "memorable events"—the restoration of "peace between Indonesia and Malaysia . . . [and] resumption of diplomatic relations between the Philippines and Malaysia," *Malaysian Bulletin* No. NB 32 July, 1966.

53. From *Towards a Malayan Nation* (Singapore: Universities Press, 1961), p. 98, quoted by Frances L. Starner in "Malaysia and the North Borneo Territories," *Asian Survey*, Vol. 3 (November, 1963) 522.

CHAPTER 5

Why Federations Fail

by Thomas M. Franck*

THE COMMON FACTOR IN FAILURE

Any attempt to explain why a particular federal experiment failed is burdened with difficulties. The more so is a comparative analysis of failure in a number of federations. Unrecorded events, classified documents, logically inexplicable events, political prides and prejudices better analyzed by psychologists and humanists than political scientists, defy neat causal classification. This becomes particularly apparent when one attempts to correlate the causes of failure in four political federations so disparate as the West Indies, Central and East Africa and Malaysia.

That classical federalism is failing in so many of the new nations which have tried to implement it is an inescapable challenge to the American scholar who, because of his national identification with what is, on balance, considered a beneficent

* I am indebted to Professor Spiro for his help in the preparation of this chapter.

instance of federalism, has been inclined to assume that it could have equally salutary application to the often artificially divided and small new nations of Asia and Africa. But if history has now proved wrong the simple generalizations about federalism's curative powers, it is important that the diagnostic error not be compounded by facile generalizations about the diseases to which it has been shown to succumb.

It is, for example, difficult to establish a common terminology. Readily apparent semantic hazards attach even to the terms "federation" and "failure." This is of more than semantic significance. Thus, while it seems to be easy to get politicians to agree to "federate," it is far more difficult to get even the most general agreement as to whether a federation means something generically different from a treaty of alliance or association. As we have seen, the leaders of the West Indies Federation spent much time at the Port of Spain and London Conferences of 1961 arguing whether the component states should be allowed to retain wide economic, and even foreign-policy powers, or whether a more generous share of these should be delegated to the federal government. The leaders of Uganda, Tanganyika, and Kenya never reached genuine agreement over the many different and mutually contradictory ideological concepts of federation. While all spoke of "federation," there was little real agreement as to the type of union to be established; and even where agreement seemed for a moment grasped, it soon trickled through hands clenched in personal animosities and ambitions.

The three federations which did come into existence further illustrate the definitional problem for the perfectly valid reason that as they represented a confluence of sets of circumstances—political, social, economic—which, while dissimilar, produced three different kinds of federation. The stages of constitutional development in Northern and Southern Rhodesia and Nyasaland required a different form of federation from the distribution of political power in the Malaysian Federation. These significant differences illustrate the importance and difficulty of defining the term "federation" so that it would adequately encompass the political unions studied. Professor Friedrich's definition, a "union of groups, united by one or more common objectives, but retaining their distinctive group character for other purposes," is wide enough to include these three very different federations—but it is also wide enough to be embraced by those Ugandan leaders who believed that one could be a federalist and at the same time insist that each of the component parts of the federation be allowed to conduct a separate foreign policy.

What this definitional problem suggests is not that a single, highly structured definition of federalism is needed. Rather, it is that there be greater understanding of the nearly infinite number of variations that can be played on the federal theme and that the difficulties of engineering a union of nations only *begins* when the leaders agree to federate and their subalterns sit down to work out what is too often called "the details." It also suggests that the content of a federal arrangement need not be governed by a historically fixed pattern, that the concept of federalism is malleable enough to bend with the realities. Indeed, it is when the realities are bent to fit into some rigid, historic but unsuitable federal pattern that trouble often begins.

And what is meant by the term "failure"? If "failure" is generally the non-achievement of certain goals, in this study, failure is specifically a non-achievement of the necessary conditions for survival of a federation as initially conceived.

But again, as with human beings, failures are seldom absolute. An old British army saying has it that "No man is ever a complete failure—he can always serve as a horrible example." Besides the lessons failed federations teach, they also frequently accomplish some very important objectives during their brief lifetime—objectives which could arguably be said to be more important than the continuation of federation itself. The three federations and the East African association were successful in reaching at least some of the economic, social, and cultural objectives they were designed to pursue. In the case of Central African Federation, certain important goals were achieved, willy-nilly, in the awakening and mobilization of African national self-awareness. In the case of Malaysia, the separation of Singapore did not end the federal association between the remaining units, suggesting that as to these territories, at least, some of the federal vaccine had, in any event for the present, "taken." Unhappily, even attainment of goals proclaimed in a Preamble to the Constitution, or of goals expressed or unexpressed by indigenous political leaders or by the British Colonial Office, has not necessarily been inconsistent with a federation's dissolution. And, where a federation has been founded to achieve secondary goals—that is, to achieve given economic, social or political goals rather than to respond to a shared federal ideology or system of values—the achievement of these goals can even make that federation redundant. (Failure to achieve the goals, on the other hand, can make such a federation irrelevant.)

It is thus important to note that the "failure" or "success" of a federal scheme is not only relative but that failure in one sense may be—and even be attributable in part to—success in another, equally important sense, and *vice versa.*

When, however, we use the term "failure" in this chapter, we are merely invoking a historical fact: the discontinuation of a constitutional association between certain units of the union, or the end of the negotiations designed to produce such a constitutional arrangement.

It is significant that the actual moment of failure—in this sense—of each of our federations was marked by a constitutional act, like federation itself. It is not without significance that it did not, in the four cases studied, occur by revolution or rioting in the streets. This, too, is a form of success and one which, in a world of increasing violence and instability, is at least entitled to our notice. In East Africa, the failure to federate became gradually a perceptible fact emerging from orderly intergovernmental negotiations which, in one form or another, continue to this day although the emphasis is now on saving what functional ties already exist rather than on strengthening them in a political context. The Central African Federation failed in December, 1963, by orderly process of a British statutory instrument, six months after a dissolution conference convened at Victoria Falls. The Federation of Malaysia failed—although only in an important part of its totality—on August 9, 1965, when its Malayan leaders peaceably separated Singapore from the rest of the Federation.

And the West Indies Federation failed and was dissolved by the May 31, 1962 Order in Council, eight months after the citizens of Jamaica so decided in a democratic referendum.

Although these "failures" must thus be seen in shades of grey, rather than as altogether black, they remain failures nonetheless. Were there common factors which brought each of the four federations to this end? The question seems important not only because of its bearing on federalism's failures but because these negative factors may, in turn, offer some clues as to the necessary pre-conditions of success. Yet, as prescription this must only be taken with caution. If we know about certain failed federations' problems of language, of disparate cultures, of variations of standard of living among the parts, a high degree of correlation of these factors in all four federal projects would still be only a sort of *prima facie* case. And these correlations are, in fact, at most very imperfect in most instances. East Africa, Malaysia, the West Indies and even Central Africa did each have their *lingua franca*. The cultures were not all that disparate, the variations in standard of living (excepting the Baganda and the white settlers of Kenya and Rhodesia) were little more than marginal and arguable. Thus the comparison of the four federations does not lead to a list of "prerequisites" which, if not possessed more-or-less equally by all the parts of a proposed federation will assure its failure. On the contrary, it leads, however tentatively, to the conclusion that the sharing of such things as culture, language and standard of living, while helpful to the cause of federalism, is not an ultimate guarantee against failure.[1] *Figure 1* illustrates this and what follows. It divides factors making for federalism and goals sought to be achieved by federation-building into three categories: primary, secondary and tertiary. *Tertiary* goal-factors give rise to a federal condition which can be described as bargain-striking, in which a federation is formed not so much to harness a genuine mutuality of interest as to prevent a clash of disparate racial or economic interests, or to take advantage of some temporary coincidence of interests to secure an immediately achieveable objective. *Secondary* goal-factors give rise to a federal condition which can be described as a genuine coalition

Figure 1   THE FACTOR-GOAL COMPONENTS IN FEDERATION MOTIVATION

Goal-Factor Type	Factors	Goals	Contribution to Success of Federation
Primary	Ideological federalism Popular or elite charisma Supremacy of the political federal value	Federation for its own sake Manifest destiny National greatness	The prerequisite needed to ensure against eventual failure.
Secondary	Common language Similar values, culture Complementary economies Common colonial heritage Common enemies Common challenge	Federation for the sake of mutual economic advantage Security against attack "Opening up the frontier" More important role in international affairs Common services	These factors may bring federation into being and thereafter engender the primary factors. The factors of common challenge and common enemies appear to stand the best chance of effecting the transition to primary factors. If so, the federation is likely to succeed; but it is by no means certain that this sequence will occur. If it does not, the federation is susceptible to failure despite the favorable motivation based on secondary factors and goals.
Tertiary	Ethnic balance Hope of earlier independence Colonial power's need to rid itself of uneconomic colonial territory	Prevention of racial/tribal friction Independence Solvency	The motivation based on these factors and goals may bring about a federation but, unless rapidly replaced by secondary and primary goal-factor motivation, these tertiary goals can be said to contain the seeds of their own defeat. In themselves, these factors rarely engender the development of secondary and primary factors.

in which a profound coincidence of parallel interests is advanced through cooperation and merger. *Primary* goal-factors give rise to a federal condition which elevates the federal value above all other political values and in which the ideal of the federal nation represents the most important political fact in the lives of the people and leaders of each part of the federation.

The correlated data of the four studies thus support the following tentative hypotheses:

1. The presence of certain secondary factors, such as the common colonial heritage, a common language, the prospect of complementary economic advantages, which traditionally have been identified as necessary for federation may be *useful,* may even be *necessary,* but are not *sufficient* to ensure success. The failure of the federations studied suggest that within a hierarchy of necessary elements for federation, these conditions, although frequently cited by writers and politicians as the *sine qua non,* are actually secondary factors, of secondary importance.[2] Their value lies in that they *may* engender a common commitment to the primary factors and goals described in 2.

2. On the other hand, the absence of a positive political or ideological commitment to the *primary* goal of federation *as an end in itself* among the leaders and people of each of the federating units did in all four instances, make success improbable, if not impossible. This was the one consistent factor found in the four federal failures. The inverse inference to be drawn from 2 is that, for a federation to be able to resist failure, the leaders, and their followers, must "feel federal"— they must be moved to think of themselves as one people, with one, common self-interest—capable, where necessary, of overriding most other considerations of small-group interest. It is not enough that the units of a potential federation have the same idea of "the Good" but that "the Good" for any *one* must be consciously subordinate to or compatible with "the Good" for *all.* This, then, is tantamount to an ideological commitment not to federation only as means—such as, for example, a means to gain independence or financial stability, to utilize secondary or tertiary factors—but to federation as an *end,* as good *for*

its own sake, for the sake of "answering the summons of history."

In a developed community, the impetus for successful federation can come either from the ideological commitment of charismatic *leaders* transmitted to the people (*elite charisma*) ; or from the broadly shared values of the people, culminating in a *federal* value, originating in charismatic *events* and transmitted to the leaders (*popular charisma*), or built gradually out of common secondary factors. In a developing or underdeveloped community, the former is far more likely to provide the necessary impetus than the latter, and in the absence of either, the chances of success for the federal cause are slight.

3. If the political commitment underpinning a federal system is only a commitment to short-term goals based on *tertiary* factors, federal institutions survive so long as the tertiary goals continue to be important or new goals are substituted, but once the tertiary goals are attained, this very achievement—the securing of independence, for example—becomes in a sense a factor making for disintegration.

4. Where there is no paramount ideological commitment to the federal ideal, the mere creation of federal institutions will not resolve the conflicts which will arise within the federation, nor will it of itself transform *secondary* or *tertiary* into the requisite *primary* goal-factor motivation.[3]

Let us now examine these hypotheses more fully. The study indicates that the presence of certain secondary and tertiary factors, superficially favorable to a "climate of unity," does not ensure success.

For example, each of the units of each of the federal experiments studies shared a common heritage of British colonial authority and practice which ought to have conduced to the requisite sense of community, of cultural unity. Decades of rule of British-appointed governors and allegiance to the Crown resulted in a broad field of legal and administrative uniformity among the constituents of each federation. The rule of law as conceived in Great Britain and transplanted with a good deal of intelligent pragmatic adaption to Asia, Africa, and the Caribbean provided a common lego-political framework. In Kenya, Uganda, and Tanganyika both elements of statutory uniformity and common bureaucratic procedures existed, and yet the East African Federation failed to emerge. To a lesser extent, the states of the Malaysian and West Indian Federations also shared this common heritage. The parties to the Central African Federation, Southern and Northern Rhodesia and Nyasaland had the benefit of similar systems of British colonial administration, statutory law and, except for Southern Rhodesia's adherence to British-influenced Roman-Dutch jurisprudence, shared the British common law (although, constitutionally, the three component territories were more disparate). The elite, for the most part, received their education in a common classical British system of higher education.

Yet, that each of the federations here studied had a common colonial past and was a product of the colonial system did not suffice to save any of them. On the contrary, in the opinion of many, the leaders and institutions of the federations were handicapped by having had about them a whiff of "neocolonialism." In East Africa, Great Britain went to great lengths to avoid its Rhodesian mistake of imposing federalism. But the federal ideal seems to have had the worst of both policies. When it was strongly urged by Britain, as in the West Indies and Malaysia, or when it was imposed, as in Central Africa, it seemed to be discounted by the charge of neocolonialism. It failed to capture the active support of the population. It failed to make the transformation from colonial policy to popular ideology. When, on the other hand, Britain avoided all overt support for the federal ideal and allowed the local political leaders to work it out among themselves after their independence, as in East Africa, they were unwilling or unable to do so and even blamed Britain for not making the horse drink after leading it to the water's brink.[4]

Then, too, in each of the federations there existed a significant degree of similarity of economic condition among the participants which would, superficially, seem to conduce to successful federalism. In the nations which were to comprise the East African Federation the advantages of institutionalized functional unity—the common services and a customs and

currency union—were in existence for several decades and
their utility, despite shortcomings, had been tested and veri-
fied. And yet this shared experience of economic cooperation
was not enough to hold the common market together, let alone
serve as a base for federation once political direction passed
from colonial to African hands. Nyasaland, Northern and
Southern Rhodesia also profited economically from trade and
investment during federation. Indeed, the most impressive
gains of the Central African Federation were economic. The
three economies substantially complemented each other, indicating that an integrated common market would benefit each
of the participants, although it has been suggested that the
economic benefits flowed downhill to Southern Rhodesia and
had to be pumped uphill to everyone else, just as those in East
Africa accrued unequally to the benefit of Kenya. That the
benefits were not equally distributed is not, however, to say
that functional or federal union did not bring benefits but
only that the pumping, the political system for the internal
distribution of the total gains, was, in Central Africa, inadequate and in East Africa nearly nonexistent.

The experience of Malaya and Singapore in Malaysian
federation is somewhat analogous. While neither state was
completely dependent upon the other for economic survival,
their respective economies are complementary—Malaya providing markets for Singapore's industry; Singapore being a
market for Malaya's natural resources. The visible flow of
trade across the causeway connecting the two symbolizes this
economic interdependence.

Only, perhaps, among the islands of the West Indian Federation might it be suggested that the island economies were
not complementary, and that this was a factor in that federation's failure. Jamaicans feared that federation would assist
Trinidadian commercial interests at Jamaica's expense. And
yet Jamaica's decision to quit the federation was made *after*
the 1961 London Conference at which she (as well as Trinidad) had gained substantial economic concessions at the expense of the smaller islands. Furthermore, it was evident
during the referendum campaign that Jamaican opinion was
sharply divided as to the economic effects of federation on

Jamaica's economic interests. And, of course, considerations other than economics must have entered Dr. Eric Williams' calculations when he, too, withdrew Trinidad from federation, for Trinidad would almost certainly have had much to gain, economically, from continued union with the remaining members of the federation after Jamaica's departure. Again, economic logic was not sufficient to hold a federation together.

The principal cause for failure, or partial failure, of each of the federations studied cannot, it thus seems, be found in an analysis of economic statistics or in an inventory of social, cultural, or institutional diversity. It can only be found in the absence of a sufficient political-ideological commitment to the *primary* concept or value of federation itself. How one can account for the absence of this primary commitment is left to be discussed in a later part of this chapter in which the four failed federations are for this purpose compared to the classical federations of Canada, Australia and the United States. Suffice it here to repeat that such a commitment might spring from the people—charismatically caused by events or gradually by a growth and confluence of secondary values and factors—or be generated by charismatic national leaders, and that the former appears to occur rarely except in a situation of overwhelming common threat from external forces or other passionate historic challenge to the collective imagination. It is, however, important to stress that, in each of our studies, this commitment to primary goals appears to have been shown not to exist at the moment of federation and not to have been generated subsequently.

Instead, the four federations are studies in leadership non-charisma and in the non-challenge of historic trivia. In East Africa and the West Indies there never existed any semblance of political agreement over the goals of federation, and the only leaders able to engender a federal ideology remained at their local posts. To the leaders of Uganda, Tanganyika, and Kenya, federation never succeeded in being more than a vague aspiration based on many varied and contradictory concepts, most of them reflecting not community but local interest, or personal self-interest. Four distinct movements—the mercantilist, centrifugal, regional, and pan-African—favored federalism in the vague abstract, but were unable to establish sufficient common ground to support a viable scheme for federal union. Instead of charisma, the East African leaders gave their people top-secret haggling, as if federation were a matter too esoteric to be submitted to the masses. In fact, the negotiations were anything but esoteric. The East African politicians were simply loathe to gamble the national powers which independence had placed in their hands on the chance of getting even greater power in a strong federation. Kenyatta was a man of great fame but he feared his stamina and mental agility to be no match for the younger leaders of Tanganyika and Uganda. Dr. Obote of Uganda was a man of great political astuteness, but he ruled a politically divided country. He was not yet ready for a power contest with the leaders of a united Tanzania who could count on a two-million-member political movement and tightly-controlled *de facto* (and later *de jure*) one-party system.

Nor could the non-charismatic leaders be pushed into resolving their pedestrian quarrels by an aroused, informed public opinion, for none existed to champion the cause of federalism. Federation was never a mass movement and, therefore, such commitment as there was to be, would have had to be engendered by the leaders. It was only from a minority: Julius Nyerere, Tom Mboya, James Gichuru, that any such leadership was forthcoming, and it was not enough. It remains to be said by way of mitigating East Africa's failure that the lack of overriding ideological commitment and of shared values was at least revealed by negotiations prior to federation rather than by federal trial and error.

Commitment to the concept of federation as the primary community value was also noticeably lacking during the formative stages of the West Indies Federation. As Dr. Eric Williams of Trinidad indicated, the federation suffered from "the absence of a comprehensive conception, the lack of clear economic perspectives, the inability of anyone to grapple with this problem of inter-territorial jealousies."

"This problem" did not diminish substantially in the period between the first discussions leading to federation and the final campaign during the Jamaican referendum which

marked the beginning of the federation's dissolution. During
the pre-federation period, the leading advocates of unity
rarely spoke of federation as the anglophonic Caribbean's
ideal, as a destiny of solving common problems by sharing
common assets and liabilities. Instead, the representatives of
Jamaica and Trinidad came and went, speaking of grants-in-
aid and tariff rates. Jamaica argued for a customs union in
which federal authority would have limited powers and financial resources; Trinidad and Tobago proposed a strong central
government with substantial financial, developmental, and tax-
ing power. In itself, such horse-trading at the time of federation is not unusual, but neither is it a substitute for an ideological commitment to a primary ideal of federation. As for
the remaining major advocate of federation, Great Britain, it
was not able substantially to modify the course or tone of the
discussions. Even the colonial office's interest in federation
seemed all too evidently focussed on the tertiary goal of finding a decent home for the several of its smaller and uneco-
nomic colonies in the Caribbean and effecting the savings that
were to result from a more centralized system of colonial administration.

The economic dialogue continued to dominate the Port-
of-Spain and London Conferences of 1961, and particularly the
Jamaica referendum of December, 1961. During the referendum campaign "both parties failed to put the important political concepts of Federation and separatism" before the electorate. The debate took place entirely in narrow terms of
economic self-interest, which made it both inconclusive and
certainly uninspiring to the average voter, rather than in terms
of commitment to a federal ideology. No doubt there were
those whose thoughts were of a manifest destiny, of pan-
Caribbeanism, of the challenge to be big and great. But the
politicians only challenged the voters to decide whether federation would cut administrative overhead and whether Trinidad
or Jamaica would glean the benefits of new markets in the
smaller islands.

In Malaysia and the Central African Federation, while
there existed in each case a greater commitment among a
small group to the primary goal of federalism, this commit-

ment was, again, not sufficiently widespread. Again, the
secondary and tertiary goals or reasons for federation were
not enough to sustain a successful federal union, for these
placed before the political ideals of nation-building such
"practical" objectives as the amelioration of racial problems.
Again, Britain's interest was primarily in finding a respectable
"home" for the bits and pieces: Singapore, the Borneo territories, Nyasaland.

Both federations soon learned that the machinery of federal institutions is no substitute for shared national ideological commitment as a means to racial harmony. As soon as
this lesson was driven home, the experiment was over.

Initially, Singapore was excluded from the Malayan Federation for the "single over-riding reason" that the addition
of a Chinese-dominated island "would jeopardize the delicate
distribution of population and control within the Federation."
The Malays, already slightly out-numbered in their own land
by immigrant groups, were not anxious to have their economic
and political power further diluted by addition of the overwhelming Chinese majority of Singapore. Yet, in 1963, six
years after formation of the Malayan Federation, Tunku Abdul Rahman and his Alliance Party did agree to federate with
Singapore, because the Island's leader, Lee Kuan Yew, had
redressed Malaya's concern with the racial issue by stressing
the dangers of keeping Singapore out of Malaysia. What if a
Chinese Communist group came to power in Singapore and
then used that base to rekindle the Communist insurrection
within Malaya? What if Singapore were to side with Indonesia
in its "confrontation" with Malaya, Sarawak and North Borneo? In terms of immediate racial and military problems,
Singapore seemed likely to be a troublesome factor, in or out
of a Malaysian federation, but to be less troublesome in than
out.

Lee Kuan Yew and the Tunku both thought of federation as the answer to immediate problems rather than as a
long-term ideological commitment to unity. Lee's argument
that merger would be the most effective way to prevent a Communist threat arising from across the causeway convinced important Malay leaders. Lee, moreover, appealed to his own

party with the argument that Singapore's merger with the Federation was a "sure and early route" to the rapid realization of merdeka (freedom) for his island-colony.

Thus, the Malaysian Federation was created to serve tertiary goals which contained the seeds of self-defeat and secondary goals which were insufficient to save it. Singapore's principal goal, the acquisition of independence, required only the creation of federation and not its survival. Tunku Abdul Rahman's desire to maintain the racial balance between Chinese and Malays caused him to grasp Lee's hand in friendship —but also to keep him an arm's length away. Lee, however, would not be kept at a distance and the Tunku soon ran head-on into the former's active intervention in Malay politics and desire to expand his political influence throughout Malaysia but particularly among its Chinese citizens. Almost from the beginning it became apparent that, to some extent, all the key leaders of Malaysia had seen federations as a marriage of convenience rather than as a genuine commitment to unity-above-all between the territories and between the races of the Straits region. Unfortunately, the convenience of one proved the discomfiture of another, and *vice-versa*.

The Central African Federation's failure in many ways parallels that of Malaysia-Singapore. Again, racial "balance" was an avowed tertiary goal. It soon became clear that the whites' ideas of balance had little in common with those of the Asians or Africans. Again, federation was regarded by some who favored it as a means to rid themselves of British colonial rule—a short-term tertiary objective and thus an unstable base for a permanent union. Again, Britain saw federation primarily in tertiary accountancy terms of being released from her colonial obligations. Again, too, political-ideological inspiration was totally lacking. It could not be replaced by economic growth statistics nor even by such gigantic good works as the federal power dam at Kariba, or such sound secondary goals as the profitable economic union of the Rhodesias.

Despite the federal Constitution's announced goal of racial partnership, the creators of the Central African Federation failed to deal effectively with the racial issue. Through-

out the life of the federation, its white leaders continued to
dismiss the seriousness of the Africans' claims for a greater
role in the political process. Racial balance or partnership
seems rarely to mean the same thing for long to parties to a
federation in the absence of a more primary ideological commitment to federation itself.

As in the other federations here studied, federalism in
Central Africa was seen by its proponents primarily as a device to accomplish certain short-range objectives; and as in
the other federations these short-term objectives of different
interest groups and their spokesmen were not infrequently incompatible one with another. The white minority, politically
dominant in 1953 when the Federation was created, was primarily interested in reducing British colonial office control,
expanding their own economic paramountcy, and consolidating
their political power. The British government viewed federation as a convenient political barrier between the increasing
white racialist threat from South Africa on the one hand and
the all-black independence movements of East Africa on the
other. Opposed to these forces, but unable to exert any political pressure but boycott, were the leaders of the black majorities, particularly in Northern Rhodesia and Nyasaland.

The experience of both the Central Africa Federation and
Malaysia indicates that the mere creation of federal infrastructure not only does not provide a substitute for a federal
ideology but also cannot long contain basic political and social
conflict. Federation can provide the mechanism for resolving
such problems only if the political leaders have first themselves
embraced federalism as a goal good in itself, and have per-
suaded the populace to accept an ideology of union not—or
not merely—because of short-run benefits returnable in money
or power.

If there is, indeed, a common factor in the failures of
the four federations here studied it is this: federations are apt
to fail when they are justified to the participants only in
terms of immediately realizeable practical advantages. If the
practical advantages accrue, the need for federation may be at
an end. If, as more often proved the case, they do not, the
federation stands exposed as a fraud. And the supposed short-

run advantages expected by each unit and each leader of a
federation are likely, on investigation or implementation, to
prove different and contradictory one to another, thus giving
rise to destructive conflicts. It has been said by J. P. Morgan
of a certain expensive yacht that if you have to ask its price,
you can't afford it. Something comparable may be said of federalism. If one has to justify it in terms of specific secondary
and tertiary short-term benefits: tariffs, subventions, votes,
jobs, racial balance, it probably cannot succeed. A nation can
neither be fully explained nor constituted in accountants'
terms. Where what is wanted is not a new *nation* but a pragmatic solution to certain problems of trade and marketing,
population movement, defense or foreign policy, some other
solution different from classic federalism may be more realistic and so, more successful.

POST-FEDERALISM

Newly independent nations, wishing for the realities of
economic and political sovereignty and not merely its cere-
monial trappings, turn frequently to some kind of a federal
aspiration. The historic successes of the United States, Canada,
Australia, Switzerland and, to some extent, even the Soviet
Union in making one out of many, lend credence to federalism
as a solution to the common contemporary problems of units
which, standing alone, are frail, uncompetitive and economically nonviable.

Why have our four federations not succeeded in the way
the old federations did? Why did these contemporary instances of federalism not call forth a commitment to the primary ideal of federalism comparable to that of their classical
antecedents? The answer, simply, is that they did not. And so
the use of the classical analogies is likely to be harmfully
misleading to new nations in search of viability through a
mode of mutual accommodation. Certainly, some of what the
successful, older federal experiments have to teach is relevant
to the new nations. Even the problems encountered in the

American Confederation of the 1780's has a ring so familiar
as to be ghostly. One can almost hear Alexander Hamilton,
as the Spirit of Federations Past, warning young African
and Asian idealists that "Among the most formidable of the
obstacles which (they) will have to encounter may readily be
distinguished the obvious interest of a certain class of men in
every State to resist all changes which may hazard a diminution of the power, emolument, and consequence of the offices
they hold under the State establishments. . . ."[5]

Yet the similarities which it bears to the present do not
necessarily equip the past to be our guide to the future. Experience can overteach. Much of the superficial analogy drawn
between the successful applications of federalisms of the past
and the present needs of the developing nations is apt to be
misleading, and reliance upon it has already led to dissappoint-
ment both among well-wishers in the old states and among
intellectual leaders of the new nations. It has led to the creation of false-analogy federalism in circumstances, to quote
Professor McWhinney, "where the legal (or social) scientist
might advise against it on the score that a sufficient minimum
value consensus does not yet exist to base a viable federal
union."[6]

What made the "classic" federations possible? Speaking
in favor of a federation of the former American colonies, John
Jay, later to become the first Chief Justice of the United States,
pointed out one important reason: "Providence has been
pleased to give this one connected country to one united people
—a people descended from the same ancestors, speaking the
same language, professing the same religion, attached to the
same principles of government, very similar in their manner
and customs, and who, by their joint counsels, aims and efforts, fighting side by side through a long and bloody war,
have nobly established general liberty and independence."[7]
The common "Volksgeist" is what Jay is describing, and its
added ingredient, which the four new federations did not
have, is the experience of winning "general liberty and independence" by virtue of "joint counsels, aims and efforts" including even "fighting side by side through a long and bloody
war."

The American colonists had not only their shared culture, but were also exposed to the shared charisma of a common war of liberation. Their union, even if in the imperfect form of the Confederation, came into being immediately, before separate sovereignties had time to crystalize and the memories of the common struggle began to fade. They formed that union, Jay said, "almost as soon as they had a political existence; nay, at a time when their habitations were in flames, when many of their citizens were bleeding. . . ."[8]

Canadian confederation occurred with only few sporadic rebellions instead of a real war of national liberation, but Canadian confederation took place in the face of a common enemy threatening to impose an unwanted manifest destiny from the south. The Canadian fear may have been myth or exaggeration and misinformed fact, but it was an effective spur to charismatic togetherness among the disparate colonies. According to the Canadian historian, Professor Stephen Leacock, writing (perhaps somewhat tongue-in-cheek) as late as 1941, this factor was crucial. The idea of Canadian confederation, he said, had seemed all but dead in 1865, with four of the five potential constituents, Nova Scotia, New Brunswick, Prince Edward Island, and Newfoundland all opposed to it on economic and ethnic grounds: "Then came destiny and altered everything. The Civil War in America ended virtually at Appomatox. As its echoes ceased, the new tumult of Fenianism was heard across the border; men killing in thousands, unimpeded, Washington Government looking the other way. There was to be an invasion, and with it a Republic of Canada to avenge the wrongs of Ireland. The invasion came, its raids across the border meeting an inglorious end. But with invasion the heart of the Loyalists stirred again within their grandchildren."[9] By 1867, a pride of prudent provinces were finding each other unexpectedly comforting company, despite economic and ethnic differences of outlook and short-run interest.

It is important to realize how much times have changed. Except for India and the Indo-Chinese states, no new nation is today seriously threatened with external aggression by a major power, as were the provinces which became Canada. Indeed, it may well be the danger posed by Chinese and Pakistani militance which is holding the Indian federation together. And what drives the Indo-Chinese states apart is that the external threat comes to them not from one but from two great outside powers pulling and pushing them in opposite directions. Even Indonesian confrontation proved not to be a sufficiently serious threat to save the Malayan-Singapore federation—perhaps because fifty thousand British troops guarded Malaysia's frontiers while 77,000 more stood ready at Aden. And with the nuclear stalemate and Afro-Asia's firm neutralist resolve, there is today little reason for the new nations to fear the superpowers or feel compelled to draw closer to each other for strength and shelter. This security allows ethnic, racial, and economic differences to come to the fore.

The classical federations thus had the benefit of a passionate negative challenge to the collective imagination of their people: the charisma of the common *Angst*.

This is a familiar and confirmed psychological phenomenon. The French biologist, Felix Le Dantec, insists that every social unit from the family to the nation could exist only by virtue of having some common enemy.[10] In a series of studies of the effect of a stranger entering a group of nursery school children, Susan Isaacs reports, "The existence of an outsider is in the beginning an essential condition of any warmth or togetherness within the group."[11] Professor Gordon Allport, the Harvard psychologist, noting this, stated that "There is no denying that the presence of a threatening common enemy will cement the in-group sense of any organized aggregate of people."[12]

History provided the classical federations also with a positive charisma: the vision of almost limitless conquests and wealth. This secondary factor challenged the people of the classical federations to join together in realizing the great vision which became the primary factor. Thus the United States, Canada, and Australia became, in an important sense, unions of affluence leading to an ideological commitment to an affluent society. Where, as in the wooden shipbuilding industry of the Canadian maritimes, sporadic economic clouds had begun to gather, they were expected to be dispelled by the diversification and general prosperity of a confederation which would, in time, include not only the mature agriculture of Ontario and Quebec but phenomenal mineral empires of British Columbia and the Yukon. In all three classical federations it was presumed—and with sound reason as well as pioneering optimism—that in the economic tug-of-war the barely conceivable strengths of the whole would always easily outpull the weaknesses of some parts.

But principally, for the pioneers of Australia, Canada, and the United States, there were the great frontierlands to conquer. This was the center of the common vision, the common ideal, so big that it could accommodate within its infectious, exciting ethos liberals and conservatives, slaveholders and abolitionists, French and English, Catholics, Anglicans and nonconformists. The vast, vacant, lucrative frontiers not only gave a common cause to the diverse, but provided the space and riches that make diversity easier to accommodate. "Opening up the land"—financing railways, roads, bridges, and schools in sparsely settled regions—was a secondary-type goal of federation, but in practice the challenge of the land was so vast, so charismatically exciting as to transform itself quickly and smoothly into the primary goal of building a great federal union for its own sake, a tower of Babel in reverse, in which the soaring dimensions of the project made one out of many.

In Africa, as in Europe, on the other hand, a frontier is not a challenge but a barrier to a nation's expansion. In Australia, Canada, and the United States the frontier could absorb, in full, the creativity, ambition and libertarian instincts of generations of pioneers. The more the better, and the faster progress. Speaking of the westward push in America, Professor D. W. Brogan said, "It was one of the most decisive campaigns in world history; won in nearly three hundred years of ceaseless battle. And the unity of the great, central, fertile, and fantastically rich mass of North America had been fought for desperately, successfully."[13] The same kind of battle engaged Canadians and Australians. The wide, empty, uncivilized frontier provided a challenge to unite the people and inflame the passions; as well as a place to which, when unity and civilization seemed stifling, men could escape to realize their individual potential.

In the sense in which it is used in the American, Canadian and Austarlian context, Asia has no such challenge of the frontier. Overpopulated Singapore's union with Malaysia did not create a new hinterland for Singapore's Chinese millions searching for room to expand. Indeed, safeguards against such an expansion were made part of the federal compact. Africa has uncrowded areas, but for the most part their value for agricultural or mineral exploitation has yet to be proven. Neither Africa nor Asia is being replenished by waves of tired, huddled masses escaping from the industrial leviathan of Europe, drawn by mystery, romance, and ambition to the undeveloped bush and veld. On the contrary, the great magnets of Africa are the relatively developed towns. The African pioneers of the 1960's and 70's are those African men and women who stream out of the remote bush to open little shops in Nairobi, work in factories in Ndola or attend the university at Ibadan. In Africa and Asia, nation-building tends to be a movement inwards, not a push against widening perimeters. Naturally, the response is different. In Canada, Australia, and America, nation-building was an adventure which originated in the interaction of ambitious people and rich, empty, beckoning continents. In Asia and Africa it tends to be an aspect of urbanization and, significantly, it is not geographic, but social mobility, which defines the goal of the new Afro-Asian pioneers.

These differences are not without their implications for the success of a federal experiment. The frontier did not merely provide a gigantic common charismatic dream, which is perhaps the essential ingredient, but it provided limitless opportunity for the courageous, the intelligent and the resourceful to make their own way according to their ability, so that no man or group of men needed fear or resent the success of another. In most of today's new nations, the perimeter of the charmed circle of success has no such potential for unlimited expansion, and there is a tendency to feel that a newcomer generally enters it only when someone already within falls away. In such circumstances, ethnic, racial and other historic distinctions are likely to assert themselves at the expense of unity, and secondary and tertiary goals remain secondary and tertiary and often become divisive.

The wealth of the frontier also allowed the colonists to create for themselves a standard of living which, though arduous, was higher than any they might have enjoyed at home. Insofar as they turned to their neighbors, theirs was a union of the increasingly affluent, joining together for the achievement of even greater wealth than could be attained alone or under continued control of the European colonial motherland. On the other hand, the potential units of regional unions in Africa, Asia and the West Indies are, compared to contemporary America and Western Europe, still very poor. Malaysia's annual per capita income of about 350 dollars is high by Afro-Asian standards only. Naturally, these new nations feel themselves drawn for aid, investment or markets not to their poor neighbors but to a favorable relationship with one or more of the industrial nations of the northern hemisphere. These nations may be more distant, they may be ethnically and culturally alien, but they alone are sources of the capital and markets to which the developing nations must have access. Thus it is not surprising that much of francophonic Africa and Nigeria have opted to associate with the European Economic Community despite cries of "neoimperialism" from the spectators' stands. Thus, too, Puerto Rico resists the natural tug of Caribbeanism to tie itself to the United States. Speaking of West Indian federation, Professor McWhinney notes that "the empirical observer of the Caribbean community can hardly avoid concluding that the individual islands and their mainland counterparts have little to offer each other economically. Their interests, indeed, seem not so much complementary as competitive; and all of them would seem to have much to gain economically and even politically, by being linked with Europe, or with the United States, or even Canada. . . ."[14] It is probably true to say that the four failed federations had good economic reasons to unite; but that economic "take-off" could, in each case, be achieved not by regional union, but only by an effort actively joined by one or more developed states

outside the region. To this extent the secondary economic expectations motivating the classic federations are importantly
different from those economic goals motivating the newer
ones.

Having stated the matter thus, it is necessary to add modifications. On the one hand, the golden challenge of the frontier
and the bloody charisma of war did not lead to the liberation
of the southern slaves and it is thus not wholly true that these
events invariably made for a sense of national unity through
a common identity and vision—not, in any event, as far as the
negro was concerned. On the other hand, it should at least be
noted that in the United States' and Australian federations,
the people who were drawn together by the charisma of events
were, a great many of them, already originally and consciously
conditioned for unity by virtue of their being of a common
stock. In Canada, except for the French Canadians, who were
still in a sense a vanquished people, this was equally true.
Thus these classical federations were to some extent born out
of a reunion of people many of whom had previously, in
Europe, already been part of the same nation. We have noted
that similar culture, language, and colonial experience has not,
in the new nations studied, been successful in preventing the
failure of federation. But we also noted that this was because
these secondary factors did not alone add up to the primary
factor of a sense of nationhood, of political manifest destiny.
A majority of Canadian, Australian, and United States settlers
came to their new homes from Britain with this primary sense
already in their bones and genes.

Of course, even in the West Indies, and in Anglophonic
East and Central Africa there have evolved among the new
nations some important cultural and even ethnic links. The
Malay federation (as distinguished from the Malaysian), too,
is butressed by such ties. But in many new nations these frail
links are constantly in danger of being snapped by tribalisms
which not only divide one new state from another but constantly threaten the break-up of existing states.

All this does not argue that contiguous territories in
Africa, Asia, and the West Indies ought not to unite, but
merely that there are fewer factors operating for, and more

factors operating against, unity among these nations than, for example, in the America of the 1770's. There are fewer instances of paramount primary goal-factors motivating federation-building; more instances of dominant tertiary motivation; and where secondary goal-factors predominate, they do so in circumstances less conducive to charismatic translation into primary goal-factors. Plans for unity in the new nations are thus likely to lead to disappointment if they do not take these differences into account.

There will, of course, continue to be a use for federalism in the centrifugal context, as a system for holding existing sovereign entities together while giving freer rein to local tribal, ethnic, religious or economic interests. Thus, in India, federalism, paradoxically, is primarily a tool responsive to the need to contain *divisive* factors. As centrifugal local feelings assert themselves, new states of the Indian Union are created out of the subdivision of older ones. Except for the federal solution, these new units might break away altogether. Generally, however, centrifugal federalism is likely to save the federal state only where the cause of centrifugalism is not a local revolt against the idea of the nation as a whole, but against the idea of a particular formulation of the local unit. Thus the Bengalis and the Maharashtrians did not dispute the validity of their Indianism but only the viability of the local state which grouped them into a single political unit (Bengal). The operation of centrifugal federalism in this instance did not threaten the Indian state because the validity of the idea of the Indian nation was not at issue. Centrifugal federalism generally threatens the federal state only when it gets out of hand, creating too many sub-units unviable in the role assigned to local government, or when it produces an overemphasis on local loyalties which eventually erodes the idea of the larger nation. The once-unitary Congo has been particularly subject to this kind of centrifugal federalism.

But subdividing federalism is, in any event, a special case. As a device for grouping newly-independent sovereign states into larger unions, traditional political federation is unlikely to be a successful device for overcoming the odds against it in contemporary Africa and Asia in the absence of an over-

whelming primary ideological commitment to the federal ideal
and value, one widely shared by the leaders and the people.

None of this argues that new forms of association may not
succeed where classic federalism fails. Complex, highly pragmatic infrastructures are likely to develop, which do succeed
in uniting nations in certain functional ways, albeit not into
the neat packages of classical federalism. Thus it would be
wholly realistic for regional groupings of states to create
quasi-federal regulation of trade within a free trade area, to
market common products jointly, and to encourage the growth
of market and money areas large enough to attract investment
and credit. This suggests a degree of regional growth-plan-
ning. Defense, too, is a problem susceptible of regional solutions. But at the same time it is also realistic to think of *non-
regional* forms of association, particularly among all the
producers of a primary commodity, such as petroleum, coffee,
cocoa, copper and tin. Supranational authorities for pricing
and marketing these commodities could help to emancipate
them from the tyranny of market conditions over which the
producers now have almost no control.

It would also be realistic for the developing nations to
overcome both geography and history to evolve some functional *quasi*-federal bonds with one, or a grouping of the developed nations, for marketing, for investment, and for technical assistance. Most Francophonic nations of Africa already
have a form of economic association with the European Common Market ("The Six" or E.E.C.). And within a group of
nations which share a common jurisprudential legacy, common *quasi*-federal judicial institutions can enrich the law and
broaden its horizons while making the judiciary secure against
local political intervention. The Judicial Committee of the
Imperial Privy Council still plays this role to some extent
in hearing appeals from some smaller nations of the British
Commonwealth, although its history and membership unfortunately do not make it a truly Commonwealth, but a more
limited institution.

Then, too, there are the so-called "mini-states" which are
likely to evolve a form of sovereignty which nevertheless allows a stronger power, usually the "mother country," to look

after external affairs and defense at the new nation's own request. Certain "overseas territories" of France already have this form of association, as does West Samoa (in modified form) with New Zealand. Comparable arrangements are being made between Great Britain and some of its smaller former colonies in the Caribbean.

These projected developments, some of which are already in a rudimentary stage of evolution, contain a "federal" ingredient—although with a clear understanding that the concept no longer is limited to the classical definition of a structured system with a common representative assembly, executive and judicial or arbitral body.[15] Instead, the concept, best called *quasi*-federal can now be taken to include any form of association between sovereign states (1) in which the relationship is a continuing one; (2) regulated by an established system of normative rules and roles; (3) executed in an impartial and flexible manner consonant with those rules and roles. Such a continuing relationship generally features not a parliament and an executive, although it may have these as well, but a treaty and an administration. (Instead of a treaty, there may be a mutually agreeable statute of the protecting power with the proviso that it can be annulled like a treaty by an agreed process of the protected state.) The treaty or law then fulfills a role analogous to a constitution and is generally executed by an administration the role of which is, within defined limits, independent of the governments of the constituent states. Such treaties, in particular, are becoming an accepted part of the world system of sovereignty and they differ from the ordinary *ad hoc* treaty designed to settle a specific problem (such as the location of a boundary or the rights of passage of migratory birds) in that they have added a new word and a rejuvenated concept to the dictionary of sovereignty: the *treaty organization*.[16]

Functional *quasi*-federal arrangements not only have certain of the attributes of sovereignty—the Rhine Commission, for example, could even amend its *Reglement* and exercised substantial judicial as well as legislative power—but they can also marshall these attributes to achieve beneficial results not ordinarily attainable by more conventional *ad hoc* agreements between states. *Ad hoc* agreements must generally embody specific reciprocity of benefits, which is to say that an agreement by which a state is to lower a specific tariff or purchase a particular commodity must contain a balancing, reciprocal *quid pro quo* in money or in kind. On the other hand, the functional, *quasi*-federal agreement which sets up a treaty organization generally operates as a clearing-house of benefits. A continuing relationship, frequently covering various matters and several states, is established which operates sometimes to the benefit of one party, sometimes to the benefit of another. But, without requiring the specific consent of the parties to each individual transaction, the *quasi*-federal treaty establishes a *regimen* which *on balance* and *in the long run* is to the benefit of all the parties. The more states and the more functions are included in the arrangement, the more the exchange of benefits can be operated on the basis of the clearing-house rather than the *quid pro quo,* and the closer, of course, one comes to the federal ideal in which federation, by itself rather than any specific short-run advantage, is the primary group-value.

Functional *quasi*-federal experiments can also operate between equal, and not only between underdeveloped or *mini*-states and the superpowers: particularly in matters of defense and foreign policy. To some extent this is true of the *Union Africain el Malagache,* the Organization of African Unity, the Arab League, the Organization of American States and, of course, the defense pacts like NATO, SEATO, METO and the Warsaw Pact. The United Nations Charter Article 52, obliges all states entering such regional arrangements to "make every effort to achieve pacific settlement of local disputes through such regional arrangements or by such regional agencies before referring them to the Security Council." Most regional treaties themselves reenforce this obligation by making provision for conciliation, arbitration or even adjudication of disputes with other members. The Pan-African Freedom Movement for East, Central, and South Africa served during the crucial inceptive years of African nationalism as a sort of intergovernmental union for the freedom struggle. The African bloc at the UN informally but effectively enforces a duty on all members to submit any proposed diplomatic initiative to a meeting of the bloc before introducing it into the appropriate organ of the United Nations. In his recent article on "New Tendencies in Federal Theory and Practice," Professor Friedrich lists first among the three primary areas of innovative federalism "the field of foreign policy and related efforts at regional unification."[17]

Foreign policy and, for that matter, economic policy are not readily separated from political policy. Yet the significant innovative feature in these functional associations is that they tend to leave the *political* organs and prerogatives of national sovereignty largely, or, in any event, superficially unaffected by the unity they bring to less-jealously guarded prerogatives of economics, justice and even foreign relations. The structure of unity is thus designed to follow the contours of secondary objectives such as collective bargaining in world trade or economizing on the cost of diplomatic representation abroad and, so designed, is likely to be successful where a political federation would fail for lack of a widely shared common primary ideological commitment.

Even when sovereign political prerogatives are, in fact, restricted by such a functional relationship, usually an effort is wisely made to minimize and disguise the restriction. We have noted that certain tiny islands which are the remnants of Britain's empire are opting for a form of functional associate status which leaves control over defense, foreign affairs, and even certain "stand-by" residual domestic powers with Britain. But the jealous sense of political sovereignty is placated by an arrangement that permits this relationship to be terminated by unilateral act of the parliament or referendum of the people of the associated state. Even Antigua, St. Kitts, and Nevis, while prepared to surrender a certain measure of sovereignty, want it left clearly within sight and reach.[18]

Thus, while insistence on political independence has swept all before it in the 1960's, including a number of the neoclassical political federations designed by Britain for her former colonies—a complex network of functional associations ranging from the *ad hoc* to the relatively permanent is in process of springing up. To the outside observer, especially to students of government and constitutional law, all of this tends to look highly irregular and even "messy," particularly in comparison with symmetrical classical federalism. It cannot easily be reduced to tables of organization. Frequently, these arrangements seem to muddy the conventional international legal definition of "sovereignty."

Moreover, the flexibility and functionality of these new arrangements, combined with a hortatory, aspirational quality which characterizes the agreement establishing many of them, sometimes leads the Western observer to conclude that they do not truthfully describe political realities at the moment of time when they are drafted, proclaimed, or ratified. Such hard-nosed realism is itself, however, quite unrealistic in judging the new *quasi*-federal associations by the values of classical federalism. Insofar as the treaties or normative laws of the new associations describe accurately, if not neatly, the variegated topography of common interest among its adherents, they are more realistic, better structured, and more likely to succeed *in the circumstances* than the constitutional laws of classical federalism. Insofar as they sometimes seems hortatory and aspirational—the Organization of African Unity is one instance; even its title is still largely wishful thinking—it is not lack of realism which is the motivation but a realistic attempt by the elite to create, in what is known to be a long uphill struggle against history and vested interest, the ideal, the ethos of unity, a common currency of values culminating in a primary institutional value.

What can we learn from our four failures to insure future successes in federation building? Mainly what we can *not* learn, or the dangers of false analogies. East Africa is not like Australia; nor are the Rhodesias and Nyasaland like the United States in 1788, or Canada in 1863. East Africa is not even like Central Africa, and the British West Indies are not like Malaysia. The four studies do, however, support the view that neither economic complementarity nor its opposite can be said to be essential to failure or to success. The same seems true of common institutions, of common language and systems of education and government. What was essential, and also lacking in all four federations, was commitment to the primary political ideal of federation itself, and charismatic leaders or events to generate such commitment.

Now the new nations must invert their own variations on the theme of federalism. That the federal form had a fixed meaning in the days of Western paramountcy should not inhibit Africans and Asians from redefining it, although in all probability the new definition will also reflect Western influences: perhaps not those of Canada or the United States so much as the Danube Commission and the Treaty of Rome.

Nor should one mourn excessively the failure of traditional federalism in some of the new nations. Each people must build with the stuff at hand. Africa has the clay of tribalism and the twigs of nationalism. The real loyalties, the genuine enthusiasms which are so essential to a successful modernizing effort are often still to be found at the local level. The real heroes are often still the local leaders of tribal democracy and the regional "freedom-fighters" of the independence campaigns. In many cases these, and not the figures known in the far-off national capital and on the world stage, are the men who have "visibility" in the villages, where it really counts. These politicians are known to their constituents, people poor in education, communication, and transport. It is often they who are respected by and capable of mobilizing the people. They may not always be the most competent or the best-educated leaders. Their standards of public morality may sometimes be nepotistic by Western standards. But there is much to be said for retaining and even reenforcing the emphasis on that unit of political government which has the loyalty and attention of the people and, equally important, which listens to local wishes and discontents. The political remoteness of national leaders from the places where the real, the basic action is, may be more of a danger to Asian and African nations' stability than is centrifugalism. For their stage of development, some states trying to act like European nations, may be overstructured, overendowed with the machinery of centralization. And the unsuitability of this machinery to the social material on which it operates may be a prime cause of break-down.

And so new machinery is being invented to somehow patch together a pragmatic pastiche of functional unity and interdependence in fiscal and technological matters with a mobilizational system of decentralizing local political dynamics; of local politicians and centralizing bureaucrats in pragmatic tandem rather than in neatly hierarchic relationship. It is, at any rate, far too early to say that it cannot be done.

NOTES

1. For a different emphasis, see Karl W. Deutsch, "Social Mobilization and Political Development," *American Political Science Review*, Vol. LV, No. 3 (Sept. 1961).

2. Indeed, R. L. Watts has pointed out that "While the economic claims . . . suggest that, with only a few exceptions, economic unions are generally advantageous, none of these arguments actually requires full political integration." *New Federations* (Oxford University Press, 1966), p. 47.

3. Despite his occupation with secondary or tertiary factors, perhaps R. L. Watts has hinted at a similar theory in writing that "Common to all these cases was the conviction of the constitution-makers that federal institutions were 'unavoidable'—the only possible compromise in the particular circumstances." R. L. Watts, note 2, p. 99.

4. Kenya's John Keen is reported to have told the Central Legislative Assembly of East Africa in November, 1964, that one of the great tragedies of British rule in East Africa was the granting of independence without first bringing about federation. *Uganda Argus*, Kampola (Nov. 27, 1964), p. 7. Cf. Rothchild, Force, and Consent in "African Region-Building," *Makerere Journal*, No. 11, 1965, 23 at 24.

5. Alexander Hamilton, *The Federalist*, No. 1 (Cambridge: Belknap Press, 1961).

6. Edward McWhinney, *Federal Constitution-making for a Multi-National World* (Leyden: A. W. Sijthoff, 1966), p. 2.

7. John Jay, *The Federalist*, No. 2 (Cambridge: Belknap Press, 1961).

8. *Ibid.*

9. Stephen Leacock, *Canada: The foundations of its Future*, (private printing, 1941) pp. 152–53.

10. Gordon Allport, *The Nature of Prejudice* (New York: Anchor, 1958), p. 40.

11. Susan Isaacs, *Social Development in Young Children* (New York: Harcourt, Brace, 1933), p. 250.

12. Allport, p. 40.

13. Deris Brogan, *The American Character* (New York: Knopf, 1944), p. 24.

14. McWhinney, p. 110–11.

15. Carl J. Friedrich, *Constitutional Government and Democracy* (Boston: Ginn, 1950), pp. 193–97.

16. The modern history of the treaty organization can probably be dated from the founding of the Rhine Commission by a convention of the Congress of Vienna in 1815.

17. Carl Friedrich, Jahrbuch des offentlichen Rechts, Vol. 14 (1965) p. 1 at 6.

18. Cf. Report of the Antigua Constitutional Conference, 1966, Cmnd. 2963, April 1966, London.

BIBLIOGRAPHY

EAST AFRICA

Carter, Gwendolyn. *African One-Party States*. Ithaca: Cornell University Press, 1962.

Cox, Richard. *Pan-Africanism in Practice*. London: Oxford University Press, 1964.

Davis, John, and Baker, James. *Southern Africa in Transition*. New York: Praeger, 1966.

Franck, Thomas M. *East African Unity Through Law*. New Haven: Yale University Press, 1964.

Hughes, A. J. *East Africa: The Search for Unity*. Baltimore: Penguin, 1963.

Ingham, Kenneth. *A History of East Africa*. New York: Praeger, Rev. 1965.

Legum, Colin. *Pan-Africanism*. (Rev. ed.) New York: Praeger, 1965.

Lofchie, Michael. *Zanzibar: Background to Revolution*. Princeton: Princeton University Press, 1965.

McWhinney, Eduard. *Federal Constitution-Making for a Multi-National World*. Leyden: Sitjthoff, 1966.

Oliver, R., and Matthews, G. *History of East Africa*. Vol. I. Oxford: Clarendon Press, 1963.

Harlow, V., and Chilver, E. M. *History of East Africa*. Vol. II. Oxford: Clarendon Press, 1965.

Economic Development of Kenya. Report of the Mission of the International Bank. Baltimore: Johns Hopkins Press, 1963.

Economic Development of Tanganyika. Report of the Mission of the International Bank. Baltimore: John Hopkins Press, 1961.

Economic Development of Uganda. Report of the Mission of the International Bank. Baltimore: Johns Hopkins Press, 1962.

THE FEDERATION OF RHODESIA-NYASALAND

Barber, William J. *The Economy of British Central Africa: A Case Study of Economic Development in a Dualistic Society.* London: Oxford University Press, 1961.

Franck, Thomas M. *Race and Nationalism: The Struggle for Power in Rhodesia-Nyasaland.* New York: Fordham University Press, 1960.

Gray, Richard. *The Two Nations: Aspects of the Development of Race Relations in the Rhodesias and Nyasaland.* London: Oxford University Press with the Institute of Race Relations, 1960.

Hazlewood, Arthur, and Henderson, P. D. *Nyasaland: The Economics of Federation.* Oxford: Basil Blackwell, 1960.

Leys, Colin. *European Politics in Southern Rhodesia.* Oxford: Clarendon Press, 1959.

Mason, Philip. *The Birth of a Dilemma: The Conquest and Settlement of Rhodesia.* London: Oxford University Press with the Institute of Race Relations, 1958.

Rogers, Cyril A., and Frantz, C. *Racial Themes in Southern Rhodesia: The Attitudes and Behavior of the White Population.* New Haven: Yale University Press, 1962.

Rotberg, Robert I. *The Rise of Nationalism in Central Africa: The Making of Malawi and Zambia 1873–1964.* Cambridge: Harvard University Press, 1965.

Spiro, Herbert J. *Politics in Africa: Prospects South of the Sahara.* New Jersey: Prentice-Hall, 1962.

Weinberg, S. *An Outline of the Constitutional Law of the Federation of Rhodesia and Nyasaland.* Salisbury: Federal Government, 1959.

Welensky, Sir Roland. *4000 Days.* London: Collins, 1964.

WEST INDIAN FEDERATION

NOTE

Useful bibliographical references pertaining to the dissolution of the West Indian Federation can be found in:
Institute of Jamaica, West India Reference Library: *A List of
   Books on West Indian Federation.* 2nd edition by Anne
   Benewick. November, 1962. (Kingston, Jamaica—mimeographed), pp. 23–24; and in "Federation in the West Indies" by Jesse Harris Proctor, Jr., a leading authority in
   the field whose contribution appeared in: *Federalism in
   the Commonwealth.* A Bibliographical Commentary edited
   by William S. Livingston. Published for the Hansard Society by Cassell, London, 1963. Especially pp. 83–84.
This author has made acknowledgements in the text to the
following monographs:
Hugh W. Springer: *Reflections on the Failure of the First
   West Indian Federation.* Cambridge: Harvard University
   Center for International Affairs. Occasional Papers in International Affairs, No. 4, July, 1962; and Amitai Etzioni,
   Political Unification. A comparative study of leaders and
   forces. New York: Holt, Rinehart and Winston, Inc.,
   1965.

THE MALAYSIAN FEDERATION

NOTE

The literature in English on Malaya and Singapore is indeed rich, especially since Francis Light became the first Su-
perintendent of Penang in 1786 and Thomas Stamford Raffles
acquired in 1819 the virtually unpopulated island of Singapore.
The general reader may well begin with Wang Gungwu, (ed.)
Malaysia, A Survey, New York: Frederick A. Praeger, 1964,
and then proceed to consult the fifty pages (405–55) devoted
to bibliographical notes to its widely ranging chapters.
   In preparing this chapter I have found the documents,
books and articles mentioned in the footnotes to be especially

valuable. There is no need to reprint their titles here. Additionally, the following may be profitably consulted.

DOCUMENTS

Federation of Malaya. *Official Yearbook.* Vols. I–V. Kuala
    Lumpur: Government Printer, 1961–65.
Federation of Malaysia. *Citizenship of Malaysia.* Kuala Lum-
    pur: Government Printer, 1964.
————. *Malaysia's Case in the U.N. Security Council, Docu-
    ments reproduced from the official record of the Se-
    curity Council proceedings.* Kuala Lumpur: Government
    Printer, 1964.

BOOKS

Brackman, Arnold. *Southeast Asia's Second Front: The Power
    Struggle in the Malay Archipelago.* New York: Frederick
    A. Praeger, 1966.
Ginsburg, Norton, and Roberts, Chester. *Malaya.* Seattle: Uni-
    versity of Washington Press, 1958.
Groves, Harr. *The Constitution of Malaysia.* Singapore: Ma-
    laysia Publications, Ltd., 1964.
Hanna, Willard. *The Formation of Malaysia: New Factor in
    World Politics.* New York: American Universities Field
    Staff, 1964.
————. *The Separation of Singapore from Malaysia.* New
    York: American Universities Field Staff, September, 1965.
Hanna, William. *Sequel to Colonialism: The 1957–60 Founda-
    tions for Malaysia.* New York: American University Field
    Staff, Inc., 1965.
Lee Kuan Yew. *The Battle for a Malaysian Malaysia.* Singa-
    pore: Ministry of Culture, 1965.
Means, G. P. *Malayan Government and Politics in Transition.*
    Seattle: University of Washington Press, 1961.
Mills, Lennox. *Malaya: A Political and Economic Appraisal.*
    Minneapolis: University of Minnesota Press, 1958.
Osborne, Milton. *Singapore and Malaysia.* Ithaca: Cornell Uni-
    versity Data Paper. No. 53, 1964.
Purcell, Victor. *The Chinese in Modern Malaya.* Singapore:
    Eastern University Press, 1960. 2nd ed. revised.
Tilman, Robert. *Bureaucratic Transition in Malaya.* Durham:
    Duke University Press, 1964.
Tregonning, K. G. *Malaysia.* Singapore: Donald Moore, 1965.

ARTICLES

Starner, F. L. "Malaysia and the North Borneo Territories," *Asian Survey*, Vol. 3, No. 2 (November, 1963), 519–34.
Tinker, Irene. "Malayan Elections: Electoral Pattern for Plural Societies?" *Western Political Quarterly*, Vol. 9 (June, 1956), 258–82.

Index

About the Authors

THOMAS M. FRANCK is Director of the Center for International Studies and Professor of Law at New York University. He received his B.A. from the University of British Columbia in 1952 and his J.S.D. from the Harvard Law School. A well-known expert on constitutional law, he has been adviser to the governments of Tanganyika, Zanzibar, Kenya, and Maritus. His previous books include *African Law, Comparative Constitutional Process,* and *The Structure of Impartiality.*

GISBERT H. FLANZ is Professor of Political Science at New York University. Born in Czechoslovakia, he has degrees from European universities and a doctorate from Princeton. A specialist in political theory and comparative politics, he has served as constitutional adviser in Korea and in Vietnam. He is presently completing a book on the constitution of Vietnam.

HERBERT J. SPIRO is Professor of Political Science at the University of Pennsylvania. He did his undergraduate work at Harvard and received his Ph.D. there in 1953. He was Fulbright Research Professor in Africa during 1959–1962. His recent books include *Africa: The Primacy of Politics, Patterns of African Revolution,* and *World Politics: The Global System.*

FRANK N. TRAGER is Professor of International Affairs at New York University, where he earned his Ph.D. He has divided his career among teaching, the federal government, and non-profit agencies, and has traveled extensively in Southeast Asia. His books include *Why Viet Nam?, Burma: From Kingdom to Republic,* and *Marxism in Southeast Asia.*

213